NEUROTIC
Parent's
Guide to
College Admissions

*Strategies for Helicoptering,
Hot-housing & Micromanaging*

by *J.D. Rothman*

Published by Prospect Park Media
969 S. Raymond Avenue
Pasadena, California 91105
prospectparkmedia.com

Distributed to the trade by
SCB Distributors
scbdistributors.com

Library of Congress Cataloging in Publication data
Rothman, J. D.
The neurotic parent's guide to college admissions : strategies for helicoptering, hot-housing & micromanaging / by J.D. Rothman. — 1st ed.
    p. cm.
ISBN 978-0-9834594-1-5
1. Universities and colleges—Admission—Humor. 2. Parenthood—Humor. I. Title.
PN6231.C6R68 2012
818'.607--dc23
    2011047727

First edition, first printing

Designed by Joseph Shuldiner

Production in the United States of America; printing in South Korea

Education is not filling a bucket, but lighting a fire.

— WILLIAM BUTLER YEATS

~

In certain cases, arson is justifiable.

—THE NEUROTIC PARENT

contents

Table of

contents

....

ORIENTATION TO COLLEGE ANGST

Back in the day, before the existence of the expression "back in the day," you took the SAT once. When you got a 1260, your relatives thought you were a genius. That was when the most difficult high school class was trig, a "B" meant "good," and the initials AP stood for Associated Press. Your main extracurricular was sitting with a sun reflector on the beach. You filled out applications for three colleges and didn't bother to visit any. Even if you were lucky enough to know your guidance counselor, it never would have occurred to you to ask her to proofread your application, which you sent in by registered mail.

You can barely remember why you selected the college where you ended up, but it probably had something to do with where your ex-boyfriend or ex-girlfriend was or wasn't attending. Then, when it was time to leave, your parents dropped you off at a train station with a duffel bag, and that began your college career.

At the Neurotic Parent Institute, we have followed the trends carefully. We can say definitively that everything has changed. Today's kids need to begin prepping for college by age 2, when they get admitted to a selective Mommy and Me group, which leads to the right preschool. Then, starting at age 5, they need tutors, coaches, and homework helpers. In their spare time after that, they must choose 20-hour-a-week activities that will become their passions by middle school. If they're actually having fun rather than excelling, there's something wrong.

This guidebook presents our findings about today's college process. It will prepare you for the fourteen standardized exams, 39 essays, and 27 supplements that your son or daughter will tackle—and all the money you will spend making sure they're on target. If you're reading this when your child is a junior or senior in high school, we're sorry to let you know that you have started agonizing way too late, and we suggest you supplement this experience with a strong cocktail or an Ativan.

We will also present popular blog entries by the Neurotic Parent, which follow the journey of her older son, Cerebral Jock (CJ), during the period when he was ultimately accepted early decision to a top-ten school. This anxious blogger is now in the middle of overseeing the application process of her younger son, Good Conversationalist (GC), so if you happen to be a college admissions officer at one of the schools on his list, please promise not to be offended by anything you read here…and admit him.

And whether you have a kindergartener or twelfth grader, may your child's college search be full of multiple acceptances, generous merit scholarships, and chill roommates.

THE MOST
DIFFICULT
TIME
TO GET INTO COLLEGE
IN THE
HISTORY
OF THE WORLD

*Frightening statistics, shocking
pie charts, depressing bar graphs*

WHAT'S GOING ON?
WHY CAN'T MY GENIUS CHILD GET IN?

Feel guilty. Clearly it is all your fault. While you were letting your child engage in normal activities like summer camp, babysitting, and bowling, other kids were interning for their senators, training seeing-eye dogs, and starting hedge funds in Sri Lanka.

As a result, for every impressive kid, there are 50 even more outstanding ones. Here are the phenomena that have changed everything:

WEIGHTING	Previously, you couldn't earn anything higher than a straight-A average or a 4.0 GPA. Now, thanks to APs, honors, and other "weighted" courses, you can have a 5.8. And because of the power of infinity, for every kid who has taken 17 APs, there is another who has taken 18.
APP-LIFICATION	Once upon a time you couldn't apply to more than five schools. Now, because of the online Common App, all it takes is a click to apply to 49.
GAMING THE TESTS	Before, it was impossible to get higher than a 1600 on the SATs. Now, not only can you get a 2400, but you also can keep retaking and combining your highest subscores from the various test sections, ending up with a Superscore. And if you don't like the SAT, its cousin from Iowa, the ACT, has become just as highly regarded.
EXTRA-SPECIAL EXTRACURRICULARS	Remember when karate seemed exotic? Not any more. Never before could kids become contortionists, foreign correspondents, or bunion-surgery assistants.
ALUMNI CONNECTIONS	Our own parents might or might not have done the college thing—either way, it was all good. Today we have a generation of parents who have all attended college, of which quite a few went on to get medical degrees, law degrees, Ph.Ds, and MBAs. And many, at least before the fall of Lehman, have been sending big bucks to their alma maters for years.
HOOKS	Athletic Recruits, Legacies, the Rich, the Poor, the Exceptionally Talented, the Famous, and the Infamous make up the majority of each admitted class. We can't all be related to a celebrity, of a mixed race, or best friends with the admissions officer. Or can we? There are now all sorts of application boosters who, for a price, will get you in, by hook or by crook.
CONSULTANTS/ TUTORS	Even though everyone is broke and our economy has crashed, some tutors are raking in $900 an hour.
VALEDICTORIAN-REJECTION BRAGGING RIGHTS	Whatever you do, don't let your kid become the valedictorian! Just about every top college likes to brag that they reject two-thirds of the vals who apply.
BOGUS B-LIST SYNDROME	There are 4,000 colleges in this country alone. Of those, probably 2,863 are just fine. But everyone wants to go to only 17.

WHICH SILLY METAPHOR ARE YOU?

Who is this book for? Helicopter parents, of course. But it can also prove valuable for those who have taken on the role of other vehicles, appliances, and household items.

The Neurotic Parent Institute has completed an important study for moms and dads who have not reached full-on 'copter status but still cannot keep themselves from hovering.

Recently in the press we've heard about Velcro parents and spider-web parents. But we've also identified many other kinds of parents who are overly involved in their kids' lives.

SAFETY NET PARENTS	DUSTBUSTER PARENTS
Let them fall, but catch them before they go to jail	No need to feel guilty about this kind of behavior; necessary to deter bed bugs
SCRAPBOOK PARENTS	BFF PARENTS
Cannot let go of all those homemade pencil holders and smelly ballet slippers	They share clothing and dispense too much information about premarital adventures
SPELL-CHECK PARENTS	LITTLE LEAGUE PETER PAN DADS
"I never read Olivia's essays, but I do go over her punctuation"	They attend every all-star game in the community, even after their kids are in college
IT TAKES A VILLAGE MOMS	"WE" PARENTS
They offer to do double duty in carpool, then gossip about how the other parents aren't involved enough	They cannot talk about the college process without using the first-person plural: "We are looking into merit aid at Clark," or "We are getting the Princeton supplement done today"

And aren't we all: *ATM Parents*

WHY DOES EVERYONE CARE SO MUCH?

It used to be enough to say your kid went to a decent state U. But now most boomer parents, once laid-back hippies, view their kids' college results as the ultimate Parenting Badge. Most importantly, they need to feel good about all the money they've spent on tutors.

UNIVERSITIES OF HOPE, CHANGE & FAME

You wouldn't be reading this book if you really believed that it Doesn't Matter Where You Go. We all know that the Unabomber attended Harvard and Oprah went to Tennessee State. But there is comfort in discovering that many people you have heard of attended colleges you've never heard of.

With that in mind, the Neurotic Parent Institute has researched the alma maters of many of our planet's notables. (Disclaimer: Research was conducted on Wikipedia, which college students are not allowed to cite, but everything seems believable to us.)

IVY/STANFORD/MIT SUCCESS STORIES

Lisa Birnbach	Brown
Bill Nye	Cornell
Timothy Geithner	Dartmouth
Conan O'Brien	Harvard
Barack Obama	Occidental, Columbia, Harvard Law School*
I.M. Pei	MIT
Philip Roth	Penn
Brooke Shields	Princeton
Diane Feinstein	Stanford
Maya Lin	Yale

*Many "transcripters" claim that he never actually attended Columbia or Harvard

NON-IVY SUCCESS STORIES

Neil Armstrong	Purdue University
Mario Batali	Rutgers, Cordon Bleu
Joe Biden	University of Delaware, Syracuse Law School
Wolf Blitzer	SUNY Buffalo

Warren Buffett	Transferred out of Wharton; got his degree from University of Nebraska
Connie Chung	University of Maryland
Stephen Colbert	Northwestern
Rahm Emanuel	Sarah Lawrence
Will Ferrell	USC
Google creators	University of Maryland, University of Michigan
Lady Gaga	NYU (dropped out)
Ashton Kutcher	University of Iowa
Bernard Madoff	One year at University of Alabama; graduated from Hofstra University
Janet Napolitano	Santa Clara University, University of Virginia
Iggy Pop	University of Michigan
Condoleezza Rice	University of Denver
Amy Poehler	Boston College
Harvey Weinstein	SUNY Buffalo

FAMOUS & SEMI-FAMOUS PEOPLE WHO ATTENDED SCHOOLS YOU'VE NEVER HEARD OF

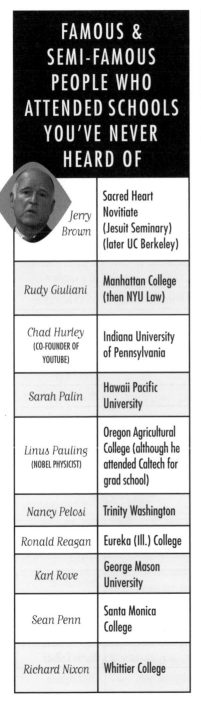

Jerry Brown	Sacred Heart Novitiate (Jesuit Seminary) (later UC Berkeley)
Rudy Giuliani	Manhattan College (then NYU Law)
Chad Hurley (CO-FOUNDER OF YOUTUBE)	Indiana University of Pennsylvania
Sarah Palin	Hawaii Pacific University
Linus Pauling (NOBEL PHYSICIST)	Oregon Agricultural College (although he attended Caltech for grad school)
Nancy Pelosi	Trinity Washington
Ronald Reagan	Eureka (Ill.) College
Karl Rove	George Mason University
Sean Penn	Santa Monica College
Richard Nixon	Whittier College

FALLEN POLITICIANS

John Edwards	North Carolina State, UNC Law
Arnold Schwarzenegger	Santa Monica College, University of Wisconsin-Superior
Anthony Weiner	SUNY Plattsburgh

HARVARD REJECTS

Lee Bollinger, president of Columbia University	
Tom Brokaw	
Warren Buffett	rejected from Harvard Business School
Art Garfunkel	
Matt Groening, creator of The Simpsons	
John Kerry	(he settled for Yale)
Scott McNealy, founder of Sun Microsystems	rejected from Harvard and Stanford business schools
David Remnick, New Yorker editor	
Ted Turner	
Harold Varmus, winner of Nobel Prize in Medicine and president of Sloan-Kettering	twice rejected by Harvard Medical School
Meredith Vieira	
Jann Wenner	

FAMOUS PEOPLE WHO WERE EXPELLED

Woody Allen	expelled from NYU for poor grades
Humphrey Bogart	expelled from Phillips Academy for throwing headmaster in the lake
Marlon Brando	expelled from Shattuck Military School for fighting and cigarette smoking
Dick Cheney	flunked out of Yale—twice
Salvador Dali	expelled for rudeness to his teachers
Albert Einstein	expelled from high school for rebelliousness
Harrison Ford	expelled from Ripon College for failing a philosophy class
Buckminster Fuller	expelled from Harvard twice, once for partying with a vaudeville troupe, then for "general disinterest"
Robert Frost	expelled from Dartmouth for poor performance and daydreaming
William Randolph Hearst	expelled from Harvard for giving his professors personalized chamber pots
Samuel L. Jackson	expelled from Morehouse College for his involvement in a black power protest during which a trustee was locked in a building for two days
Ted Kennedy	expelled from Harvard for paying a classmate to cheat for him
Charlie Sheen	expelled from Santa Monica High for poor attendance and sub-par grades
Kevin Spacey	expelled from Northridge Military Academy for behavioral problems
Ted Turner	expelled from Brown for having a girl in his dorm room

FAMOUS PEOPLE WHO WERE REJECTED FROM THEIR FIRST-CHOICE SCHOOL

Katie Couric	rejected from Smith; attended the University of Virginia
Steven Spielberg	rejected from USC Film School; attended Cal State Long Beach
Gloria Steinem	rejected from Cornell and Stanford; attended Smith

THESE ACCOMPLISHED GUYS & GALS NEVER ATTENDED COLLEGE AT ALL

Julie Andrews		Lucille Ball	David Bowie	Harry Truman
Richard Branson	Albert Camus	Charlie Chaplin		Cher
Simon Cowell	Tom Cruise	Walt Disney	Duke Ellington	William Faulkner
Aretha Franklin		Whoopi Goldberg	Paris Hilton	Jay-Z
Ray Kroc	Fran Lebowitz	David H. Murdock	Quentin Tarantino	
Princess Diana	John D. Rockefeller Sr.	George Bernard Shaw	H.G. Wells	Neil Young

ACCEPTED: THEN & NOW

We promised you all sorts of scary charts. Here's one.

	1997	2009	2011	2020 *projected*
Columbia	24%	10.4%	6.4%	1.3%
Northwestern	29.4%	26.8%	23%	6%
Penn	33%	17.1%	12.1%	4.6%
WashU	56%	22.2%	20%	12%
USC	70%	24%	23.8%	11%
U Chicago	71%	26.8%	18%	9%
Yale	20%	9.7%	7.4%	-0.3%*

*you'll have to go to Yale to figure out what that means.

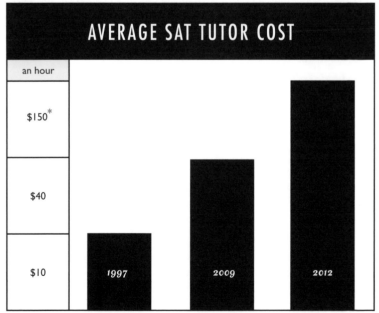

AVERAGE SAT TUTOR COST

an hour

$150*

$40

$10

1997   2009   2012

* but 100-minute sessions are required

HAPPINESS: A MATTER OF DEGREES?
We randomly polled 100 readers of the Neurotic Parent Blog, with these results

Percentage of readers who attended Harvard, Yale, or Princeton	*21%*
Percentage of above who could get into Harvard, Yale, or Princeton today	*2%*
Percentage of readers who went on a spring-break tour to visit colleges before they matriculated	*1%*
Percentage of readers who took an SAT prep course	*4%*
Percentage of readers who have used calculus, physics, or philosophy in the last 30 years	*8%*
Percentage of readers who consider themselves financially successful because they bought a home in 1993, not because they went to college	*96%*
Percentage of readers who consider themselves interesting because they listen to NPR, not because they went to college	*92%*
Percentage of readers who attended top colleges yet waste time reading shallow, humorous books	*83%*

THE LATEST TRENDS

SAFETIES ARE NO LONGER SAFE

Most of the "likelies," once known as "safeties," are now considered "matches" or "targets" by the college counselors.

REACH SCHOOLS ARE NO LONGER WITHIN REACH

Many of the "long shots," previously known as "reaches," have been reclassified as "impossibles." For example, for the class of 2006, Brown was a reach for anyone. By 2009, it was a long shot. Now, when anyone discusses Brown, it is considered a "crapshoot." That makes a school like Cornell a long shot, and Berkeley and Michigan reaches. Skidmore, once a "likely" for many kids, has become a target. And so on.

EACH NEW YEAR IS THE MOST DIFFICULT YEAR IN THE HISTORY OF THE WORLD TO GET INTO COLLEGE

Every year from now on will be the toughest college admissions year—ever. This is not because the population has increased, but thanks to the Common App and essay recycling, it is now relatively easy to apply to 38 schools instead of three.

IT'S EASIER TO GET INTO HARVARD THAN THE UNIVERSITY OF BEIJING

Despite the crash of the economy and our plummeting logic skills, international students are enamored with American schools. And they're hard to turn down—they pay full price.

GRADS CANNOT GET JOBS, REGARDLESS OF THEIR SCHOOL OR MAJOR

Although many find this trend upsetting, it can actually be comforting to those who are concerned about where their kid will be accepted. At the end of the day, all of our kids will soon be competing for a handful of Teach for America positions and MTV internships.

SAT RESULTS HAVE GONE THROUGH THE ROOF/PARENTS ARE SPENDING MORE ON GETTING THEIR KIDS INTO COLLEGE THAN THE COST OF COLLEGE ITSELF

Scores have risen, not because kids are smarter but because their parents are more competitive and have spent more on tutoring. In fact, every penny of their disposable income is now allocated toward getting their kids into college—and then goes to tuition.

KIDS HAVE THEIR EYE ON THE PRIZE

Thanks to the success of *The Social Network*, a new role reversal has emerged. Young people are obsessed with getting rich, while their parents just want to have fun playing video games. Yes, middle-aged guys are the ones who are now addicted to their iPads. They play Angry Birds while the kids scheme about how to become internet billionaires.

WHEN THEY GET INTO THEIR DREAM SCHOOL, IT'S JUST TOO DARN HARD

"I finally made it to Dartmouth," says one bright student we know, "only to find out I have to study all the time." Many are unhappy in Organic Chem—they wish they were at Fun State U tailgating and taking a course in Street Art.

LET THE ANXIETY BEGIN

Why you need a bunch of expensive helpers to get your kid to write a decent two-page essay

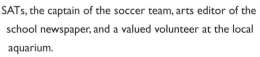

The Neurotic Parent Answers Your Questions

BWRKS—FAQS

Q: What is a BWRK?

A: Rumored to be used by admissions officers, this acronym stands for a Bright, Well-rounded Kid—for example, a high school student with a 3.8 unweighted GPA, 2150 SATs, the captain of the soccer team, arts editor of the school newspaper, and a valued volunteer at the local aquarium.

Q: If I've raised a BWRK, shouldn't I be proud and content?

A: No way. Über-selective colleges these days are averse to BWRKs. They want Nobel Prize winners, published novelists, and Olympic champions. Or any of the following:

• Children of unusual minorities
• Children of famous parents or gay parents or inmate parents (gory, heartbreaking felonies are preferable to white-collar crimes)
• Children of alumni parents who show up at the helipad for their interview with the development office
• "First-generation" families with no previous college attendees and no indoor plumbing

Q: Uh-oh. I'm a bland, boring suburbanite, and I think I inadvertently raised a BWRK. What should I do?

A: Clearly, you cannot go back and change

your sexual orientation or marry that goat herder from Zimbabwe you dated in graduate school. Or enroll your 3-year-old in a fencing workshop rather than T-ball. So you have to figure out how to make your child's credentials **jump off the page**. In other words, start marketing and branding your student at as early an age as possible.

Q: Oops! I didn't do that either. I screwed up and raised a nice, normal, smart student with kid-appropriate interests. Help! What should I do?

A: One quick fix might be **crew**. Almost every student we know who perfects his or her ERG score ends up at a top school. The bad part is you have to spend most of your time rowing in freezing water at 5:30 a.m.

Q: My child is not strong enough/too lazy for crew. What other options do I have?

A: The other quick fix is **academic research**. If you can bribe your college-professor sister-in-law to let your child help conduct a study about curing psoriasis by eliminating pesticides in nightshade vegetables, your kid is golden.

Q: Forget it. The only research my child will do is about hip-hop artists.

A: In that case, my friend, you will need to resort to **packaging**. And for that, you will need to hire all sorts of specialists to guide you through the process. They will help your son or daughter seem as if he or she is a GHAK (Genius, Highly Accomplished Kid), one whose accomplishments sound impressive when they are introduced by the president at the incoming freshman convocation.

LINING UP YOUR SUPPORT STAFF

Parents often ask when to become angst-ridden about the college process. Most experts agree that the right time is the last Wednesday in April of your child's sophomore year in high school. If it happens to be that Wednesday, here is a handy checklist of essential resources:

☑ **SAT Tutor** The best ones must be booked by eighth grade. But lots of luck finding out who the good ones are (parents don't like to share—fear of competition and fee inflation). Although the super tutors have no qualifications other than being smart kids who performed well on their own SATs, their fees are similar to what you would be charged by a junior partner in a corporate law firm. $150 to $550 an hour.

☑ **ACT Tutor** Few trends start in the Midwest, but the ACT is now spreading like gangbusters. If you live in NY or LA, you must find someone in Des Moines who is willing to work by Skype. $100 an hour (until they find out how much the SAT guys are charging).

☑ **Highlight Reel Producer** (for athletes). Bring this guy a pile of blurry videos and he will edit them to make it look as if your kid has better ball skills than David Beckham. $2,500 for the ones who add "Hey There, You're an All-star" as the soundtrack, more for those with better musical taste.

☑ **Audition Coach** (for actors). Although the Neurotic Parent Institute is based in Southern California, where there are thousands of audition coaches, it is necessary to fly one in from Dallas so our children won't come off as "too Hollywood." (We swear, this is true.) In just three two-hour sessions, this expert middle American will help your young thespian seem more conservative. She will provide hair and wardrobe advice, as well as a recommendation for a headshot photographer from Oklahoma. Once the Texan receives her kickback, the Oklahoman will make sure your child looks wholesome in his or her photos. Fees are very reasonable: $1,500 for the audition coach and $800 for the headshot photographer (plus airfare and lodging at The Standard).

☑ *Waitlist Specialist* Arguably the most important resource on this list. Call her immediately after your senior is deferred. She will help you bombard each college with heartfelt letters about how that school was your child's absolute first choice. $500 per letter.

☑ *Independent College Counselor* Many parents like to hire an independent counselor so they won't have to nag their kids about deadlines or make phone calls to get them internships at cancer-research facilities. Parents who say they "never even glanced at any of Tyler's eighteen applications" used independent counselors. Book by ninth grade. $1,500 to $40,000.

☑ *Co-dependent College Counselor* Similar to an independent counselor, but instead of relieving anxiety, they create more. Fees vary.

Of course, ninth-grade parents, there might be a light at the end of the tunnel. This madness could end, and maybe there will be a dip in the difficult years for admissions. So just enter your 14-year-old in a biorobotics competition and try to relax.

APPLICATION BOOT CAMP:
A MERE $3,500 A DAY

*I*f you have a ninth grader and some extra cash after the collapse of the U.S. economy, you might consider hiring Dr. H, an independent college counselor. For $40,000, Dr. H will get your children on the right track for highly selective schools. She will put them in quirky activities so they will have a hook by the time the application process comes around. Then, during senior year, she'll offer essay-writing help, including brainstorming and unlimited revisions.

In a recent NPR interview, Dr. H said that many parents who think college prestige will give their kids better lives seek out her services in today's difficult times. "How many newspaper articles do you read about the valedictorian with the 1600 who did not get in?" she asked.

If you don't have 40 grand to spare or are starting late, your student can attend her four-day application boot camp for only $14,000. Dr. H claims that this experience is so beneficial that Dartmouth chose one of her attendee's essays as one of its six best essays of the year. She acknowledges that this never would have happened if Dartmouth (where she used to work as an admissions counselor) had known she worked with the writer of the essay. In fact, even though she "preserved the student's voice," Dartmouth might have never even accepted the student.

So not only does Dr. H give you invaluable guidance, but hiring her is dangerous and exciting—on top of all the other junior- and senior-year stresses, you have to keep your fingers crossed that nobody finds out your child has a puppetmaster.

The head of admissions from the University of Chicago told NPR that what Dr. H is doing ("retooling" essays and packaging clients) constitutes "perpetrating a fraud." "Some of my best friends are independent counselors," he said. "They offer help, but they don't go too far."

At the end of the segment, the NPR folks introduced two staffers, one who attended Yale and one who attended St. Olaf's, a school with no name recognition. Look, they said, these two ended up with the exact same job. So why are all you guys stressing? If you can stand sitting with your snarky teen for hours while they rewrite their unreadable essays at the last minute, then you can use the $40K to remodel your kitchen.

Chapter

three

THE EARLY YEARS

Yes, you really do need to kiss up to the director of the Yellow Balloon Preschool

THE ITSY-BITSY FISKE GUIDE

Aa	is for Amherst/prestigious and preppy/but trying to get there/is a bit schleppy
Bb	is for Boulder/the skiing is great/you can get in/if you're from out of state
Cc	is for Caltech/this is where you will be/if you got 36/on the math ACT
Dd	is for Deep Springs/a fine two-year gig/you'll analyze Chaucer/and kill your own pig
Ee	is for Emory/Southern school-Northern folk/Salman Rushdie's a prof/his big check comes from Coke
Ff	is for Fordham/now on the west side/if you are a Jesuit/you might get a full ride
Gg	is for Georgetown/a place you will love/just take three SAT IIs/you can then be a gov
Hh	is for Harvard/you will someday be boss/of your very own start-up/just avoid Winkelvoss
Ii	is for I-U/a rah-rah state school/though it's in Indiana/the Midwest is now cool
Jj	is for Johns Hopkins/go there for pre-med/but if you want beer pong/check out Lehigh instead
Kk	is for Kenyon/this place is the bomb/sometime in your future/you'll write a sitcom
Ll	is for Lawrence/where cheese-making thrives/it appeared in a book/of schools that change lives
Mm	is for McGill/Montreal is très nice/and the best part by far is/the fees are half price
Nn	is for Northwestern/many would kill/to matriculate there/despite the wind chill
Oo	is for Oberlin/you can play the French horn/and pursue social justice/in a field filled with corn
Pp	is for Princeton/a top learning hub/you'll soon rule the world/with your whole eating club
Qq	is for Quinnipiac/a nice LAC/for those who missed Yale/with a low SAT
Rr	is for RISD/in Providence town/you'll conceptualize/and take classes at Brown
Ss	is for Stanford/you know the name well/too bad that it looks/ like a huge Taco Bell
Tt	is for Tufts/not very much sun/but there's global studies/and a naked quad run
Uu	is for U-T/'cause Austin is green/and liberal (for Texas)/with a cool music scene
Vv	is for Vassar/once just for the gals/now guys can sign up/for their many chorales
Ww	is for WashU/in St. Louis, that is/be sure to apply/if you're a bio-med whiz
Xx	is for Xavier/not far from Tulane/just bring a good raft/for the next hurricane
Yy	is for Yale/your kids might get in/if they win Intel awards/and have noteworthy kin
Zz	is for Zane State/this is where you might go/if your GPA is/below 3.0

EXCERPT FROM A B+ SUCKS

The sun shone outside
But I could not play
I was thinking ahead
To a high GPA

I sat there with Tyler
(He's 5 and a loser)
I'm sure when he grows up
That he'll be a boozer

While Tyler was shrieking
"Weee, weee, weee, weee,"
I worked on my skills
For the PSAT

Now is the time
To line up my ducks
I have to start now:
'Cause just one B+ sucks

From the annals of the Neurotic Parent blog

THE RIGHT PRESCHOOL = THE RIGHT COLLEGE

My son CJ graduated from Blue Dolphin Preschool in 1995. Last night we had a reunion barbecue with five other BD families, all with sons who had been CJ's friends when they were 3, 4, and 5.

Our get-together was a celebration of the high school graduation of the three older boys, who were born in the summer of 1990. The three younger boys, including CJ, were born in the fall, so they started elementary school a year later than their friends because they missed the cut-off date for kindergarten.

One parent put together an emotional video of BD highlights, which we watched twice. Wiping away tears, we saw our wide-eyed sons on a field trip to the fire station and proudly wearing jeweled crowns on their birthdays. The boys looked so tiny and adorable that it was almost impossible to believe that the big, hairy men sprawled on the couch were the same people.

The evening was not just nostalgic, but it also provided hope. The graduates' list of college acceptances was so impressive that one would never guess that this is the most difficult year to get into college in the history of the world. One boy is headed to Tufts. Another will be attending UCLA. And the third has enrolled at Oberlin (turning down Wesleyan, Vassar, Reed, Kenyon, and McGill), but first he is taking an inspirational gap year—part Kerouac road trip, part Katrina volunteer.

Was it a coincidence that these kids all did so well? Probably not. Word is that all the kids who attend BD get into phenomenal colleges

years later. What could it be? This was a school that offered very little in the way of traditional academics. There was no counting, and I don't even remember the students singing the alphabet. The teachers were not particularly scholarly—one was recently sighted working as a bagger at a local supermarket. What, then, was Blue Dolphin's secret?

A preliminary study by the Neurotic Parent Institute discovered that the curriculum was primarily comprised of the following:

1) Singing
2) Cooking
3) Sand Play
4) Guinea Pig Care
5) Holiday Celebrations

Sounds like fun, but these were not the learning endeavors that led to Tufts, UCLA, and Oberlin.

Then, after more intensive research, we discovered the answer: Scissors.

Yes, Blue Dolphin emphasized cutting skills. So much so that during one of our parent/teacher conferences, CJ's teacher told us to start him on an intensive practice regime, because he wasn't cutting anywhere in the vicinity the dotted line on his worksheets. At first we contemplated hiring a scissors tutor, but fortunately we remembered enough about shears from our own preschool days to help him on our own. He worked so hard perfecting his scissors skills that by the time he started kindergarten, you'd never have guessed he'd overcome such a severe disability.

By next year, we'll find out if that early cutting instruction paid off.

LEAKED E-MAILS BETWEEN THE
NEUROTIC PARENT & THE TIGER MOTHER

We must disclose that more than a decade ago, the Neurotic Parent Institute was contacted by the controversial Yale professor who wouldn't let her kids have sleepovers and coined the phrase, "A B is an Asian F." Although her kids were then only 3 and 6, she was desperate to find a surefire way for them to gain acceptance to the top Ivy League schools. Our response to the Tiger Mother was honest but a bit unconventional. We never thought she'd go for our radical suggestions, but as the ultimate helicopter parent, she followed the advice to the letter, and now it looks as though we might have influenced the course of international parenting history. Here's the e-mail exchange:

From: **Tiger Mother**
Subject: Dear Neurotic Parent
To: Neurotic Parent

Dear Neurotic Parent,

Perhaps you can help me. Although I am a superior Chinese mother, I just realized that I have made a terrible parenting mistake. I forced my daughters to learn the piano and the violin, and they are now virtuosos. However, as you know, the Ivies will be flooded with applications from thousands of other Asian kids who have studied these instruments. Can you help?

Best regards, Tiger Mom

From: **neurotic**
Subject: Re: Dear Neurotic Parent
To: Tiger Mother

Hi Tiger Mom,

Yes, I'm afraid you have made a serious mistake. But there is still hope! Perhaps you should marry a member of an under-represented minority—an Upper Chinook would be perfect. Then the admissions committees might overlook the fact that your kids have mastered ordinary instruments like the piano and the violin.

Fondly,
The Neurotic Parent

From: **Tiger Mother**
Subject: Re: Re: Dear Neurotic Parent
To: Neurotic Parent

Oops! I'm already married to a Jewish guy (law professor and novelist). I don't think the colleges will count him as an under-represented minority. Any other suggestions?

Tiger Mom

From: **neurotic**
Subject: Re: Re: Re: Dear Neurotic Parent
To: Tiger Mother

Okay... How about this? It's a long shot, but it just might work. What if you became absurdly strict with your daughters—almost borderline abusive? You could forbid play dates and sleepovers, and perhaps even burn their stuffed animals if they don't get straight As. That would give your girls plenty of material for great college essays, full of conflict. What do you think?

The Neurotic Parent

From: **Tiger Mother**
Subject: Re: Re: Re: Re: Dear Neurotic Parent
To: Neurotic Parent

Wow! I may have two degrees from Harvard and an endowed chair at Yale Law School, but YOU, Neurotic Parent, are a TRUE genius! I'll start torturing my children right away. I will call them "garbage," threaten to throw the 3-year-old out in the snow, and maybe even give their dollhouses to Goodwill. That kind of anguished upbringing should produce the most powerful essays ever, guaranteed to tug at the heartstrings of any admissions committee. I could even publish a memoir about my extreme cruelty—I bet I could get a six-figure advance if I market the book as a quasi-parenting manual and link my absurd philosophy to my race. Then the girls will be able to use the proceeds from the book to pay for college. I cannot thank you enough for the brilliant advice, Neurotic Parent. It will be a LOT easier to abuse my children than to have them start all over with less-common instruments like the trombone or the harpsichord. You can bet I will be back in touch when they're applying to law school.

Your #1 Fan,

Tiger Mom

HOW TO SUE YOUR PRESCHOOL

It's not so easy to get into the right preschool. But if you don't like it once you get in, there's always litigation.

From the *Wall Street Journal*: "A Manhattan woman is suing an Upper East Side preschool, arguing that its classroom environment didn't challenge her 4-year-old daughter or adequately prepare the child for the exam that elite private schools require for admission."

The suit, filed by Nicole Imprescia, claims that the selective, $19,000-a-year York Avenue Preschool perpetuated "a complete fraud" when it said it would prepare 4-year-old Lucia for the Educational Records Bureau exam. "Indeed, the school proved not to be a school at all, but just one big playroom," the suit alleged. The suit further said Imprescia was upset that her daughter was learning about shapes and colors at age 4. She pulled her daughter one month into the school year and demanded a refund of the $19,000.

York's website said its curriculum included weekly library visits, French lessons, and music. But Imprescia alleged that the preschool had instead placed her daughter in a classroom with kids half her age, learning those tedious lessons about shapes and colors.

Luckily, in other parts of the country, there are no entrance exams for private kindergartens. In those areas, schools stick to old-fashioned requirements—like who you know and how rich you are.

JUNIOR KUMON OFFERS BOTOX FOR PRESCHOOLERS

Goodbye bubbles, hello bubbling. The *New York Times* recently reported that there are now almost 40 Junior Kumon centers in New York, where 2-year-olds can begin prepping for the SATs they will take in 2027. The director of the Battery Park Center said space is tight, but "If they're out of a diaper and can sit still with a Kumon instructor for 15 minutes, we will take them."

We've discovered that Junior Kumon plans to offer enrichment in other areas necessary for kindergarten acceptance:

• Cello lessons (most kindergartens already have their quota of violinists)
• C++ and Python (with Java offered for those who stay after naptime)
• Calc BC flashcards during snack (extra Goldfish for those who master parametric equations)
• Dissection of the class bunny (using patented blunt-pointed surgical tools)
• Sing-alongs to Rigoletto and Götterdämmerung
• Botox injections in the dress-up corner (for those unsightly pout lines)

One of the parents quoted in the NYT piece said her children also take swimming, karate, music, art, and German—but she wouldn't think of giving up Kumon. Of course, these kids must quit playing hide and seek, digging in the sandbox, and eating Play-Doh. But hey, if you can't figure out the surface area of a prism by the time you're 3, you can kiss those MIT hopes goodbye.

PREP GOES THE WEASEL

*It is never too early to
begin padding your resume*

EARLY ACTION

If you've managed to get your child into the right preschool and then kindergarten, you can relax for a few years...NOT. Even if your son or daughter is only in third grade, this is the time to make sure he or she will have interesting passions to write about ten years or so down the line.

Here's a sneak preview of what colleges say they're looking for. This chart, adapted from the Common Data Set, lists the criteria that one top school consider for admissions, as well as the importance of each category rated with stars. It should be sufficient to help you screw up your kids' childhoods, starting as early as the second grade.

ACADEMIC CRITERIA	
★ ★ ★ ★	Rigor of high school classes
★ ★ ★ ★	Class rank
★ ★ ★ ★	Academic GPA
★ ★ ★ ★	Standardized test scores
★ ★ ★ ★	Application essay
★ ★ ★	Recommendation(s)
NON-ACADEMIC CRITERIA	
★ ★	Interview
★ ★ ★ ★	Extracurricular activities
★ ★ ★	Talent/ability
★ ★ ★ ★	Character/personal qualities
★ ★	First generation
★ ★	Alumni/ae relation
★ ★	Geographical residence
★ ★	State residency
★	Religious affiliation / Commitment
★ ★	Racial/ethnic status
★ ★	Volunteer work
★ ★	Work experience
★	Level of applicant's interest

ADMISSIONS CRITERIA KEY			
★ ★ ★ ★	Very Important	★ ★	Considered
★ ★ ★	Important	★	Not Considered

Whether or not "geographical" is actually a word (shouldn't it be geographic?), we feel that this chart can alleviate stress down the road. It is never too early to think about curriculum rigor, to conjure up an unusual talent or ability, or to change one's geographic(al) residence.

Of course, since this is an insiders' guide, we feel compelled to share with you a chart that illustrates colleges' *real* admissions criteria—like any school, they just want to accept kids whose parents will not complain. The fewer questions you ask at information sessions about the issues listed below, the more likely that your child will be accepted.

ADMISSIONS CRITERIA—
NO PARENTAL COMPLAINING ABOUT:

	ACADEMIC CRITERIA		
✶ ✶ ✶ ✶	*Grade deflation*		
✶ ✶ ✶ ✶	*Professors who don't speak English*		
✶ ✶ ✶ ✶	*Not getting into classes*		
✶ ✶ ✶ ✶	*Lack of research opportunities*		
✶ ✶ ✶ ✶	*Hard tests*		
✶ ✶ ✶	*Classes taught by TAs*		
	NON-ACADEMIC CRITERIA		
✶	*Faulty A/C in the dorm*		
✶ ✶ ✶ ✶	*High cost of attorneys for drinking violations*		
✶ ✶ ✶	*Naked runs*		
✶ ✶ ✶ ✶	*Freshman 15*		
✶ ✶	*Freshman 30*		
✶ ✶	*Eating disorders*		
✶ ✶	*High-gluten lunches*		
	ADMISSIONS CRITERIA KEY		
✶ ✶ ✶ ✶	Very Important	✶ ✶	Considered
✶ ✶ ✶	Important	✶	Not Considered

The Neurotic Parent Answers Your Questions

WII ARE THE WORLD—THE WORLD OF WARCRAFT HONORS SOCIETY, THAT IS

Q: Dear Neurotic Parent Institute,
I trust your opinion. Please tell me right away if I can list my passion for video games as an extracurricular on my Common App? I play very strategic online games, and my gaming is a true passion. I sometimes practice up to eighteen hours a day. Plus, there is more leadership in games than there is in sports, since in   sports it's hard to communicate over the whole field. What do you think?

A: Yes, absolutely. Be honest. Be yourself. Let your *you* shine through. College counselors will be thrilled to learn about your passions, even if they're a total waste of time and eventually lead to antisocial, violent behavior. (This advice is particularly applicable if you're applying to the same schools as our children.)

COLLEGE CONFIDENTIAL:
THE SCARIEST PLACE ON THE INTERNET

After a Neurotic Parent Institute board meeting, we almost decided to give College Confidential its own chapter in this book. Never mind that 96.3% of the parents on the site have lost their senses of humor. And every time we log on we feel guilty about investing in progressive education instead of Mensa flashcards. Or that *Urban Dictionary* calls it the "douchiest website on the internet."

The bottom line is that if you are a neurotic parent, it is not a bad idea to stay away from the web watering hole for the super kids who are stealing places right and left from bright, normal students.

But if you need any college-related information at all—from which schools superscore the ACTs to lists of merit scholarships for left-handed students—you should establish an account by the time your student is in fifth grade. Then you can post any sort of question about college admissions and receive multiple answers in minutes. And it's a great place to hang out if you've already alienated all your friends by discussing nothing but the C word for a year.

Here is a typical query from a student:

Today, 01:24 PM	#1
512774442 New Member Join Date: Jun 2011 Posts: 4	should i retake 2330? **I just got 2330 in the may test, CR800, Writing 770, but only 760 on math, should i retake the test???**

And if you think the students on the site are rare birds, check out what the parents concern themselves with:

Today, 09:05 PM	#x
prd1992 New Member Join Date: Jun 2011 Posts: 4	College that looks like Harvard/Yale/Princeton **My daughter is a high school soph, and an A- student. She will not qualify for an Ivy League school, but she wants to go to a college or university that looks like Harvard, Yale, or Princeton. You know the look—old stone or brick buildings, lots of big trees. Are there schools that accept A- students that have that look?**

THE CCBS APP

It has come to the attention of the Neurotic Parent Institute that many posters on College Confidential are just not telling the truth. The nerdy kids who ask for their "chances" at top schools often lie about their SAT scores and exaggerate their extracurriculars. And the desperate parents who spend their weekends giving inaccurate advice are even more unethical.

Recently one poster told a poor orphan in Mumbai to give up his dream of going to Princeton.

Here's the exchange:

Today, 01:24 PM	#1

prd1992
New Member

Join Date: Jun 2011
Posts: 2011

Do I stand a chance?

**Hi I'm just about to start my senior year at school (Aloo Gobi School for Boys, Mumbai) and I'd like to apply to Princeton. I am a nine-toed orphan who lives in a ditch with no electricity. (Planning to write my essay about how I lost the other toe.) Please have a look at my stats and tell me if I stand a chance...
SAT: CR - 750, Math - 800, Writing -780 (2350) SAT 2: Math 2 - 800, Litrature (sic)– 740 (I know, I'm a moron, will retake) Class Rank: 1 GPA (unweighted): 3.93 APs: 17 (my school offers 18, but I had a conflict)**

Senior Year Courses: AP Chaucer, AP Neuroeconomics, AP Multivariable Calculus, AP Mongolian History, AP Computer Science (online course with Mark Zuckerberg as personal tutor).

Sports: Water Polo (Olympics): 2 gold, 1 silver – 35th Junior National Aquatic Championships 2008: 2 gold, 1 bronze – Selected for the national level swimming coaching camp for the preparation of Bengali Swimming Team for the Commonwealth Youth Games.

Debate: Participated & secured 3rd position at the Inter-School debate on "Refugees & Internally Displaced Persons Are the Same People" conducted by West

continued	#1
	Bengal Federation of United Nations Associations and the United Nations High Commissioner for Refugees.

Model UN: Was instrumental in the staging of the first-ever Model United Nations in Eastern India. Built a replica of the real United Nations out of mud, then populated it with 250 delegates from 167 countries. Participated at the Harvard Model United Nations Pakistan, held in Abbottabad, and was declared Outstanding Delegate in the UNSC.

Other: Ranked second in West Bengal in the BFD National Scholarship Test. Regular contributor to several newspapers in Mumbai. Student guest anchor on the morning news.

Please let me know if i have even a slim chance and tell me where i need to improve in order to get into Princeton... |

Today, 01:24 PM	#2
Mauve
Senior Member

Join Date: Jun 2011
Posts: 2,225 | Sorry, dude, but you don't stand out enough. Everybody swims and does model UN. And if it's your pinky toe that's missing, the adcoms see hundreds of essays on that topic. Plus, didn't they even teach you how to spell literature? No wonder you only got a 740. I hope you have some safeties. |

To dispel this kind of irresponsible online behavior, the NPI is proud to offer the **CCBS App**. Just install the app and roll your cursor over any post with a negative response, and you will see what the poster was really thinking.

Here is an example of how the app works: When you place your cursor on Mauve's post above, you'll see what he/she was really thinking:

Today, 01:24 PM	#2
Mauve
Senior Member

Posts: 2,225 | Oy. I have no shot if this guy applies. Better convince him to try for Muhlenberg instead. |

CLAM FARTING

Just when you wish the College Confidential server would explode so you could stop reading about those kids who want to retake their 2340 SATs, CC redeems itself. It is invaluable, of course, for finding out anything you need to know about colleges: median SAT scores, which schools count the writing, what other kids wrote for their supplemental essays, and even the best place to store your stuff over the summer once you get into college. But occasionally, something priceless crops up—the kind of concern that a cultural anthropologist could write a thesis about. Of all of those threads, one in particular deserves a shout-out.

As a joke, a student wrote on his Common App that his primary extracurricular activity was "clam farting." And, if you can believe him, he was accepted to Yale.

03-14, 01:24 PM	#1
SillBill **Junior Member** **Join Date: Aug 2007** **Posts: 234**	Clam fart!!!!!!!! Oh my God... What did I do?! I just realized that I listed "clam fart" as an extracurricular activity on my application to Yale. *dies* I was filling it out while one of my friends was over at my house, and she was intently watching as I filled it out (which was annoying me). So, as a shocker, I typed in "clam fart" and she started laughing hysterically. BUT I FORGOT TO DELETE IT!!!!! What's worse is that I wrote that I had been doing it for 17 years!!!!!!!!!!!! I don't even know what a clam fart is!!!!! It's already submitted (obviously), but I didn't re-read the printed version of my application closely until today. Should I call the office of admissions??

03-14, 01:28 PM	#2
BedHead **Senior Member** **Join Date: Nov 2006** **Posts: 1,494**	I think the most serious issue here is the perceived lying that you have been involved in clam fart for 17 years. That kind of lying gets even those granted admission rescinded. Less important, but still not good for you, is the fact that you left clam fart activities on your application simply because you didn't proofread carefully enough. Good luck. I hope you've learned something from this.

03-14, 02:01 PM   #3

SillBill
Junior Member

Join Date: Aug 2007
Posts: 234

Learned something? No, I didn't learn anything. I was joking around with my friend, and I made a simple mistake by missing it when I proofread. Do you want me to get rid of my personality? You don't have to be rude.

03-14, 06:27 PM   #4

somni
Member

Join Date: Feb 2008
Posts: 962

17 years? at least they'll think you're devoted to it.

03-14, 07:53 PM   #5

strandlib
Junior Member
Join Date: Jul 2007
Posts: 123

Asking whether Yale reviews their applications thoroughly now makes me question the validity of your claim. Besides, clam fart, while funny, simply does not sound like a legitimate EC. I mean, maybe if you said you were clam farting with low-income children, or feeding clam farts to the poor at a homeless shelter, it would sound legit, but clam farting on its own sounds ridiculous.

03-14, 07:58 PM   #6

Sligh_Anarchist
News Editor

Join Date: Jul 2007
Posts: 1,916

Does it really matter that you have been participating in clam farting for 17 years? The real question is whether you have achieved anything in clam farting! Where are your clam farting leadership skills?

03-14, 8:39 PM   #7

A-Card
Member

Join Date: Oct 2007
Posts: 667

don't you know? clam fart is one of the most popular activities at yale. They are know (sic) for it throughout the world.

04-03, 09:40 PM   #8

Sligh_Anarchist
News Editor

Join Date: Jul 2007
Posts: 1,916

Has this guy said if he has gotten accepted or not? I believe decisions are out, right?

04-03, 11:38 PM	#9
SillBill Junior Member Join Date: Aug 2007 Posts: 234	**I got in. I CANNOT believe it.** **Clam farts for everyone!!!!** **Thank you all for your support** **throughout my meltdown!**

04-04, 02:05 PM	#10
febreze88 Junior Member Join Date: Feb 2008 Posts: 94	**CLAM-GRATULATIONS!!!!**

04-04, 02:11 PM	#11
doctordestiny Member Join Date: Jul 2007 Posts: 321	**I think you've found a new hook to put in** **those college admissions books.**

04-04, 10:44 PM	#12
somni Member Join Date: Feb 2008 Posts: 962	**Maybe they don't even read applications.**

VETTING THE CLAM FART KID

The Neurotic Parent Institute felt compelled to check the validity of this whole thread, so we called Yale Admissions. Here is a transcript of our conversation:

THE NEUROTIC PARENT: Hi—Is this Yale Admissions?

YALE: Please listen carefully because our menu has changed. If you're calling to find out if you should retake the SATs if you got a 2350, press 1. If you're calling because you think our admissions video is lame, press 2. If you're calling to authenticate the validity of the Clam Fart Thread on College Confidential, press 3.

THE NEUROTIC PARENT: (presses 3)

YALE: Please enjoy the music while your party is reached (plays the Whiffenpoofs).

THE NEUROTIC PARENT: Hi, I'm writing a book about college admissions.

YALE: Great. Please tell your readers that we don't care if they got a 2350 or a 2400.

THE NEUROTIC PARENT: Will do. But I'm mostly interested in the clam farting kid. Did he really get in, or was he an internet troll?

YALE: Yes, he is here, studying crustaceans and enjoying life in one of our residential colleges (bursts into song, tune of the Yale admissions video):

When he was a student in Pre-K
Every kid there was just the same.
He'd often beach comb
not far from his home,
clamming was his claim to fame.
Then when he went through the options
Of how to stand out in his class,
He sent some mail to a college called Yale.
They said, "train your shellfish to pass gas."

THE NEUROTIC PARENT: Wow, thanks so much. Good to know.

YALE: Any other questions?

THE NEUROTIC PARENT: Yes. How about a 2320? Does that warrant a retake?

From the annals of the Neurotic Parent blog

LIST YOUR AWARDS

I, the Neurotic Parent, have been tracking (obsessed with) our older son CJ's college admissions process for over a year. But that does not mean I have forgotten that I have a younger son, GC, a ninth grader. Even though I have neglected GC for the last nine months, he has remained focused on his extracurriculars, and last week he came home with his first high school–level award, which we will save in a folder and report on his college apps in just three short years.

The Award? The Triple King Challenge. Here's what the certificate says:

CONGRATULATIONS ON CONQUERING
THE TRIPLE KING CHALLENGE
(We deem you King of all Carnivores)
Awarded to: GC
At: Brentwood Fatburger

Yes, my son, completely on his own, with odds stacked against him at 5'7" and under 115 pounds, managed to consume an entire Fatburger triple cheeseburger in one sitting. Okay, he did leave off the pickles and onions, but nonetheless it's an achievement! Now he has a head start on this significant EC—and I wouldn't be surprised if there's a Quadruple King Challenge in his future.

UPDATE: As we go to press, GC, now 5'11 and 140 pounds, has confessed to the unthinkable: He cheated on the Triple King Challenge by slipping bites of burger over to his buddies when nobody was looking. But the good news is that his disclosure to us after all these years could make for a good essay topic.

SAMPLE ACTIVITY SHEET

In case you don't have enough room to list your many extracurriculars and awards, the Common App invites you to attach a resumé. This is where you get the admissions committees (or, as they are called on College Confidential, adcoms) to feel bad, by showing them that your kids have more accomplishments at age 17 than the admissions officers do at age 42.

We are pleased to offer a sample activity *sheet. Feel free to use it as a template.*

Your name:
Your address:
Your name: **Your e-mail address:**
Belcherville High School, Class of _____

ACADEMIC ACHIEVEMENTS/AWARDS
- Second Place Spelunking (12)
- Excellence in Sustainable Turnip Farming award (11)
- Excellence in Fire-breathing award (9)

LEADERSHIP
- President and founder of Collagen for the Homeless Club (12)
- State Advisory Bingo Conference (12)
- Acne Council (9, 10, 11, 12)

ACTIVITIES
- Varsity Badminton (10, 11, 12)
- Varsity Badminton co-captain (11, 12)
- D.A.R.E. badminton (9, 10, 11, 12)
- Freshman/junior varsity badminton (9)

COMMUNITY SERVICE
- Volunteer at FML Talent Show (9, 10, 11, 12)
- Volunteer as tour guide for FML open house and orientation (9, 10, 11, 12)
- Jumpstart Molecular Physics Program for Preschool (12)
- 15 hours raking lawns (11)
- Toys for Twitter (11)
- Alex's Red Bull Stand (11)
- Walk for Herpes (10, 11)
- Tacos for Tennis Elbow (9, 10)
- Bottle and clothing drive for FML athletics (9)

EMPLOYMENT
- Salmon Breeder & Spawner, Upstream Salmon Farm
  (seasonal, 20 hrs/wk) (10)
- Translator, Tagalog/Swahili (weekends, Cascade Mini-Golf)

[REAL TEEN ACTIVITIES TO LEAVE OFF]

LEADERSHIP
- Captain, Fantasy Football League (11, 12)
- Vice-president, Mean Girls Club (7, 8)

BODY ART
- Most Hidden Tattoos Award (12)
- Multiple Piercing Certificate (11)

DRIVING
- Frequent Customer Award, FenderBenders.com Traffic School (12)

RETAIL EXPERIENCE
- Shopping (9, 10, 11, 12)
- Shoplifting (9)

From the annals of the Neurotic Parent blog

I WANT TO BE, LIKE, ACADEMICALLY CHALLENGED

Last Thursday was College Night at CJ's school, and he was invited to be a member of a student panel for rising seniors. The intent was to demystify the college application process and provide sage advice for those about to embark on the journey.

A few hours before the panel, CJ received an e-mail from his dean listing possible topics of discussion. One was "What I did during the summer between eleventh and twelfth grade." Because that summer was a full seven months ago, CJ had trouble remembering, but once I reminded him about his eight-hour a day summer job at a major concert venue, he felt prepared to serve on the panel.

I asked if I could attend (after all, I always need blog material), but of course, I was the last person he wanted in the audience.

CJ said the evening went well, but I had to rely on the parents of juniors for details. One mom said her son thought the student panel was the highlight of the entire event, even better than essay advice from the University of Chicago admissions representative. The mom said that the panel consisted of kids who had been accepted early to NYU, Vassar, MIT, and CJ's school, plus four who were waiting to hear.

Her son reported that although the students on the panel provided him with great tips, one panelist constantly used the word "like."

I immediately assumed that CJ was the culprit because of his eight years at summer camp with (San Fernando) Valley kids. How will he survive a freshman seminar at his prestigious college? But when I confronted him with the news that kids were critiquing his diction, he laughed and admonished me for jumping to conclusions. He said that one of the other panelists said "like" so much that it was, like, out of control. That student is waiting to hear about a full scholarship at Berkeley, where they do not require interviews.

From the annals of the Neurotic Parent blog

THE MOST TIME-CONSUMING EXTRACURRICULAR

People often ask what it takes to play club soccer. For kids, it's speed, agility, and fortitude. For their parents, it is a willingness to spend eleven years driving four to eight hours every weekend.

These drives involve finding your way to places you've never visited but have heard mentioned on the news when there are gang killings or extreme weather. The games are scheduled for 7 a.m. and 5 p.m., leaving you with six hours to kill in cities with few offerings besides a Denny's and a Walmart.

Club soccer, of course, is not the only interest that prevents kids—and their parents—from having a life. There are other sports, like volleyball, which means spending weekends at the Comfort Inn in Reno. There are also dance competitions, horse shows, and chess tournaments, all of which require giving up all your free time, as well as all your exercise time—the result is watching your kid get the exercise while you eat Kettle Korn.

Until recently, the Law of Inconvenient Youth Logistics ensured that if your child became interested in an activity, it would never be available at a normal hour within a 20-mile radius of your place of residence. But now, thankfully, more and more students are pursuing a challenging extracurricular that can be practiced right in their own homes, often for as long as six hours a day, seven days a week. And it is an activity that teaches the importance of individual accomplishment rather than the clichéd lessons of teamwork.

That activity is Facebook.

I didn't appreciate the enormous skillset necessary for Facebook until I signed up. Even a beginner needs talents in computer science, graphic arts, photography, creative writing, and pretending to like photos of their childhood friends' cats. Unlike sports and other popular extracurriculars, Facebook requires no uniforms, costumes, or equipment. It is cheap, convenient, and injury free.

And the networking potential is so immense that Facebookers might never need to go to college. They can recruit thousands of friends who will invite them places and even get them jobs, not to mention send annoying Farmville requests without ever having to actually speak to them. They can even become famous, like GC's friend's sister, who is an "Internet It Girl" with 4,243 friends.

But Facebook is an activity that is appropriate only for the most focused, driven kids. You cannot dabble—three hours a day is the bare minimum required for the child who chooses this as his or her passion.

So give away the cleats and sell the horse. This is the activity you want your kids to excel at. And it is essential that they start when they are very young—although I like to consider myself reasonably computer literate, I still cannot figure out when it's my turn at Scrabble.

FACEBOOK FACELIFT

facebook   Search | Q

About You (Before)   ✎ Edit

Recent Activity

You joined the group Friend of Spark Notes

You joined the group I Don't Remember Getting this Bruise

You joined the group I Have Junioritis

You added Ocean Park Medical Marijuana Clinic as your friend

You are attending the Malibu Goth Naked After-party

You have 13,864 unanswered SAT questions of the day

> Has anyone seen my wallet? I had it just before I
> blacked out in the taxi.
> August 30 at 3:21pm · Like

> Dude, I think you left it at Bevmo.
> August 30 at 3:21pm · Like

> LOL – it's gonna be a fortune to replace that fake id
> August 30 at 3:21pm · Like

Activities & Interests   I'm studying my ass off right now...LOL jk, I'm on Facebook liking everything; The Librarians at my School Take Their Job Way Too Seriously; Not Wearing Pants; Every Girl has a Slutty Friend; I Hate Mondays, Tuesdays, Wednesdays, Thursdays, and Half of Friday; Summer Needs to Come Already; I may be going to hell but at least all of my friends will be there; That awkward moment when a girl brings you the wrong kind of sandwich; The 3 B's: Brews, Bitches, and Blunts; "Why yes, I AM a Pokemon Master"; I LOVE YOU...lol jk I'm drunk

Religious views   Pastafarian

Movies   Superbad, Pineapple Express, Anchorman, Zoolander

Activities   Super Smash Bros., the Legend of Zelda, Sexual Tension, Performing Satanic Rituals, Fist Pumping

Favorite Quotations   "Sometimes you just gotta toot it and boot it"
                        "I'll be the one on the corner in the trenchcoat who looks like a bag lady"
                        "Even when I'm on my back, I never back down" — Lil' Wayne
                        "If we're all going to hell in a handbasket, we might as well make it a party on the way down."

College admissions officers are very busy people. The reason? In addition to reviewing applications, meeting with prospective students and parents, reading essays, ensuring that the college has a diverse student body, and singing in admissions videos, they are also analyzing your Facebook page.

Many teens think it's enough to change their name so they cannot be found (particularly to something clever—like Emma Newsom might become Emma Nem). But admissions officers have a knack for tracking down kids' pseudonyms.

With this in mind, the Neurotic Parent Institute is proud to offer a new service to help your child look like a desirable candidate.

Here are Before and After screen shots.

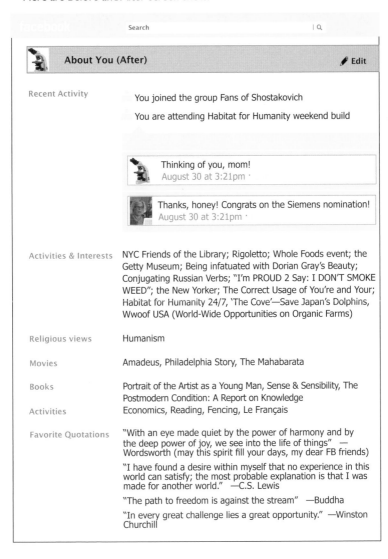

Facebook   Search | Q

About You (After)   ✎ Edit

Recent Activity

You joined the group Fans of Shostakovich

You are attending Habitat for Humanity weekend build

Thinking of you, mom!
August 30 at 3:21pm ·

Thanks, honey! Congrats on the Siemens nomination!
August 30 at 3:21pm ·

Activities & Interests   NYC Friends of the Library; Rigoletto; Whole Foods event; the Getty Museum; Being infatuated with Dorian Gray's Beauty; Conjugating Russian Verbs; "I'm PROUD 2 Say: I DON'T SMOKE WEED"; the New Yorker; The Correct Usage of You're and Your; Habitat for Humanity 24/7, 'The Cove'—Save Japan's Dolphins, Wwoof USA (World-Wide Opportunities on Organic Farms)

Religious views   Humanism

Movies   Amadeus, Philadelphia Story, The Mahabarata

Books   Portrait of the Artist as a Young Man, Sense & Sensibility, The Postmodern Condition: A Report on Knowledge

Activities   Economics, Reading, Fencing, Le Français

Favorite Quotations   "With an eye made quiet by the power of harmony and by the deep power of joy, we see into the life of things" — Wordsworth (may this spirit fill your days, my dear FB friends)

"I have found a desire within myself that no experience in this world can satisfy; the most probable explanation is that I was made for another world." —C.S. Lewis

"The path to freedom is against the stream" —Buddha

"In every great challenge lies a great opportunity." —Winston Churchill

From the annals of the Neurotic Parent blog

PASSIONISTAS

Yesterday, when I picked up my younger son, Good Conversationalist, he had just come from a meeting with his dean. He is starting high school next year and had to select his ninth-grade electives. He showed me the catalog and said that for a sport, he wanted to try cross-country.

I was horrified. He has always been a baseball player. Why was he suddenly thinking of trying something new?

Then he let the other shoe drop. "Mom," he said. "There is so much I want to try. I might want to stop doing graphic arts and take a semester of photography. Then maybe I'll do a year of speech and debate, and a summer program in creative writing. I'm going to run for Student Council and start a ping-pong club. And I want to take music composition, kayak lessons, and maybe even two languages: French and ancient Greek."

At that point I was too agitated to drive and had to pull over. How dare he become enthusiastic about so many different pursuits! What kind of kid had we raised?

"Stop right there," I said. "You cannot study all those things. How would that look to the admissions committees at the colleges where you're applying to four years from now? They want to see that you have just one passion, two at the most. Top candidates choose something they love in third grade and stick with it."

"But how am I supposed to have a passion now?" he asked. "I'm only 14!"

"Most 14-year-olds bound for selective schools already have won awards in their field of choice," I explained. "They know it's a terrible idea to have more than a few interests. So give it up."

He looked down. "But how am I going to know if I like something if I don't try it? Can't I be passionate about learning itself?"

Here it was: my worst parenting nightmare coming true. I shook my head and told myself it was all hormones, and he soon would return to baseball. But in my heart I knew he might be on the road to giving into his temptations. Any day, I imagined, I would be getting a call from the Dean of Students, letting me know that he was experimenting with both photography *and* Greek.

This was something that needed to be nipped in the bud. I dropped him off at Little League practice and went home to look into intervention programs.

COST OF COMMUNITY SERVICE

All of these are *real* programs for teens. And by now, the prices will have gone up.

Himalayan Adventure

A rugged journey intersecting the remote nomadic and mountain cultures of Ladakh's Zanskar Region. Collaborating with a number of internationally supported aid and development groups such as the Tibetan Nuns Project, we actively contribute to constructive development while also critiquing the work of the NGO community. Furthering our focus on environmental and naturalist studies, we visit with experts who run snow leopard conservancy projects and sustainability projects that promote cultural integration of renewable energy development, innovative land-use, and the use of traditional medicinal plants. We visit prominent monasteries and explore the cultural heritage and religious traditions by living with families in nearby mountain communities.

COST: $6,700. **FLIGHT**: $1,800

WHAT $8,500 WILL BUY IF YOU DONATE THE MONEY AND STAY AT HOME:
Homes for 50 villagers; textbooks for 1,500; vitamins for 5,000.

Bali Service Trip

Live in a small village in the hills of Nusa Penida, and work directly with our host community to complete a series of projects identified by the village council. In past years, we have made repairs to the island's many sacred temples, helped subsistence farmers tend their fields, organized a recycling and composting program, run an arts-based program for local children, and taught conversational English. You can also choose an independent research project based on your interests. Projects include learning a traditional Balinese dance, creating a cookbook of local recipes, working with a farmer to tend cows and pigs, or learning to play the gamelan. After our day of work is finished, we spend late afternoons exploring the beauty of the surrounding areas, playing pick-up games of Frisbee, soccer, or volleyball with village friends, or attending traditional ceremonies.

COST: $5,890. **FLIGHT**: $1,408

WHAT $7,298 WILL BUY IF YOU DONATE THE MONEY AND STAY AT HOME:
Vaccinations for 200,000 islanders; bicycles for 432 schoolchildren.

Ghana Service Trip

Study dance and music, participate in Twi language classes, and attend lectures on Ghanaian history, culture, and economics. Feast your eyes on colorful kente cloth in vibrant street markets, take a tro-tro minibus to the beach and experience the richness of Ghanaian wood carving, drum making, and weaving during a whirlwind introduction to Ghana and her people. Dig clean water wells; paint community buildings; repair and refurbish village schools; work at an orphanage.

COST: $6,600. **FLIGHT**: $1,682

WHAT $8,282 WILL BUY IF YOU DONATE THE MONEY AND STAY AT HOME:
Malaria prevention for 142,000; breakfasts for a year for 30,000 preschoolers.

Ecuador Visions

For three and a half weeks Patate is your home, where participants have constructed preschools, kiosks for central marketplaces, community cisterns, traditionally built ethnographic museums, and potable water systems. We teach English, arts and crafts, and sports to school children, have prepared greenhouse space for communal gardens, assisted reforestation efforts, and helped families milk cows, feed rabbits, and harvest crops.

COST: $5,440. **FLIGHT**: $988

WHAT $6,428 WILL BUY IF YOU DONATE THE MONEY AND STAY AT HOME:
A vacation at the Four Seasons on the Big Island for your parents, who deserve to travel this summer more than you do.

SUMMER CONUNDRUM

*E*verybody knows that colleges care about more than GPAs and standardized testing. They look at curriculum strength, essays, teacher recs, and, in particular, extracurriculars. It is no secret that the admissions committees are very concerned about what you do with your spare time, be it volunteering with lepers in India or interning as a trapeze artist with Cirque du Soleil.

And it is equally important that you do not begin a brand-new extracurricular activity during your junior year. The committees will not be impressed with your story unless you have demonstrated a lifelong passion for your extracurricular of choice.

This makes it a challenge to choose an activity for the summer between junior and senior year. Many neurotic parents struggle for months evaluating programs that will help their children's college chances. Theoretically, it is best to be selected for a prestigious, competitive program related to your passion, a program that you can categorize as an award or scholarship on your application. Unfortunately, there are only seven of these programs, and four are for New Jersey residents only. And, if you're anything like our son, you missed the deadlines, and your hang-gliding skills are so rusty that you probably wouldn't have qualified anyway.

That means you will have to choose between the following:

A CHALLENGING SUMMER COURSE AT AN IVY

Schools like Brown, Columbia, and Cornell offer fascinating classes for pre-college students—courses in great books, genomes, or globalization. Unfortunately, these programs cost $5,000 to $8,000, and although the colleges like keeping their dorms filled, they are not particularly impressed when they see these classes on your resume. They assume you're a rich kid who settled for genome studies because you couldn't get into a more prestigious program.

A LIFE-CHANGING TRIP TO A WAR-RIDDEN, DEVELOPING COUNTRY

These excursions, which often involve performing bunion surgery in Mongolia or training villagers in Guam to grow sustainable kale hydroponically, take high school students out of their comfort zones. The participants live with local families in mud huts and come back with a new appreciation for the after-parties they attend at home. Sadly, however, the colleges don't like to hear about these adventures. They want you to wait until you're actually in college to go on expeditions to the rain forest, because then the profits will go to their own institutions. (For proof of this, take a look at a recent University of Delaware catalog: Both the front and back covers feature two smiling students, one riding an elephant while wearing Ray-Bans, motorcycle boots, and a fashionable poncho, accompanied by a barefoot *mahout*. The tagline says "Dare to be first™," and the mist in the background is clearly not the kind you would find in Wilmington.)

AN OUTWARD BOUND EXPERIENCE BACKPACKING BLINDFOLDED IN WEST VIRGINIA

Again, the colleges once respected students who spent their summers eating bark. But now they look at these programs as magnets for troubled teens.

AN INTERNSHIP ON YOUR UNCLE BRAD'S NEW PILOT FOR FOX

Don't even think about it. Stinks of privilege, especially if the show becomes a hit.

That leaves just one desirable summer activity:

A JOB AT JAMBA JUICE

This, dear friends, is what the colleges want to see. All the better if you don't actually get to blend the juice and instead spend eight full hours a day peeling carrots and mopping up. But landing one of these coveted assignments is not as easy as it sounds. We're sorry to report that all of next summer's Jamba Juice positions have already gone to recent cum laude neuroscience grads from UCLA.

That's where the Neurotic Parent Institute comes in: For a mere $6,500, less than it costs to go to Ghana or Cornell, we will personally arrange an UNPAID INTERNSHIP at a Jamba Juice for your high school student. There is no compensation, but we will ensure that your son or daughter encounters severe traffic, rude customers, and rancid protein powder—in short, a plethora of excellent essay material. This is the kind of experience that jumps off the page. Apply soon; opportunities are limited. You don't want your kid to end up spending his or her summer studying international relations at Columbia!

WHERE YOU DIDN'T GO THIS SUMMER

If you have a high school student, your son or daughter
is likely to visit one of
the following destinations this summer:

✈ Kerala
✈ Vietnam
✈ Costa Rica
✈ The Altiplano
✈ Yosemite
✈ The Appalachian Trail

✈ Guatemala
✈ Malawi
✈ New Orleans
✈ Buenos Aires
✈ The Grand Tetons

And here is what the moms and dads of the teen travelers will do in June, July, and August:

Stay home and work so they can pay for these programs.

To respond to this shocking situation, the Neurotic Parent Institute has formed an emergency task force, as well as a new foundation—**Martyrs Anonymous**—and we're asking for your generous contributions. This benevolent organization will provide psychological support for parents who are stuck at home while their children travel the world, boosting their resumes. Please don't let these selfless individuals be forgotten—provide them with the hope that some day they will have the means and self-love to finance their own exotic adventures.

JUST IN CASE THIS CHAPTER HASN'T GIVEN YOU ENOUGH ANXIETY: ANOTHER REAL CC POST

Today, 01:24 PM	#1
ThreeToSend	8th grade SAT score vs 11th
Join Date: Apr 2011 Posts: 7	**Hi, my 8th grade son just took the SAT. Would people mind posting their kids' 8th grade scores vs. 11th grade? If there is already a thread on this, please point me to it. Thanks!!**

THE COLLEGE LIST

How to narrow down the possibilities to 29

THE POWER OF VOWS

Often we are asked, "Neurotic Parent, how does a school become prestigious?" Excellent question. Many of you see your children getting mail every day from fabulous-sounding colleges that nobody has ever heard of. Some of these fine schools even say they have merit scholarship money available for your child, although they found him or her by purchasing a mailing list.

The answer is one you might not want to hear. Although there are more than 2,300 four-year colleges in the country, there are only seventeen that people want to attend.

"How does a college get on that list?" you might ask. "Strong academics?"

No, college prestige does not just come from strong academics; in fact, you can get an excellent education at hundreds of schools. And, despite what is commonly believed, not even the *U.S. News & World Report* rankings are the real measure of a school's status.

We are here to reveal the truth: It is "Vows," the *New York Times* wedding section, that determines the desirability of a college. Thousands of *Times* readers have graduated from college and gone on to get married. But if you want the paper to report your wedding, and you haven't attended a top-twenty, name-brand school like Wellesley or Williams or Dartmouth, good luck. Occasionally a Purdue grad manages to sneak in, but only if he or she is a member of the House of Representatives or the general manager of the American Ballet Theater.

We have sent the *New York Times* the Neurotic Parent Institute's list of new Vows-worthy universities. But for the time being, most college grads will have to send their wedding announcements to the *Sacramento Bee*.

A TYPICAL VOWS PIECE

Blake Polk and Kendall Advil

Blake Hobbs Polk and Kendall L. Advil were married Saturday at Feldenkrais Manor, a 1914 mansion in Yonkers. Mr. Polk's third cousin, Wendell Phelps Polk, a retired Unitarian minister, officiated.

Ms. Advil, who will keep her name, is a production assistant on MTV's "13 and Bulimic." She graduated cum laude from Barnard, received her M.A. from Princeton, and earned a law degree magna cum laude from Yale. Her father, Byron Advil, a graduate of Johns Hopkins and Harvard Medical School, is the retired inventor of Ibuprofen. Her mother, Hillary Tufts Advil, teaches Ethics and Modern Manners at Hampton-Fielding Country Day Preschool in Westchester.

Mr. Polk, the son of Richard H. Polk and Meredith Whitney Polk of Arlington, Virginia, dropped out of the University of Colorado, Boulder to become a ski instructor in Vail. Luckily, he is a descendant of President James Polk—otherwise, his marriage would not be Vows-worthy.

WESLEYAN: THE NEW BROWN

According to the *Los Angeles Times*, many kids are not getting into their first-choice universities! How proud we are to have this level of intrepid journalism in our city. The piece, "College Rejection Isn't the End of the World," states that many kids who expected to go to the Ivies are actually content at their second-choice schools.

Now there is hope for other kids who have been and will be rejected from their top choices. According to the Neurotic Parent Institute, a whole new crop of institutions have assumed the status of the Ivies and their peers:

Wesleyan	is the new Brown
Northwestern	is the new Penn
Vassar	is the new Yale
Bard	is the new Amherst
U of Wisconsin	is the new U of Michigan
U of Indiana	is the new U of Wisconsin
Eugene Lang / The New School	is the new NYU
UC Davis	is the new UC Berkeley
UC Merced	is the new UC Davis
Vanderbilt	is the new Duke
Tulane	is the new Emory
Bowdoin	is the new Williams
and, in a shocking development:	
Pitzer	is the new Stanford

This is just a partial list. Consider American University, because in five years it will be the new George Washington University. Fordham in the Bronx (which is the new Brooklyn, which is the new Manhattan) will be the new Boston College (which is the new Georgetown). Chapman will be the new USC, and USC will become so selective that even Annenberg's grandchildren won't be able to get in.

GUIDE TO THE COLLEGE GUIDES

We all remember the Barron's guide, which still exists, although these days everyone seems to use Fiske, Insider's, College Prowler, and the fabulous, iconoclastic book about amazing schools you've never heard of: *Colleges that Change Lives*. Barron's used to list some mid-range SAT scores and a few majors and call it a day. Now the guides go into detail about everything from the quality of hot chocolate in the student union to the number of Precor stairmasters at the gym...make that the fitness center. They also pepper their blurbs with quotes from students. Each lists 300 or so schools, including 30 that you'll never get into and 60 that you've never heard of.

Which guide should you buy? Each and every one, of course. If you have a girl, she will memorize them all and, with some luck, become incensed that College Prowler rates students by looks. If you have a boy, leave one of the books in the bathroom, and he just might glance at the page about the club scene in Hanover, NH.

Here are some real quotes from the Fiske Guide, which all the college counselors tell parents to buy. And we wonder why kids make snap judgments about schools.

Deep Springs:	*"Unless a tractor runs over you, you're fine."*
Drew University:	*"It's a nice college town according to my parents, but not to students."*
Emory University:	*"My friends and I jokingly call ourselves 'the students formerly known as gifted.'"*
Grinnell College:	*"It's like a cruise ship...the students all stay in one place and entertainment is brought to us."*
Hampden Sydney College:	*"It's called Farmville...need I continue?"*
Harvard:	*"I gauge myself by how many allusions in the* New Yorker *that I understand."*

Iowa State:	"We have a lot of farmers…this is a pretty white campus."
Scripps College:	"The salad bar is gourmet, the bread comes from a local bakery… don't even get me started about the hot cookies!"
SUNY Binghamton:	"The nearest Walmart is infested with students no matter what time of day."
Susquehanna:	"It is not uncommon to see an Amish family go by in their horse and buggy."
Tufts:	"Who wouldn't want to see a bunch of cold, naked kids running around?"
UConn:	"You will never go hungry here."
Vanderbilt:	"It even sounds expensive."

We are in the final stages of publishing our own guide, **Colleges That Won't Change Your Life Because You Won't Get In**, which we promise will be more realistic and not full of quotes by smug students who are trying to sound witty. Here are some student quotes from our honest book:

The food's not so great, but who cares? I'll get a job and you won't.

Why are you even wasting your time reading about our biomedical engineering program?

Intramurals are huge at our school, but it's unlikely you'll make the cut.

The professors have always shown genuine concern for the top 1%.

We love traditions and have a cushy alumni club, which you'll never see.

FROM MUNCIE TO CHELSEA

The *Wall Street Journal*, in an effort to cheer up its depressed readers, has published a humorous piece about New Yorkers who are attending Indiana University, presumably because they couldn't get into Northwestern or Cornell in this difficult, difficult year. The story states that a record number of students from Manhattan's prestigious Dalton school have chosen to move to America's heartland for the true collegiate experience.

The article, with the headline "From Bloomingdale's to Bloomington," features a photo of a girl in a black Chloe mini-dress, talking on her Blackberry Pearl as she walks across the Midwestern quad. Undoubtedly inspired by the Neurotic Parent blog, the author of the piece refers to Indiana as "the new Wisconsin." There are quotes from Hoosiers who resent the New Yorkers' accents and shopping addictions, but most view the migration as a fascinating cross-cultural exchange.

In a related story, the Neurotic Parent Institute has learned that students who have been waitlisted at Purdue are now heading east, enrolling at downtown Manhattan's Eugene Lang (The New School) in droves. In fact, there are rumors that to accommodate the influx of all-American palates, there will soon be an Applebee's in Tribeca.

JESUITS ARE NICE, AND THEY KNOW HOW TO NAME A COLLEGE

We weren't prepared to like Georgetown, because two years ago, a couple of girls from CJ's school got in trouble for passing Coffee Nips to each other during the information session. The admissions officer actually called their high school to complain, and needless to say, the girls were not admitted. (Luckily the infraction did not affect their chances elsewhere—they now attend Yale and the University of Chicago.) However, we were concerned that the Georgetown admissions people would remember the incident, so we left our Altoids in the car.

But instead of a place full of Mint Nazis, we found Georgetown to be lovely, an oasis of interesting people investigating worldly pursuits (and playing serious basketball) in the middle of the most livable part of our nation's capital.

And it has the best name of any college we have visited.

THE NAME GAME

Vanderbilt	Sounds too elitist.
Duke	Should be the name of Labrador Retriever rather than an institution of higher learning.
The George Washington University	It has a pretentious, annoying "the" in its title. What other college uses a definite article? Just imagine: The Princeton University or The Notre Dame.
Colgate	They've got to be kidding. Is it in an athletic league with Oral B University and Listerine State?
Northwestern	The "North" part has some logic for a college located in the northern city of Chicago. "Western" might have worked in 1807, but it doesn't quite cut it today.
Georgetown	This, however, is a fantastic name. It sounds like Downtown or Motown or Funkytown—a theme park of sorts inspired by our favorite founding father, where you can join the Ultimate Frisbee club or get an internship at the Mongolian Embassy. The name looks fabulous on sweatshirts and girls' boxer shorts.

OTHER COLLEGES WITH QUESTIONABLE NAMES

Rice	A grain
Colby	A cheese
Bates	An ominous motel
Emory	Nail care
Harvey Mudd	No annotation necessary
WashUStL	Not to be confused with the state or the District. You'd think the folks at the Harvard of the Midwest could have come up with a less confusing name

BLAME OHIO

The great state of Ohio has the nicest citizens in the country, but if its universities are trying to attract students from the coasts to attend its colleges, it has a long way to go. An institution with any of the following names is going to have a tough time attracting sophisticated and/or logical students:

Bowling Green State	Makes one wonder how many strikes and spares are required for admission.
Kenyon	It sounds like "Canyon" when you say it, and "Kenyan" when you write it.
Miami University of Ohio	Duh? Is this an exercise in faulty logic?

In Miami of Ohio's Defense

Believe it or not, it was founded in 1809, 87 years before the city of Miami, Florida was incorporated, and 116 years before the University of Miami was founded. Of course, the University of Miami isn't even *in* Miami—it's in Coral Gables. But that is no excuse for Miami University of Ohio, which is in Oxford, to adopt the name "Miami." For one thing, it leads one to expect everyone to have tans and look like J. Lo, when in fact it is nicknamed "J. Crew U."

THE COLLEGE WITH THE MOST RIDICULOUS NAME OF ALL

The Neurotic Parent Institute kindly requests that you cut one college from your son's or daughter's list and send the money that you would have spent on that application to cure world hunger instead. If you are unsure about which college to eliminate, I would suggest Case Western Reserve, the college with the most ridiculous name of them all. Is it a naval militia or a university? Or is it a bank, like Chase Manhattan? And how, by any stretch of the imagination, is it "western"? Even compared to the geographically misleading Northwestern, it is soooo east.

SINCERE APOLOGIES TO CASE WESTERN RESERVE

After proclaiming that Case Western Reserve's name was "ridiculous," the Neurotic Parent Institute received this e-mail from the wife of a prominent brain surgeon:

My husband, one of the top neurosurgeons in the world, did his internship at Case Western. It was the most memorable learning experience in his amazing academic career (Williams, Mt. Sinai, Case Western).

Oh dear. Although we did state that Case had a dumb name, we really didn't mean to diss the quality of education. The NPI position is that even if you can get over the military-sounding "reserve" part, nothing about Cleveland is remotely western, unless you consider that it is west of Connecticut.

It turns out the university's name is a combo of the Case Institute of Technology, founded by philanthropist Lawrence Case, and the Western Reserve College. Where is it situated? In the area formerly known as the Connecticut Western Reserve. (Back in the day when CT was 500 miles wide—this explains why there are so many Talbots stores in Cincinnati.)

Case does seem to be a wonderful school. *U.S. News* ranks its undergraduate program #1 in Ohio, and its medical school is ranked #21 in the country. The *Princeton Review* is not so kind, however, naming it #19 for unhappiest students.

Clearly those students are unhappy about the name. According to Wikipedia (which we use all the time, but don't endorse for college students), a "naming controversy" transpired on campus in the '90s, when the administration attempted to emphasize the Case and downplay the Western. Purist alums and professors rebelled. After some key staff quit, the branding campaign was declared a disaster and the trustees went back to giving equal weight to "Case" and "Western Reserve."

As a goodwill gesture, the Neurotic Parent Institute has just completed a task-force investigation of this matter. After much analysis, our recommendation is that the university simply use its initials, CWRU, which sound very collegiate—almost like "crew." As a bonus, that would attract more students from Eastern Europe and other regions with limited vowels.

From the annals of the Neurotic Parent blog

WE KNOW WHERE YOU LIVE

Every day, CJ gets mail from colleges. All sorts of cool brochures appear in our mailbox, along with personalized letters inviting him to come to a local information session or even a special day on campus for athletes. He has even been getting mail from highly competitive schools that turn town 88% of their applicants and would probably deny him admission as well. But they still want him to apply, so they can become even more selective.

On Friday, an oversize glossy postcard arrived from a fine institution: Indiana University. The front of the card had a photo of a Jason Bateman lookalike, with a five o'clock shadow and Prada glasses. It said, in multiple cutting-edge fonts: "CJ, There's Life After 1040 Franklin Street" (our address).

Here is the text on the other side of the card:

CJ,

We think you should have an amazing life. See the world. Be an Olympian. Learn new languages. Write new laws. Create your masterpiece. Save the environment. Discover a cure. Meet the Dalai Lama. Start your own business. Win the Nobel Prize.

Indiana University students get more than just college degrees. Our brilliant faculty, innovative programs, incredible facilities, and rich resources inspire and nurture new ideas, creative visions, and awe-inspiring achievements.

Where will you go from 1040 Franklin Street? We invite you to start your journey in Bloomington.

Wow. I rushed into CJ's room and found him trying on beanies, because his friend had inadvertently created a checkerboard pattern on his scalp while trying to give him a buzz cut.

"Look!" I said. "This came from a great school that not only thinks you should get a life and move out of here but will also help you save the environment, meet the Dalai Lama, and win the Nobel Prize."

"Don't I have to win a Nobel Prize *before* I apply?" he asked.

Not at all, I answered. Not only did the people at Indiana view him as more than "Dear Occupant," but they also seemed realistic about the timeline for when kids are supposed to do great things. If he went to Indiana, he wouldn't have to start his amazing life until *after* he leaves home.

The Neurotic Parent Answers Your Questions

NAVIANCE FAQS

Q: *What is Naviance?*

A: Although it sounds as if it's a new fragrance by Chanel, Naviance is an online college-planning tool. Elite high schools pay for the service, and students get personalized pages, where they can fill out surveys, look for scholarships, and access graphs that compare their personal GPA/ACT/ SAT statistics to those of "recent" applicants from their high school. This could be a terrific service if it gave actual data about legacy connections and athletic hooks, but unfortunately, the little squares on the chart that indicate "acceptance" all too often give kids false hopes.

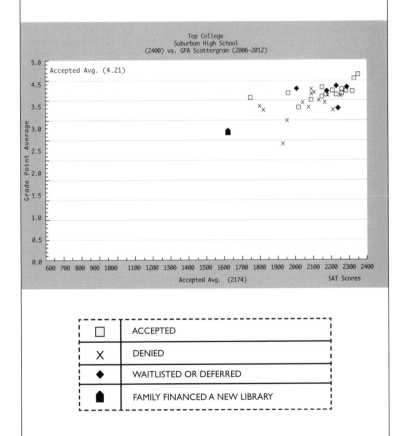

☐	ACCEPTED
✕	DENIED
◆	WAITLISTED OR DEFERRED
⬛	FAMILY FINANCED A NEW LIBRARY

COLLEGES THAT WILL IMPRESS THE GRANDPARENTS

If your son or daughter gains acceptance to Washington University in St. Louis, he or she will be thrilled, because WashU is a phenomenal institution that sometimes even gives prospective students plane tickets to visit the campus. The father of a recent admittee tells the story of how his daughter, upon getting the news about her acceptance, "screamed for two minutes straight," texted all her friends, and finally called her grandfather, who will be helping with tuition. The grandfather was happy, but he assumed she was talking about the University of Washington in Seattle.

Of course, all of us obsessed with the college process know that WashUStL is the Harvard of the Midwest—duh! But, unfortunately, the rest of the world is oblivious about its level of prestige. In fact, most people think there are only seven top colleges: Harvard, Yale, Princeton, Cornell, Columbia, Berkeley, and Stanford. Most don't know the difference between Penn and Penn State, and many have never even heard of Williams—or even the University of Chicago.

The Neurotic Parent Institute has just completed a significant market research proposal that promises to benefit the Colleges that Change Lives as well as the countless kids who cannot get into the seven most competitive schools during these trying times. And grandparents will be able to brag to their hearts' content.

Instead of going through the futile steps of applying to colleges with 6% admission rates, consider the schools on the right.

WHAT THE FISKE?!?

The NPI has learned of a disturbing college-search-related vandalism incident that transpired on the Upper East Side of Manhattan. An involved mother recently consulted her Fiske Guide to research Lewis & Clark, a fantastic liberal arts school in the very cool city of Portland, only to find that the page was gone.

In horror, the astute mom checked the S's and discovered that the page for Scripps, another fine West Coast liberal arts school, was also missing. She then concluded that the perpetrator was a houseguest who had mentioned that her daughter was interested in small West Coast liberal arts schools.

This, dear friends, sets a record for both extreme college angst and rude houseguest behavior. It's one thing to steal magazines from the dentist's office, but never, ever tear pages out of your host's Fiske Guide.

Berkeley College

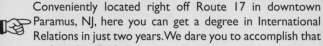
Conveniently located right off Route 17 in downtown Paramus, NJ, here you can get a degree in International Relations in just two years. We dare you to accomplish that at the other Berkeley.

Brown College

This school in Minnesota offers degrees in hot fields like radio broadcasting and criminal justice. Best part—it's half the price of Brown University, and Grandpa gets to say you got into Brown.

Columbia College of Chicago

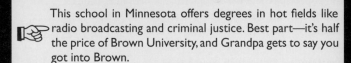
Here you can study something hip and practical like fashion studies, acoustical engineering, or marketing communication. Best part: There's no need to read Plato for two years, but you can still impress the relatives with your Columbia car decal.

Cornell College

This place, in Vernon, Iowa looks awesome, has a 44% acceptance rate and no dangerous gorges. And Grandma can tell her friends you go to Cornell.

Northwestern Oklahoma State University

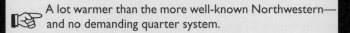
A lot warmer than the more well-known Northwestern—and no demanding quarter system.

Wesleyan College

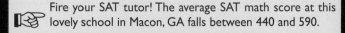
Fire your SAT tutor! The average SAT math score at this lovely school in Macon, GA falls between 440 and 590.

THE MATTHEW WEINBLATT FACTOR

Every day our postman brings CJ five or six pieces of college-related mail, most of which comes from the same prestigious Midwestern university.

Why does such a selective school feel the need to bombard prospective freshmen with an endless stream of viewbooks, catalogs, pre-apps, and invitations to information sessions?

Oddly, they are the result of one disgruntled student named Matthew Weinblatt. (Okay, that isn't his real name, but read on, and you'll see why I have to protect his identity.)

Matthew is a young man from a large West Coast metropolis. His story dates back to several years ago when he applied to Penn and was waitlisted. He was pleased to get into his second choice, but apparently he hadn't quite gotten over Penn, because upon arrival he instantly decided that all his fellow students had lousy taste in music. He came home for his first Thanksgiving and shared his observation with everyone: The academics at his school were fine, but the entire student body had terrible playlists in their iPods.

Thanks to Facebook, this shocking news spread quickly. Soon, high school students all over the country—including my son—refused to even read the catalog from Matthew's university, let alone apply there. The school was forced to embark on an expensive ad campaign, but because none of its brochures mentioned iPod playlists, it will take years to get back on track.

So if your child needs to add a great school to his or her list, think about choosing one that has faded in popularity in your community. Matthew Weinblatt now has an unpaid internship at a music company known for its cutting-edge roster), but his legacy lives on. According to a recent NPI study, 70% of students in blue states still acknowledge that the Matthew Weinblatt Factor will stop them from applying to his alma mater because attendance there could endanger the quality of their iPod libraries. Urge your child to apply now, before Matthew Weinblatt returns for graduate school and changes his mind.

CLUB SCOUTS

In case your son or daughter has other criteria for choosing a school besides academics, a cappella groups, or the kind of shoes students wear, here are some popular clubs around the nation:

➡	Bard Squeegee Collective
➡	Boston University Cigar Aficionado Society
➡	Brown University Lion Dance Team
➡	Carleton Vaginas Against Violence
➡	Colorado College Carnivore Club
➡	Columbia Bartending Agency and School of Mixology
➡	Cornell Quidditch Club
➡	Georgetown Grilling Society
➡	Grinnellians in Favor of Buying a Machine with Foam (BAMF)
➡	Harvard Wisconsin Club
➡	Harvey Mudd Gonzo Unicycle Madness
➡	Ithaca College Beatbox Crew
➡	Macalester Kilt Klub
➡	Middlebury Flying Fists Juggling Brigade
➡	Pitzer Balancing Club
➡	Princeton Bee Team (beekeeping)
➡	Reed Bagel and Schmear Club
➡	Swarthmore Motherpuckers (Recreational Hockey Club)
➡	University of Michigan Broomball Club
➡	University of New Mexico Society of Creative Anachronism
➡	UNC Bollywood Club of Carolina
➡	Washington University in St. Louis Troll Club ("We are trolls. Help us live with it.")
➡	Wesleyan Pizza Club
➡	Williams College Chocolate Appreciation Society

A CAPPELLA MATCHING QUIZ

For many students, only one collegiate activity counts: a cappella singing. This matching exercise can help students narrow down which wacky group they want to join.

A Cappella Group	**College**
A. Spizzwinks	1. Bowdoin
B. Purplehaze	2. University of Michigan
C. Kosher Pig	3. Harvard
D. The Hangovers	4. Northwestern
E. The Logarythms	5. MIT
F. The Din and Tonics	6. Princeton
G. Compulsive Lyres	7. Yale
H. Harmonic Motions	8. Tufts
I. Nassoons	9. Cornell
J. Beelzebubs	10. University of North Carolina
K. The Meddiebempsters	11. Brown
L. Vocaholics	12. William & Mary
M. The Clef Hangers	13. USC
N. Cleftomaniacs	14. NYU

THE MUSICAL TASTE OF GENERATION Y
(or *Whatever They're Called*)

The Millennials may have discovered classic rock, but because of their childhood overdoses of TV and video games, their a cappella tastes are suspect. No "Dock of the Bay" or "Lion Sleeps Tonight" for them. Here are five popular a cappella choices:

♫ *Friends' Theme*   ♫ *Stacy's Mom*
♫ *Gummi Bears Theme*   ♫ *Whip My Hair*
♫ *Pokemon Theme*

	M. 10	J. 8		C. 13
	L. 14	I. 6	G. 2	E. 5	B. 4
N. 12	K. 1	H. 11	F. 3	D. 9	A. 7

Answers

From the annals of the Neurotic Parent blog

ALL ROADS LEAD TO WESLEYAN

Many of you have asked which schools I will be visiting with our son GC on our ten-day, nine-state tour. I cannot yet reveal that list because every day there is minor tweaking and/or major restructuring. But I can tell you that we will be paying a visit to Wesleyan University in Middletown, CT.

Wesleyan is quite different from most of the other colleges that GC is checking out. In fact, he added it to his list only because I insisted that he visit one smaller liberal arts college. At first he resisted, because he thinks he wants a larger university with big-time sports. But now that we have planned his Wes visit, he's actually looking forward to spending a night in the dorms with a freshman pal from camp and attending a Terrorism class with an upperclassman family friend.

Maybe he'll like Wesleyan. But that would be a problem, because I have just discovered that *all* the other juniors in his school are also checking it out. Last night, at the junior-class potluck, I had the occasion to speak to at least 40 parents about college tours. And no matter what sort of qualifications and passions their kids have, every single one is considering Wesleyan.

Here are some of their tour itineraries:

Harvard ➡ *Brandeis* ➡ *Yale* ➡ *Tufts* ➡ *Brown* ➡ *Wesleyan*

Oberlin ➡ *Kenyon* ➡ *Sarah Lawrence* ➡ *Vassar* ➡ *Wesleyan*

Barnard ➡ *Bard* ➡ *Skidmore* ➡ *RISD* ➡ *Wesleyan*

Those all make a lot of sense.
But then the lists got weirder and weirder:

Wisconsin ➡ *Indiana* ➡ *Syracuse* ➡ *Lehigh* ➡ *Wesleyan*

and even:

SMU ➡ *Texas A&M* ➡ *Notre Dame* ➡ *U.S. Naval Academy*
➡ *Wesleyan*

Can anyone enlighten me? Why do 90% of the students in our school have Wes on their lists? Could it be the clothing-optional dorm? That's *so* 2002.

THE IMPORTANCE OF BEING A SQUIRREL

As we all know, there are other important factors in the college admissions process besides the tour guides' footwear, a cappella repertoires, and Bollywood appreciation clubs. One of the most essential considerations is squirrel life on campus. Do your kids prefer plump squirrels that will remind them of the cockapoos they left at home? Or are speedy, svelte squirrels their thing? Because of their relevance in college selection, squirrel clubs are mentioned during countless info sessions, including several times during the first five minutes at the great University of Michigan in Ann Arbor.

Once we double-check our rabies inoculations, the NPI intends to publish a comprehensive, pocket-size guidebook to collegiate squirrels. But in the meantime, for up-to-date information about sightings on top campuses, go to www.gottshall.com/squirrels/campsq. htm. The home page of this comprehensive site states, "The quality of an institution of higher learning can often be determined by the size, health, and behavior of the squirrel population."

Here's some vital info from squirrel clubs on our nation's top campuses:

🐿 *UMich:* What do we do at a Squirrel Club meeting? We feed peanuts to the squirrels and have a good time. No stress, no dues, just the pure joy of having a squirrel take a peanut out of your hand.

🐿 *Cornell:* The aim of our club is to raise awareness about squirrel diversity and lifestyles, have fun participating in squirrel-related activities, and enjoy the presence of campus squirrels. In pursuing this mission, we hope to do all sorts of fun activities including, but not limited to, watching squirrel-related movies, listening to guest speakers, and walking around Ithaca on squirrel watching adventures.

🐿 *From the Harvard Squirrel Archive:* As the nation's oldest university, Harvard naturally has the longest record of squirrel encounters. Squirrels have been scurrying around Harvard Yard since 1636! This portrait by Boston's great eighteenth-century painter, John Singleton Copley, depicts a Colonial-era squirrel.

🐿 *UCLA:* Whether chasing each other around trees or begging for (or even stealing) food, watching the squirrels at UCLA is a non-stressful diversion from studying.

🐿 *UPenn Squirrels:* At Penn, squirrels have their own Facebook page, which proclaims that they like Nuts, Scavenging, and Hibernation and that they have studied Moonlighting at Drexel.

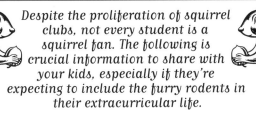

Despite the proliferation of squirrel clubs, not every student is a squirrel fan. The following is crucial information to share with your kids, especially if they're expecting to include the furry rodents in their extracurricular life.

PRINCETON

From "Beware the Ninja Squirrels" in the *Daily Princetonian*: "By some freak of New Jersey nature, the Princetonian squirrels have reached roughly the size and weight of small puppies. (Note to Paris Hilton: perfect accessory for next season's Coach tote?)." To that we say, Ms. Hilton would carry a gigantic squirrel, but *never* a commoner's Coach bag.

UC BERKELEY

In proper Cal iconoclast tradition, the squirrel Facebook group stresses the irritating obesity of campus squirrels: "This group is for people who have observed that the squirrels on the UC Berkeley campus are unnaturally fat, are disturbed by this, or contribute to the squirrels fatness by feeding the squirrels."

STANFORD

Here, there is a blog devoted to squirrel behavior: "The campus squirrels have apparently taken to bizarre suicidal death leaps into the path of oncoming student bikers. 'It's really hard to even ride your bike on campus,' said Katie Founds. 'They're always leaping in front of you.'"

UNIVERSITY OF CHICAGO

Of course, the intellectual University of Chicago has a quotable quote: "Where squirrels are more attractive than the girls, and more aggressive than the guys." We're investigating whether this, the ultimate in self-deprecation, is replacing the better-known campus slogan, "Where Fun Goes to Die."

CASE WESTERN

This institution has a chat room for students who just cannot stop talking about squirrels. Recent comments include: "they're like fucking cats," "aren't they supposed to be hibernating?" and "they are genetically modified and don't need sleep."

NOTRE DAME

ND's Facebook group not only makes observations about the species, but gives out prizes to students who join the group: "Congratulations to BD, who is our 2000th follower! Your limited-edition Squirrels of Notre Dame gift basket is in the mail, courtesy of ND Food Services! Or it would have been, except we sort of ate it before the postman came. Sorry."

SQUIRREL CULTURE AT DUKE

This top university may not have a squirrel club, but it gets the award for the cleverest squirrel Facebook page.

---

facebook | Search 🔍

Duke Squirrels 👍 **Like**

Public Figure

Wall   Duke Squirrels · **Everyone (Top Posts)** ▾

Share **Post** Photo

Ryan Nini
I see you have been hitting the gym recently!

🗏 Like • Comment • Share

Deborah Wei
Warning: Two hawks patrolling the Main Quad. Flee to your nests and gutter pipes!!!! Hide the females and children!

👍   10 people like this.

Write a comment...

Duke Squirrels
You know that awkward moment when you perform a mating ritual for a female squirrel, and then she leaves you for a squirrel with bigger nuts? Life's tough fellas.

👍   45 people like this.

Write a comment...

Latrice Coleman
People don't understand the seriousness of duke squirrels. when i first got to duke i thought i could just scare one out of my path so i stomped in its direction. not only did it not run away, that thing chased me across the west quad. and i ran away with NO SHAME. that squirrel was a G.

👍   11 people like this.

Write a comment...

Search

Jorden C. Jones

Duke squirrels are clearly bred with some form of flying squirrel and they just don't tell us.

🔥 9 people like this.

Write a comment...

Duke Squirrels

Reading period sucked...especially cuz I can't read :(

🔥 26 people like this.

Write a comment...

Nichole Nneka Ogojiaku

Literally my second day at Duke as a freshman, I was walking to Belltower. Three squirrels apparently were in some sort of meeting because they were huddled up together. Being from a place where the NORMAL thing for squirrels to do is scurry away, i kept at a normal pace.....before I knew it i was in the center of the meeting and the squirrels were straight muggin me.....maybe I phoned a friend, maybe this friend had to come all the way from belltower to shoo the squirrels away and rescue me, maybe I developed a fear of Duke squirrels.....maybe....

🔥 11 people like this.

Write a comment...

Duke Squirrels

I wish acorns were on food points!

🔥 31 people like this.

Write a comment...

Dane Huling

All I want to do is pet you. Quit playing games with my heart by scurrying away at my every approach. And one other thing—you're not fooling anyone, I know exactly why you're hiding all of those nuts. Hoarders.

🔥 14 people like this.

Write a comment...

CHOOSING A LOW-PAYING CAREER AT THE AGE OF 17

When students create their college lists, they are typically influenced by weather, sports teams (or lack thereof), and access to concerts/raves. However, some kids actually know what they want to study and seek majors in their areas of interest. A few even go for petroleum engineering, a career with a whopping starting salary of up to $155K—but one that requires taking Chemical Methods for Subsurface Characterization. It comes as no surprise that those who choose the majors that are the most altruistic, interesting, and important to society will never be able to support themselves. According to payscale.com, here are the worst-paying college degrees, along with median starting and mid-career salaries:

	Majors	Starting & Mid-career Pay
THE 15 WORST-PAYING MAJORS		
1	CHILD & FAMILY STUDIES	$29,600 - $40,500
2	ELEMENTARY EDUCATION	$32,400 - $44,000
3	SOCIAL WORK	$32,200 - $44,300
4	CULINARY ARTS	$29,900 - $46,800
5	SPECIAL EDUCATION	$34,300 - $47,800
6	RECREATION & LEISURE	$34,500 - $49,100
7	RELIGIOUS STUDIES	$32,900 - $49,700
8	ATHLETIC TRAINING	$34,600 - $50,200
9	PUBLIC HEALTH	$35,500 - $51,700
10	THEOLOGY	$35,600 - $52,000
11	ART	$35,300 - $52,400
12	ART HISTORY	$38,300 - $53,300
13	PARALEGAL/LAW	$35,300 - $53,500
14	ANIMAL SCIENCE	$33,800 - $53,700
15	MULTIMEDIA/WEB DESIGN	$40,400 - $53,900

On the other hand, we know a public health official who has three homes, a chef who has a private plane, and a web designer who charges $15K per website and is too busy to answer e-mails.

The Neurotic Parent's best advice: Worry about one thing at a time. Right now you're just finding a good college that will admit them. But if you can't stop obsessing about your child's mid-career salary, make sure his or her list includes Texas A&M, Colorado School of Mines, and the University of Tulsa, all top institutions for petroleum engineers.

THE COLLEGE TOUR

The trip of a lifetime: Quality bonding or a damaged relationship forever?

AN ICONIC ROAD TRIP WITH YOUR DISENGAGED TEEN

If your high school junior has become sassy, stubborn, secretive, unmotivated, uncommunicative, and generally impossible, there is one thing you can do to make matters even worse: Plan a spring break college tour. It is the ideal opportunity for neurotic parents.

CONS
You will spend what you would on a Caribbean vacation, yet mostly eat Chick-Fil-a.
You will see thousands of shockingly bright, polite, alert students, all of whom are vying for your son or daughter's spot.
You will have to hire a small staff to coordinate your travel plans. Immediately after booking your flights and hotels, you will find out that at least one essential university you're visiting is on spring break, and you'll have to redo the entire trip.
You will imagine all sorts of cool quality-time opportunities with your teen, and instead get to witness round-the-clock texting, embarrassing dozing during information sessions, and general negativity.

PROS
You will have numerous opportunities to brush up on your extreme driving skills in foul weather, as well as map-reading skills when your GPS fails.
You are guaranteed to meet other parents more neurotic than you. You will return home feeling refreshingly normal.

←——————————————————————→

PACKING LIST FOR SPRING BREAK COLLEGE TOUR		
Parent	*Kid (from East Coast):*	*Kid (from West Coast):*
GPS, spare GPS (for after your child loses the first one); parka, long underwear, Smartwool socks, hiking boots	Respectable outfit, hat, gloves, umbrella, Tretorn rain boots, cool scarf	Torn T-shirt, ripped jeans, filthy sneakers, hoodie

1. Should I even bother getting out of the car?
2. Do I like my tour guide's shoes?

WHAT REALLY HAPPENS ON COLLEGE TOURS:

☑ Parents take notes at info sessions while students snooze or doodle

☑ Students form impressions based on weird, illogical reasons (see pages 82–83)

☑ Some students fall in love the second they set foot on campus; others won't get out of the car. If they fall in love, it is usually with a college they will never get into or you cannot afford. If they despise the place, it's usually because the accompanying parent is too enthusiastic

WHAT YOU'RE SUPPOSED TO DO ON COLLEGE TOURS:

☑ Attend an info session

☑ Walk around with a tour guide

☑ Sit in on a class

☑ Visit the bookstore

☑ Eat in the cafeteria

☑ Check out the immediate neighborhood as well as the town/city nearby

☑ Stay in the dorm with a current student who will take you to an art exhibit, a lecture by a visiting environmentalist, and, of course, an a cappella concert

☑ Participate in an interview with an admissions rep

Ah, if I were only young again.

RECALCULATING

You will be able to get to the colleges on your list by plane, train, or rented car—everywhere, that is, except Middlebury, a stellar, must-see liberal arts school. Since it will take you dozens of hours to drive there from the nearest airport anyway, you might as well turn the excursion into a fun road trip.

❶ Before you leave, test out your GPS. To accomplish this, plug in your address and the address of Middlebury College in Vermont. If it tells you that it will take 49 hours to get there, you are on the right track.

❷ Follow the 78 steps to drive to Middlebury.

❸ After the 49 hours, don't be discouraged if your son or daughter won't get out of the car. In fact, you can celebrate, because he or she probably can't get in there anyway.

If you happen to live in Taiwan, have no fear. Google Maps can still get you to Middlebury, although it will take 39 days and 9 hours to travel a distance of 19,208 kilometers. Before you start, make sure you're up for Steps 6, 9, and 14.

1. Head **west** on 人倫林道支線 toward 人倫林道	200 m
2. Take the 1st left onto 人倫林道	26.6 km
3. Turn left to stay on 人倫林道	950 m
4. Turn right to stay on 人倫林道	1.3 km
5. Take the ramp onto 台64線	10.1 km
6. Swim across the **Pacific Ocean**	782 km
7. Turn left to merge onto 九州自動車道 **Toll road**	342 km
8. Keep right at the fork, merge onto 東名高速道路 **Toll road**	303 km
9. Kayak across the **Pacific Ocean**	6,243 km
10. Turn right onto **Kalakaua Ave**	500 m
11. Turn left onto **Kapahulu Ave**	2.5 km

12. Merge onto **HI-99 N/Kamehameha Hwy**	13.7 km
13. Turn left onto **Kuilima Dr**	800 m
14. Jet Ski across the **Pacific Ocean**	4,436 km
15. Tight left onto **N Northlake Way**	350 m
16. Take exit **164** toward **Bellevue/Spokane**	1.3 km
17. Continue the ramp and merge onto **I-90 E**	944 km
18. Merge onto **I-15 N**	12.3 km
19. Take exit **58B** to merge onto **I-94 E toward Madison**	400 km
20. Continue onto **I-90**. Partial toll road,	217 km
21. Merge onto **I-94 E**	24.7 km
22. Slight left onto **I-90 E** (signs for Interstate 90 Skyway E/ Indiana Toll Rd)	45.9 km
23. Continue onto **I-80 E**. Partial toll road,	461 km
24.Take exit **151** to merge onto **I-480 E** toward **Cleveland.** Partial toll road,	42.2 km
25. Merge onto **I-90 E**. Partial toll road,	678 km
26. Turn left onto **NY-67 E/Church St.**, continue to follow **NY-67 E**	29.9 km
27. Take exit **20** for **NY-149** toward **Fort Ann/Whitehall**	230 m
28. Turn left onto **NY-149 E/US-9 N**	800 m
29. Take the 1st right onto **VT-9 E**	18.9 km
30. Turn left onto **US-4 N/George St**, Continue to follow **US-4 N**	17.0 km
31. Turn left onto **Storrs Ave.** Destination will be on the left	150 m

GOOGLE DISCLAIMER

These directions are for planning purposes only. You may find that construction projects, traffic, tsunamis, or other events may cause conditions to differ from the map results, and you should plan your route accordingly. You must obey all signs or notices regarding your route. Bring a lot of change for the tolls. If you end up stuck in a Tokyo traffic circle or a Vermont maple forest, it might be because the editors cut out a few steps for brevity. And as you're kayaking with your kid across the Pacific, think about what an awesome essay she can write about your college tour.

50 INSANE REASONS WHY KIDS DON'T LIKE COLLEGES

1	Dislike of archways
2	No In-N-Out Burger or Chipotle within walking distance
3	Old girlfriend goes there
4	Current boyfriend could not get in
5	"I don't know anybody there"
6	"I know too many people there"
7	Tour guide too smug
8	Tour guide too outgoing
9	Tour guide too preppy (wearing sweater on his/her shoulder tied at the neck)
10	Tour guide too hipster (wearing keffiyeh scarf/Hello Kitty hoodie/neon Wayfarers)
11	Tour guide too goth ("Blame My Parents" T-shirt, black nail polish, studded headband)
12	Tour guide too granola (no bra, Birkenstocks, long skirt, flannel shirt)
13	Aversion to school colors
14	Aversion to tour guides' footwear (Crocs, Uggs on males, socks with sandals, Vibram five-toe multisport sneakers)
15	Aversion to tour guides' headwear (Sherpa caps, beanies, backwards baseball caps, Panama hats)
16	Aversion to tour guides' haircuts (buzzes, mohawks, mullets, frizzy shags, preppy ponytails)
17	Annoying bell tower
18	Mean parking attendant
19	Too much/not enough mention of a cappella groups
20	Not enough/too many food trucks
21	Pizza quality
22	Not enough/too many vegetarian options
23	Not enough/too many Harry Potter references

24	Foul odor in dining hall
25	"School rhymes with my name"
26	Aversion to architecture: too Georgian, too Gothic, too Taco Bell
27	Overuse of the following words and slogans: vegan, civic-minded, power of ideas, intellectual cross training, plugged in
28	Fellow touring students and parents overdressed
29	Too many mentions of how oceanography course changed tour guide's life
30	Tour guide's perspiration issue
31	Tour guide's eye contact issue
32	Tour guide's resemblance to sibling
33	Too many homeless people
34	Professors look like homeless people
35	Aversion to upstate NY ("Upstate NY is for camp, not college")
36	Too nerdy
37	Too cool
38	Aversion to colleges with geographic envy—e.g. Miami of Ohio, Indiana University of Pennsylvania
39	Tour guide's repeated mentions of squirrel clubs
40	Torrential downpours
41	Blizzards in May
42	Smog
43	Fog
44	Woodland creatures: deer, raccoons, skunks
45	Townies reminiscent of characters in *Deliverance, Big Love,* or *Jersey Shore*
46	Low-rider vehicles in admissions parking lot
47	Long line for the ellipticals at the gym
48	Lame Latin words in school motto
49	Emma Watson transferred out
50	School is your parents' first choice

THE INFO SESSION:
COMMON WISDOM OR OVERT HYPOCRISY?

Here is a translation of the sage advice you'll hear at most college info sessions:

1. "Be Yourself"

TRANSLATION: Yeah, right. Only the most clueless parents would let teens be themselves. Just imagine what their activities would be. Unless you want your kid to excel at sexting, better enroll him in Space Camp.

2. "Don't sign up for activities just because you think they'll look good on your app"

TRANSLATION: I defy you to show me a kid who would think about working with genomes otherwise.

3. "Challenge yourself: Take the hardest courses"

TRANSLATION: What they really mean is to sign up for courses that *sound hard*, but won't result in a GPA-spoiling B+.

4. "What matters is FIT—all of you will end up where you're supposed to"

TRANSLATION: Sucker! Your kid was always destined for Badlands U—you could have saved all that money you spent on a physics tutor.

WHAT ALL TOUR GUIDES HAVE IN COMMON

☑ Advanced skills in walking backwards.

☑ Effusive about junior year abroad.

☑ Proud to display their student ID cards, which can be swiped everywhere for cash, sports tickets, and food.

☑ Fearful of losing said cards.

☑ Have all taken a lecture class with 100 kids, and the amazing professor learned everyone's names!

☑ Have eaten less than half the food their parents paid for on their meal plans, but luckily they can donate the balance to charity.

☑ Can list six of the a cappella groups on campus, but have to think for a minute before remembering the name of the seventh.

☑ Combat boots (formally Uggs).

☑ Danceathon fanatics.

MOST OBNOXIOUS QUESTION ASKED BY A PARENT AT AN INFORMATION SESSION

Transcribed verbatim at the NYU information session:

PARENT: "I know you mentioned you had a four-year language requirement, but my son has taken every language AP and also every other AP offered by his school. So, what if he had an opportunity like... okay, I'll tell you what the opportunity is...to be the head anchor on a local news show, and the entire program revolves around him....would that be okay rather than the required four years of a language? And could we list that opportunity as a special award?"

NYU DEAN OF ADMISSIONS: (cutting her off) "Sure. That would be fine."

From the annals of the Neurotic Parent blog

DIARY OF A LEISURELY 8-STATE, 14-COLLEGE SPRING BREAK TOUR DURING THE MOST DIFFICULT YEAR TO GET INTO COLLEGE IN THE HISTORY OF THE WORLD

The Neurotic Parent and the Cerebral Jock (CJ) are setting off on a relaxing, stress-free eight-state college tour. NP is looking for an inspiring, life-changing setting where CJ will read great books, conduct fascinating research, and learn to think. CJ is looking for the perfect place to spend four to six years honing his beer-pong skills.

EXPERT COLLEGE CRITIQUES

Our original list of colleges to visit was too ambitious. But fortunately there is a girl in CJ's class traveling in the opposite direction. This compulsive texter has been providing CJ with instant feedback about every school she visits. Early on we were able to eliminate one well-situated liberal arts college from the list because Compulsive Texter told CJ that the entire student body of the highly selective liberal arts college was "stupid." Her tour guide, she reported, had a 3.3 high school GPA and was rejected by the University of Miami. Today, she sent a missive letting everyone know that all 12,000 students at Cornell are "too serious." She did say, however, that she was "obsessed" with Colgate, so apparently we still have to visit upstate New York.

UPDATE/DISCLAIMER: We are now in New York visiting friends who have kids who attend an elite boarding school in Connecticut. They say the school that this texting addict dissed is actually a very desirable place, filled with intelligent, involved students. In fact, one of our smartest friends spent his undergraduate years there and went on to attend Yale Law School. He is now working as a top litigator in Los Angeles, and would no doubt represent his alma mater if the administration decided to sue me for reporting the outrageous claims of Compulsive Texter.

A LEISURELY SUNDAY:
THREE COLLEGES, SEVEN HOURS OF DRIVING, HUNDREDS OF COWS, AND A LOT OF SNOW

After a low-key weekend in New York, we decide to make up for our hiatus by driving through three states and seeing three colleges in one day.

9 A.M.: We rent a silver Subaru Outback at Hertz on East 90th Street.

10 A.M.: First stop is New Haven, where we have breakfast with one of our favorite college students. Other than the wind chill factor, everything at Yale lives up to the hype, especially, to CJ's delight, foosball and ping-pong in the lounge. (But my omelette was disappointing.)

12:30 P.M.: We participate in a "peek" (or "drive-by," as it is often referred to in college tour vernacular) of the gorgeous Gothic architecture of Trinity College. Unfortunately, we do not see much else, because we cannot find a place to park.

2 P.M.: Tour of Amherst College. Although CJ is fairly certain he wants a school with multiple fraternities, he wants to check out a tiny liberal arts college where he could play Division 3 soccer. Amherst is supposedly harder to get into than Yale, but because there is no coffee available on campus on Sunday, I am not impressed. Our tour guide seems like a normal Uggs-clad, a-cappella-ish girl from New Jersey, but as an Amherst student, we know she will win a Nobel, a Pulitzer, or first place on *Top Chef.*

3:30 P.M.: Amherst soccer player invites CJ to watch an important March Madness basketball game with the freshmen members of the team.

3:30–5 P.M.: After an hour in the bookstores and cafes of Amherst, I decide to retire here and begin looking at real estate. CJ calls every half hour to say the game will end in "ten more minutes."

5–9 P.M.: An inspiring drive through the Berkshires. CJ and I share some incredible bonding moments and even sing "Up on Cripple Creek" together. Sadly this is short-lived, because he manages to get loud, staticky basketball reception. In the last hour of our journey, our GPS guy loses his mind and sends us onto sixteen back roads instead of taking us on an obvious direct route that we discover later when we look at a map.

We're now in the picturesque town of Hamilton, NY, covered in a blanket of pristine snow. It could be the quintessential Christmas card if it weren't almost April.

The Neurotic Parent Answers Your Questions

COLLEGE VISIT FAQS FOR THE NEUROTIC PARENT

Q: How do you like the Subaru Outback? We're thinking of getting one.

A: Thrilled with it. Just spent the day driving through an ice storm (unlikely for you to experience in LA, but with the climate change, you never know), and it performed brilliantly. Not sure if I can recommend our Garmin GPS, though. It speaks with an Australian accent and says "mmmst" for "M Street."

Q: What's your favorite college so far?

A: I cannot divulge CJ's fave because there is so much competition out there, and word has it that many juniors are reading this blog. But my favorite would have to be one of the schools where I could sit under a tree reading poetry. CJ likes to tailgate, paint his face blue, and jump in the fountain.

Q: Did CJ's high school counselor approve your college tour list?

A: Not really. The list she gave us was much more realistic. But we decided instead that it was the right time to start the torturous process of considering schools where the chance of admission is a crapshoot.

MORE QUESTIONS FROM READERS

Q: Did you look at any safety schools?

A: We did visit one safety, now referred to by college counselors as a "likely." What a relief to be somewhere where you don't need a 4.5, a 2400, and an Olympic medal to be accepted! There were some interesting programs for CJ. And the chatty roundtable info session with the charismatic dean presented a whole new way to approach this sort of trip—visiting schools where you can actually get in.

From the annals of the Neurotic Parent blog

OOPS! I JEOPARDIZED MY SON'S CHANCES AT COLGATE

Toured idyllic Colgate University during a torrential downpour. Our friendly hosts gave us giant, sturdy umbrellas, as well as fruit and Chipwiches—the only snacks we've been offered at any of our college visits. After the tour, the admissions officer recommended that everyone explore the town of Hamilton, all two blocks of it, before heading onward.

I forgot to turn on my cell phone after the tour. When I finally did, at 12:30 p.m., I heard three voice mails from the Colgate Inn letting me know that their strictly enforced checkout time was 11 a.m. I know it's a weak defense, but at this point in the trip it was difficult to remember whether I had indeed arranged a late checkout or was still counting on the one from the previous hotel the day before.

We raced back to the hotel and gathered the piles of college brochures scattered all over the room. (We hadn't had time to unpack anything else.) The people at the front desk seemed to forgive us, but when we got in the car, CJ reminded me that our tour guide said the university owned the inn. Certainly, in today's competitive environment, colleges consider not just GPAs, SATs, and ECs, but also respect for checkout policies. If anyone from the Colgate Inn happens to be reading this, please give us another chance. We'll be out by 10:59 next time—I promise.

UPDATE: You would think I learned my lesson, but three years later, when on tour with GC, we lived through the embarrassment of a similar situation at the Middletown Inn near Wesleyan University. This time I remembered to request a late checkout, but as we were dining on campus, we got a call telling us we'd better get over there within five minutes or we would be charged for an extra day.

Oops!
Missed the Tour at Cornell

Braving an ice storm, we raced through most of the country roads of Madison, NY. Arrived at Cornell with just minutes to spare before our 3 p.m. tour. But it turned out there was no 3 p.m. tour.

Planning this trip had been so time consuming that I'd contemplated quitting my job, and now the unthinkable had occurred: our first major scheduling glitch. The date was March 31st, and the 3 p.m. Cornell tours do not begin until April 1st.

I was disappointed, but CJ was relieved. March 31, it turns out, is baseball's opening day, and this meant that instead of traipsing through yet another campus, he could stay in the hotel room and watch several three-hour games.

We ended up taking a self-guided/cousin-guided tour instead, but we never did find out how many a cappella groups there are at Cornell.

From the annals of the Neurotic Parent blog

CAL

We toured UC Berkeley, where CJ spent an entire day and evening with FE (Fencing Engineer), a childhood friend (and outstanding tour guide) who is thriving there. The boys attended two classes together, and while CJ is not quite ready to switch from Undecided to Engineering, he said he "understood" the computer-programming lecture.

THE GOOD
(besides the cost, location, prestige, and weather)

1. Fires here are under control (SoCal fires rage).
2. Despite the enormity of the campus, we ran into two people we knew and were spotted by a third, who didn't say hello but called his mom to report that he saw us.
3. Frozen yogurt possibilities.
4. Great China Restaurant—New York–quality Chinese.
5. Amazing suites for freshmen.
6. Parking spaces marked "NL" are reserved for Nobel Laureates.
7. Multiple styles of mugs in gift shop. Truly, I have never seen a better selection of college mugs.

THE BAD

1. Uncomfortable cement bleachers at football stadium.
2. Our tour visited a class with 750 kids and a professor with sub-par English skills; tour guide was not certain whether class was calculus or economics.
3. Parking.
4. Political activism is presented on the tour as a piece of ancient history.

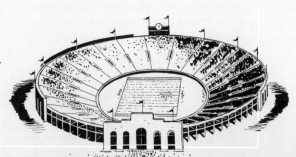

WISH THEY ALL COULD BE CALIFORNIA GIRLS

Recently a San Diego family stayed with us while on a college tour. These savvy people waited to look at schools until *after* their child had been accepted. Not only do I admire their attitude about the process, but their daughter is so impressive that I plan to hire her the second she graduates from UCSB.

Maybe the thing to do is spend the spring break of junior year studying rather than looking at colleges. Most eleventh graders are not interested yet anyway, and those who are rarely use rational criteria to evaluate the schools. One of CJ's friends said that he didn't like Amherst because the dorms, with their hardwood floors, were "too nice." Another reported that "all the students" of both genders at a top Midwestern school were unattractive. Anyone with that attitude should think seriously about forgetting the tour and attending UCSB.

NYU COMES OF AGE

We have a high school friend who dropped out of three colleges, spent a year following the Grateful Dead around, and then enrolled at NYU. In those days, you didn't have to apply, because it was a commuter school with a 100% acceptance rate. You just filled out a form, sent in your money (a comparative fortune), and you were good to go.

My friend is now a guidance counselor at a prestigious high school in New Jersey. She has her NYU diploma framed on the office wall, and her students beg her to help get them accepted at her alma mater, which now has among the most applications of any school in the world. Last year there were 33,949. And next year there will be even more, because it will be the most difficult year to gain admission to a college in the history of the world.

No surprise that our information session at NYU was Standing Room Only. Here are the reasons:

The school is located in one of the most vibrant neighborhoods in the world's coolest city. And it is gradually taking over the whole metropolitan area, like the collegiate version of Donald Trump. Soon there will be NYU flags on the Statue of Liberty and Bergdorf's.

At NYU you don't have to study an esoteric liberal art like philosophy or English. Instead you can choose a program that will prepare you for a fascinating career as a music producer or sports agent or documentary filmmaker or restaurateur. Then, in four years, after spending $250,000+ on your education, you are guaranteed a $10-an-hour internship in your chosen field.

TRAVEL ADVICE: SOUTH BY SOUTHWEST

Happily, many readers of the Neurotic Parent blog are well on the other side of the college admissions process. These smug empty nesters feel compelled to share information with us, and when they talk, we listen. We were recently contacted by a friend we'll call Compulsive Swimmer (CS). Two of her children have graduated from college, one from WashU St. Louis and one from Vanderbilt, and the youngest is a junior at Penn. CS and her husband, Triathlete Physician (TP), are enjoying life and building a spectacular second home in Jackson Hole.

CS is more than satisfied with all of her children's college choices, but absolutely raves when discussing her older daughter's experience at Vanderbilt.

"Vanderbilt," she said with authority, "is a great mid-size school in a fun city. Of the three colleges my kids went to, I would have to say it's my favorite."

She then revealed why: You can get to Nashville via a nonstop flight on Southwest Airlines.

"On Southwest," she explained, "you can rebook your flight ten times and they don't charge you anything. You can use AmEx points, and if you buy a packet of five round trips, you get free companion fares."

And there was more!

"You can check two bags for free—in this day and age, all the other airlines charge for a second bag, or even a first."

She paused. We hoped she would mention something about the academics at Vanderbilt, but all she wanted to discuss was her favorite airline. "I absolutely would not let my kids go to a school in a city that is not serviced by Southwest," she said. "Before applying anywhere, you have to go to the Southwest website and see where they fly. They have three nonstops a day to Nashville. Wash U and Penn are good schools, but there's only one nonstop to St. Louis, and to get to Philadelphia, you have to stop or change planes in Vegas."

Finally, a reasonable way to select colleges. Especially if you enjoy unlimited bags of low-cal Cheese Nips.

OVERHEARD AT BROWN

Admissions officer at a recent Brown information session:
"At Brown, we pride ourselves on being a place for original thinkers."

Student (to his mom):
"We can go now."

VARSITY QUIDDITCH

A dear friend, the mother of Latin Star, sent brief messages
from their college tour. Her e-mail wasn't working, so she contacted
us on, you guessed it, Facebook. Here are the highlights:

At the Yale info session, she experienced two direct Harry Potter
references and overheard two more.

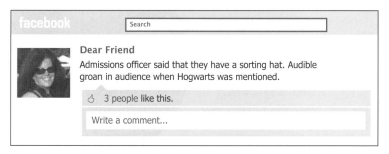

If this trend continues, we can be relieved that our children have already
read all the great books necessary for Ivy League survival.

COLLEGE TOUR APTITUDE TEST

Recently I received a call from the mom of Future Senator, asking me to recommend a hotel in Nashville. Yes, it's that time of year again—another crop of juniors are donning their North Face jackets and traipsing across the country in search of the perfect place to study the impact of globalization.

After a brief discussion about Marriotts versus Hampton Inns, FS's mom realized, in horror, that she had booked all the wrong flights on all the wrong dates, because she'd incorrectly calculated the start of Passover. This was particularly distressing because her more-competent daughter had secured the last spots on two key college tours.

FIRST CTAT SCORE: 1570 (very low percentile on the Holiday Comprehension/Calendar Reasoning Skills section).

I told FS's mom to be thankful that she'd booked all travel on Delta, which, like the SAT, gives you the option of a morning-after pill of sorts, allowing a full refund for any flight you booked within the last 24 hours. And luckily, FS is visiting only three schools on this trip—Vanderbilt, Duke, and Emory—so rebooking was not the nightmare I experienced when I had to change our entire eight-state itinerary after discovering that Northwestern was on spring break when we'd scheduled to visit. It was comforting for FS's mom to learn that arranging college tours is a challenge, even for the Neurotic Parent.

So we started over, attempting to reserve tours, hotels, and reasonably priced flights with minimal layovers. Ninety minutes later, we had a plan that would work—until we discovered that Emory didn't have room on its 3/31 morning tour, and Vanderbilt had no info-session openings on Good Friday. Plus, the only convenient flight from Nashville to Atlanta was on a tiny Cessna turbo-prop on an oddly named regional airline that neither of us had heard of, called Pacific Wings. We decided to take a break and continue our tour planning in the morning.

SECOND CTAT SCORE: 1830 (disappointing performance in Southern Tour Scheduling Skills).

The next morning, we booted up our computers and got on the phone, each with two #2 pencils and a TI calculator. Our perseverance paid off. We ended up with a not-too-hectic schedule that saved $366 on flights, $40 on hotels, and seven hours of travel time compared to the original itinerary. In the end, we had to include the Pacific Wings flight, but we decided it was okay after checking its safety record—plus, the alternative was a four-hour road trip via Chattanooga, which FS's mom refused to consider because she hates driving in the rain and was convinced that it would rain on March 30th. But other than one undesired travel leg, FS's mom was thrilled to earn this:

FINAL CTAT SCORE: 2260, good enough to earn FS admission to a tour at any highly selective college.

OFF-SEASON
COLLEGE TOURING

*C*ollege campuses, covered with slush during "spring" break, are verdant paradises in the summer with glistening ponds and gardens in full bloom But the kids that you see throwing Frisbees are mostly high school students enrolled in summer programs. And the tour guides are often from the B list.

Case in point: A tour guide at Emory, a witty and articulate young man, hit a trash can while walking backwards. And a perky leader from Penn, clad in flip flops (as were all of her colleagues), didn't even attempt to strut in reverse.

We're pleased to see that colleges no longer discriminate against tour leaders with deficiencies in walking backwards. But we hope this affirmative action trend doesn't phase out that most impressive of collegiate talents. What's next? Off-key a cappella singers?

FOUR SEASONS U

*When our kids go off to college, we are no longer there to
spoil them every day. So it's up to the colleges
to take over the pampering. Here is what to expect:*

▶▶	State-of-the-art gyms and workout rooms with shiny new equipment—the kind of places you'd pay hundreds of dollars a month to belong to on one of the coasts.
▶▶	International food courts with salad bars, sushi chefs, fresh-baked pizza, vegan entrees, and other exotic fare, often available 24/7. And if you still can't find something to your liking, just use your meal plan card at dozens of farm-to-table restaurants in town.
▶▶	Opportunities to join hundreds of clubs. Want to create your own? No problem, even if you need funds for editing rooms or sailboats or polo sticks.
▶▶	Free laptops (yes, this was an enticement at many schools).
▶▶	Dorms that look like hotel suites, with fireplaces, pool tables, and "business centers" equipped with brand-new printers and scanners.
▶▶	18-hole golf courses, Olympic-size swimming pools, art museums, sculpture gardens, plush screening rooms, complimentary airport shuttles, and free lecture series with fascinating speakers.
▶▶	Opportunities to travel to Barcelona or Capetown or Buenos Aires or Sydney, as well as other places we'd never dream of visiting ourselves, what with the cost of paying for college.

So the good news is that if your student is headed to a private school, he or she will enjoy a luxury lifestyle, much like the more prosperous parents get on vacation. Who pays for all this? A recent *Wall Street Journal* story had the answer: Surprise—it's us, the very same stressed-out parents who are working weekends so we can pay for a decent education for our children.

In "Pleading Poverty: Colleges Want Parents to Foot the Bill for Their Largess," a reporter points out that many colleges that suffered during the financial crisis considered suing their brokers or postponing new construction, but many instead have "contemplated making up their shortfalls the old-fashioned way—by increasing tuition." The reporter produced statistics about how tuition increases have outpaced inflation and wrote, "The soup-to-nuts cost (tuition, room and board, extras) of one year at a private college is already in the region of $50,000, bringing the cost of a bachelor's degree to close to a quarter of a million dollars....like buying a new BMW every year and driving it off a cliff."

The astute reporter compared modern college lifestyles to living at Versailles, with abundant food of every type available 24/7 and perks that Louis XIV couldn't have even dreamed of, including free tech support, plentiful concerts, screenings, and parties, and unlimited funds to start obscure clubs. Of course, all of this lavishness is possible because of us, the parents.

For the students, the only downside to all this luxury is that they actually have to learn something. If not, their moms and dads might get angry and make them go to community college or pay for their own health club memberships.

And they'll have to come to grips with the reality that one day it will all end. No longer will somebody pay $50,000 a year for them to play Ultimate Frisbee, take a heli-skiing course, or spend six months "studying" the villa gardens of Florence.

INVESTMENT ADVICE

If you have anything left over after spending your life savings on higher education, we recommend investing in the following companies, whose presence is ubiquitous on every campus we've visited:

North Face
S'barro (plus every other kind of fast food you find in a suburban food court)
Apple
Bed Bath & Beyond (they have the monopoly on the model dorm rooms)
J. Crew
Samsung
Chili's
Verizon
Anheuser-Busch
Red Bull
Axe
Solo plastic cold drink cups (red, from Costco)
Alitalia (Just about every junior in America spends his or her junior year in Florence)

DISCLAIMER: *The Neurotic Parent takes no responsibility for investment suggestions offered in this book. After we blogged about S'barros on campus, Mr. Neurotic Parent let us know that they'd filed for Chapter 11 bankruptcy.*

TESTING

Hands down, the worst part about the admissions process (until your kid gets a 2260)

The Neurotic Parent Answers Your Questions

SAT/ACT FAQS

Q: What does "SAT" stand for?

A: It used to stand for Scholastic Achievement Test, but in 1947, the name of the exam was changed to Scholastic Aptitude Test. Then the folks at the College Board used their Critical Reasoning skills and came to the conclusion that a coachable exam could not be called an "aptitude" test. So officially, SAT stands for nothing, although at least one college refers to it on its website as the Scholastic Assessment Test.

Q: What time does Staples close, in case your kid can't locate his TI-183 calculator the night before the SAT exam?

A: Luckily, the Staples in our neighborhood closes at 9 p.m., as we discovered the other night. (CJ, who had "just had" his calculator the day before, volunteered to pay for the new one.)

Q: What are some good snacks for the SATs?

A: A power bar, a peanut butter sandwich, and a banana. We typically procure all of these, but our sons typically leave the power bar at home and the sandwich and banana in the car.

Q: What is the ACT?

A: A standardized test that up until twenty minutes ago was popular only in the Midwest. But because there are no trick questions, they allow score cancelling and unpenalized guessing, and they have an early September test date, it is the test *du jour*. New Yorkers are now obsessed with the ACT, and it is gaining fans nationwide. In fact, for the first time ever, the number of ACT test takers is slightly more than the SAT. Poor SAT—it now stands for Sad Anachronistic Test.

Q: What is a superscore?

A: A superscore is achieved by choosing the best subscores from multiple sittings of the same test. (We know, a "sitting" sounds like you're posing for a portrait, but bear with us.) For example, let's assume you have these SAT results from these three sittings:

Sitting 1: **800M,** 500CR, 450W • Sitting 2: 600M, 410CR, **780W** • Sitting 3: 510M, **740CR**, 530W • Your composite scores would be 1750, 1790, and 1780, but your superscore would be 2320.

Q: Wow! Do colleges superscore the ACT as well?

A: Not many superscore the ACT, because they'd have to work with five separate numbers, including a composite that often has been rounded up or rounded down. That would require advanced math skills, which would be too confusing, even for colleges. Except MIT, of course. They will even cross-superscore the SAT with the ACT ... just because they can.

Q: Do you have to send in all your scores to Yale, even the ones that suck?

A: No, that's Penn. Yale's website says, "As long as you provide a complete set of score reports from one testing agency (either the College Board or ACT, Inc.), you are not required to report scores from both. You can choose to report either all of your SAT results (both SAT and SAT Subject Tests) or all of your ACT results. If you want us to have any scores from both the College Board and ACT, Inc., you must report all scores from both testing agencies."   If you're having trouble understanding this, you probably shouldn't be applying to Yale.

Q: I thought the SAT and the ACT offered Score Choice, so you can send in only your impressive scores.

A: They do, but Yale wants to find out if sitting for standardized exams was your only extracurricular activity. And they promise not to peek at your lousy scores.

Q: I heard you could cancel your scores so nobody will see them.

A: The SAT offers you a morning-after pill of sorts: If you were fooling around the night before or felt queasy during the exam, you can cancel *before* you find out your scores. But the more progressive ACT, which also allows you to guess without penalty, will let you terminate whenever.

Q: Do you really believe that Yale doesn't care about SAT Subject Tests if you send in an ACT score?

A: No—so we recommend you also submit the results of your APGAR test. That's the score babies get from their doctors right after they are born, on a scale of one to ten. Yale's APGAR average is 9.8.

Q: What's with the writing section of the SAT? Some fine colleges, like Cornell, say they don't count the SAT writing, yet if you take the ACT, they want you to take ***that*** *with writing.*

A: You're right. Some things are just not logical—or fair. Even the Neurotic Parent cannot write a decent essay in 25 minutes, especially using a #2 pencil while sitting in a stuffy classroom surrounded by smelly teenagers. But maybe we'd have success if they'd let us write about reality television.

STANDARDIZED PREPPING

We all know that the "process" is holistic, and testing is only one part of the equation…blah, blah, blah. But the bottom line is this: If your child gets a 2380, it's reason to celebrate. And if he or she gets a 1560, not so much.

ADIOS, ANALOGIES

For those of you who have fond memories of the analogies section of the old SAT, we are sorry to report that it's been laid to rest because of cultural bias. The most famous example was the analogy question above right. The correct answer, oarsman: regatta, assumed that students would know something about crew, a sport for wealthy people who live near large, cold bodies of water. 53% of white students gave the correct response, while only 22% of black students came up with the answer. Analogy questions have since been replaced with short reading passages. Unfortunately, before getting rid of the most fun section of the exam, nobody bothered to check whether taking the SAT itself is an activity for wealthy, coastal people, regardless of race.

"That's incredibly culturally centered," said a critic of the question. "You don't see a regatta in center-city L.A., you don't see it in Appalachia, you don't see it in New Mexico."

"But," says a libertarian member of the Neurotic Parent Institute, "you do see massacres, embassies, tournaments, and stables in those places—and you can train people to use the process of elimination." Instead of dumbing down the exam, how about teaching all our kids about the fabulousness of logic?

Analogy Question

RUNNER: MARATHON

- ○ **A** envoy: embassy
- ○ **B** martyr: massacre
- ○ **C** oarsman: regatta
- ○ **D** referee: tournament
- ○ **E** horse: stable

Critical Reasoning

The following sentence contains either a single error or no error at all. If the sentence contains an error, select the one underlined part that must be changed to make the sentence correct. If the sentence contains no error, select E.

Bubble This

The college admissions process

has _emerged as_ one of the most
○ **A**

stressful procedures _of_ the late
○ **B**

twenty-first century, _causing_
○ **C**

sleep loss, ulcers, _and even_
○ **D**

irreparable damage to the parent-

child bond. _(No error)_
○ **E**

CELEBRITY SAT SCORES

We've haven't spoken to these folks
personally, but this is what internet research tells us,
and we are choosing to believe it's true.

Paul Allen	1600	Stephen King	1300s
Kobe Bryant	1080	Rush Limbaugh	1530
George W. Bush	1206	Bill O'Reilly	1585
Bill Clinton	1032	Sarah Palin	841
Bill Cosby	<500	Will Smith	1600
Janeane Garofalo	950	Ben Stein	1573
Bill Gates	1590	Howard Stern	870
Al Gore	1355	Amy Tan	1100s

* based on the 1600 scale

The Neurotic Parent Answers Your Questions

ANOTHER TESTING QUESTION

Q: *The ACT sounds awesome—if you take it, some colleges let you forego the SAT Subject Tests. But I don't get those wacky science graphs. Where can I find a good ACT tutor in L.A.?*

A: Unfortunately, the ACT is still very...er...*Midwestern*. Because of this, only one test-prep company on the West Coast at this writing claims to have ACT specialists. And they charge $880 per session (not including parking validation). But the always-resourceful Neurotic Parent Institute has located the top ACT tutors in the country. They are all in Evanston, IL, and they charge $40 an hour. So for the price of one $880 session in L.A., you can fly to Chicago *twice* for tutoring *and* splurge on a Cubs game, a taxi to and from O'Hare, and a deep-dish pizza.

HOW TO EVEN THE PLAYING FIELD (SHORT OF GETTING RID OF THE TESTS)

The cruelest part of this whole exam thing is that they are just not fair. Less fortunate kids may no longer have to answer culturally skewed questions about regattas, but they also have not had access to tutors, prep books, online courses, and proctored practice tests that have been graded with detailed analyses of their strengths and weaknesses.

To even the playing field, the NPI suggests that students also be required to submit a Testing Disclosure Form. This supplement would require the following:

➡ Attach tutor receipts. Subtract 50 points on the SAT or ½ point on the ACT for each $1,000 spent on tutoring.

➡ Disclose the total amount spent on educational psychologists who have facilitated test-taking time extensions when the student has never had extra time for anything at school. Subtract 100 points for each $2,500 spent on this sort of educational therapy.

Finally, we propose an additional attachment, the Pathetic Excuse Form, which will allow all test takers to provide supplemental information about interruptions, disturbances, and illnesses that might have affected their scores: headache, hangover, got my period during the exam, calculator broke, proctor was clearing his throat, etc.

ADDICTED TO TESTING

A study has shown that the almost-four-hour SAT with the added Writing Section does not predict college success. However, it's given lots of business to tutors who claim they can teach a 17-year-old to write a decent essay about solitude in 25 minutes with a #2 pencil.

Perhaps feeling guilty about the writing, the folks at College Board have instituted Score Choice, which means students are no longer required to send in all their lousy SAT scores to colleges. As in the case of the kinder, gentler ACTs, test takers can choose which scores to share.

This means that a test-obsessed student who takes the SAT seven times a year starting in ninth grade could theoretically have as many as 24 SAT attempts from which to choose.

But before your student retakes for the eleventh time, here's a little caveat: Several top colleges have gotten hip to serial test taking and are not honoring Score Choice. For example, Penn now requires kids to send in *all* their scores, even the ones that suck. Which is better? A 2200 after six tries or a 1950 on the first sitting? The answer: probably neither.

SOLVING THOSE ANNOYING TESTING ISSUES

Among our issues with standardized testing are the logistics of it all. First, there's the scheduling problem. Both the SAT and ACT are administered when juniors and seniors are busiest, usually during midterms, finals, AP exams, playoffs, theatre opening nights, proms, etc. This ramps up the stress considerably. Second, the sign-up deadlines are terribly inconvenient. You rarely get your score in time to sign up for a retake without paying a late fee. And if you want to switch from the SAT to the ACT or visa versa, the two testing administrators seem to be in cahoots—either forcing you to continue paying tutors in case you have to retake, or to scramble to pay late fees when your disappointing scores are returned just a few days before the competitor's exam.

If standardized testing continues to be a necessary evil in the college admissions process (and it will—it is too large of a business to abandon), the Neurotic Parent Institute has a few simple ideas that will lower the level of testing neurosis:

➥ Offer exams during the summer, when kids are relaxed.

➥ Offer overnight scoring options. Charge $99. If the College Board and the ACT happen to adopt this suggestion, invest in both companies immediately. This will become the hugest money maker in the college admissions process, guaranteed.

➥ Shorten the tests. Two hours is plenty. Performance on a five-hour exam is not a predictor of college success, just of test-taking stamina.

Some colleges opt out of Score Choice and require kids to send in all exam scores from both the ACT and SAT, just so they can see which students have turned test taking into an extracurricular. This turns into a lose-lose ethical dilemma for students who have repeated the exams: Should you be honest and send in your seven scores? Or "cover up" your testing addiction (and your bad scores) and face being caught? Some schools want you to keep testing so they can report high scores to *U.S. News & World Report* and get high rankings. Others just want to keep your parents awake at night.

The Neurotic Parent Answers Your Questions

WHERE ELSE TO SEND YOUR SCORES

Q: *I've sent my scores to 27 colleges. Where else should I send them?*

A: The Neurotic Parent Institute has drawn up this handy checklist for sending scores:

➡ Grandma (framed version or wallet-size laminated card)

➡ MTV (for internship consideration)

➡ Starbucks (for barista consideration)

➡ Mensa (for membership consideration)

➡ Sperm donor bank (for cash-flow potential)

SAT IIIs

In addition to the SAT Subject Tests (formerly known as SAT IIs), the College Board is now offering SAT IIIs, which measure the sort of critical thinking and problem-solving skills that a student will actually need in college. High school juniors should take these exams in May, in the area of their greatest expertise/talent.

APTS (ADVANCED PROM TRANSPORTATION). Students are given the task of reserving an appropriate vehicle to transport 26 of their closest friends to the junior prom and after party. Then they must collect $80 per passenger, more than it costs to attend the prom itself.

FMTS (FACEBOOK MULTI-TASKING 2C). Students are expected to communicate with at least 680 friends in a five-minute period, while simultaneously studying for a pre-calc quiz, watching a Lakers game, and reading *The Great Gatsby*. (Note: The UCs have announced that they will not accept scores from the lower-level Facebook 1C Exam.)

PBRS (PEER-BASED RATIONALIZATION). Students research and present an argument that their interim grades were outstanding compared to those of their high-achieving friends.

Most highly selective colleges recommend submitting scores from just three SAT IIIs, but highly gifted students can also consider taking the **COD (CALL OF DUTY)** achievement exam in November, just to show the admissions committees that they are well-rounded and truly challenging themselves in high school.

THE MORNING AFTER: SAT QUESTION OF THE DAY

When students sign up to take the SAT, they can request that the College Board e-mail a Question of the Day to their parents. These sample questions are reminders that the Critical Reading section of the exam was designed for people in their 40s and 50s who read *The New Yorker*.

But a recent question was contemporary—and provocative. As students all over the world recovered from the stress of a test held just one day before, this SAT Question of the Day imparted a surprising message about the value of higher education.

Was the College Board, which forces kids to spend months and months studying vocabulary and equations they'll never use again in their lives, having an existential crisis?

What if this sort of question inspires hordes of 15-year-olds to drop out and become autodidacts, forgetting about college (and college prep) entirely? This Question of the Day could put the CB out of business, instead inspiring kids to go straight to becoming CEOs. That is, if the test takers could only understand the question.

> *Choose the word or set of words that, when inserted in the sentence, best fits the meaning of the sentence as a whole.*

The CEO of the computer company, who had quit school at the age of 15, was a noted _____, having taught himself everything he needed to know about computers and business, in addition to working to gain proficiency in such subjects as international copyright law.

- ◯ *pedant*
- ◯ *autodidact*
- ◯ *demagogue*
- ◯ *ambassador*
- ◯ *disputant*

VANITY LICENSE PLATE?

Spotted on Sunset Boulevard by a reader:

California
ACT 33

The Neurotic Parent Institute has tracked down the owner of the car, who said that he also had scored 2210 on the SAT. But when he tried to order those plates, SAT 2210 was already taken.

CONVERSATION WITH THE COLLEGE BOARD: CRITICAL REASONING EXPERTS

Here is a transcript of a telephone conversation we had the other day with Operator #25987653 at the College Board:

College Board Operator: Hello. You have reached the College Board. Please have your credit card ready. This call may be recorded for quality-assurance purposes.

NEUROTIC PARENT: Hi. My son is signed up to take the SAT reasoning test in June and he would like to take the SAT subject tests instead.

College Board Operator: There will be a $21 charge to change.

NEUROTIC PARENT: That's fine.

College Board Operator: And there will be a $57 charge for the new exam. What is your first and second choice for a test center?

NEUROTIC PARENT: My son just wants to change his test type, not his test center.

College Board Operator: I'm sorry. That test center is full. But we do have other centers that might be open in your area.

NEUROTIC PARENT: But he is already signed up at the center he wants. Why can't he keep the spot he has?

College Board Operator: Because he is switching test types. There might not be enough SAT subject test booklets at his test center.

NEUROTIC PARENT: Aren't you the ones who provide the booklets? Couldn't you send one to his test center? What if we paid you $42 instead of $21? That would cover the cost of postage.

College Board Operator: *That is impossible. But I can offer your son a spot at Frances Dorito High or Our Lady of the Immaculate Conception of the Sacred Heart.*

NEUROTIC PARENT: Where are those?

College Board Operator: *We don't have the exact locations on file, but our records show they are in your area. There also might be an opening in Phoenix.*

NEUROTIC PARENT: But that's 400 miles away. Why can't he just take the exam where he signed up to take it?

College Board Operator: *Once he cancels, he will lose his space.*

NEUROTIC PARENT: He does not want to cancel. He just wants to change from the SATI to the SATII. And by the way, if you're canceling and rebooking, why are you charging a change fee?

College Board Operator: *Because if $V = 21R / (r + R)$, then $R = Vr / (12 - V)$. But if you pay an additional $87, there is an opening on the waitlist at San Bernardino High. However, there are no guarantees that your son will get the exam of his choice. That means if he signs up for a subject test in U.S. History, he might have to take Korean instead. And he will have to arrive at 5:45 in the morning and take the test in the boys' bathroom.*

NEUROTIC PARENT: If he has to drive to San Bernardino at 4 in the morning, he might get stressed out and bomb the exams. And that could ruin his entire future.

College Board Operator: *Tell me about it. I've had this job for seven years, but it seems like only yesterday that my own mom got angry with a College Board Operator. Remember, this call is being recorded.*

From the annals of the Neurotic Parent blog

BOO, BOO, BOO, SQUARE ROOT OF TWO

Most people my age never prepped for the SAT, but I had the privilege of attending a series of six evening classes in a funky office above a pizza place next to a subway station in New York. There I met a girl who attended a rival high school who went on to become one of my dearest friends. And our teacher was destined for greatness: He was none other than the pioneer and guru of standardized test preparation, Stanley H. Kaplan. When asked what the "H" stood for, he would say "Higher Scores."

My primary memory about the historic course was that Stanley H. had to stop speaking whenever the subway came because the whole office rattled. And I recall him telling us, "If you girls would just shut up and listen, you'll get a 1600!"

My friend has a stronger recollection. She said Mr. Kaplan taught us a mnemonic to remember a trigonometry formula: "Boo Boo, Square Root of Two." She couldn't identify the formula, so she called her brother-in-law, who had also prepped with Mr. Kaplan and is now a successful dentist with a great memory. He too had never forgotten the phrase, but he couldn't conjure up what it was supposed to help one remember. Perhaps something related to a hypotenuse?

On to Google. All I could find on the entire information highway was a 2001 *New Yorker* piece about Mr. Kaplan, which I vaguely recall reading years ago. Fascinating stuff about the origins and sociology of standardized testing.

And sure enough, there was a "Boo, Boo, Boo" reference. (It turns out there were three "boos," which could have lead us astray during an exam, if we had memorized just "Boo Boo.") Kaplan had determined that the test makers were fond of geometric problems involving the Pythagorean theorem. So an entire generation of Kaplan students were taught "boo, boo, boo, square root of two" to help them remember how the Pythagorean formula applies to an isosceles right triangle.

A nod to the past, but alas, no explanation. Then, a short while later, when the great Mr. Kaplan passed away, all was explained in his obit. Each "boo," it turned out, referred to one of the angles. We won't be fooled again, SAT.

SO YOU THINK YOU CAN PROCTOR

It's the first day of winter break, which means 'tis the season for a four-hour practice SAT. Don't know what I was thinking when I offered our home as a venue for GC and his friends to take a grueling practice exam.

I procured the tests from GC's tutor, sent Mr. NP to Kinko's for copying and collating, and got the protein bars and water ready for the breaks. And now here I am, supervising the *ninth* section of this joyous activity. Although I have been doing little more than keeping the dog from licking the test takers' feet and running back and forth to the kitchen to set the timer, I really feel the boys' pain. As they complete the final section, I feel as if I've tortured rather than empowered them.

A few random observations:

➡ I could not figure out how long to allow for breaks between sections. My usual definitive source, College Confidential, was inconsistent: Some kids swore the pauses were supposed to be just two minutes, while others mentioned multiple five-minute rest periods. We went for the kinder, gentler five-minute breaks—which added an hour to the exam schedule.

➡ The boys had no interest in cheating, but they were very interested in chatting. They felt a need to analyze and ridicule the exam.

➡ Even if you're not taking the test, four hours is L-O-N-G. I stayed in the room, playing Scrabble online, surfing the internet, and writing Christmas cards to the guy who delivers our *New York Times*. Sort of felt as if I were in a plane with WiFi. On a cross-country flight.

➡ I'm not sure if the stamina necessary for this test is anything related to the skill set you need for college. When will one ever again be required to write an essay about creativity, then figure out the area of the shaded portion of a triangle, then find misplaced commas—all in one tightly structured time period?

And those wacky exam creators are all over the map: first, getting rid of my favorite part—the analogies—and then making the exam hours longer in order to include an "experimental section," plus writing, which many colleges don't even count. That darn College Board can't even remain consistent about what SAT stands for. Back in the day it was Scholastic Aptitude Test. Then in the '80s, it became the Scholastic Achievement Test, even though the questions remained relatively the same. And now it's just plain SAT, no longer an acronym but a word unto itself, as in "I SAT for four hours taking a brutal exam, and its biased results could define my whole future."

PRAYER FOR THE SAT

Here is a powerful, non-denominational prayer for those who wish to do well on the SAT. This can be recited aloud in the car on the way to the exam, or silently between sections.

On this occasion of my (first, second, seventh) sitting for the SAT exams, I beseech the Almighty College Board to look over me and protect me from mis-bubbling. Grant me the strength to avoid the Passive Voice in my essay. Give me the focus to remember the properties of an $f(x) = ax^2 + bx + c$ function, as well as the meaning of **paucity**. May I stay awake through the Critical Reading section, even if I get a passage about the process of refining rice husks for Tibetan wax statues. Bless my #2 pencils and protect their points; let me be forever grateful that they are not #1s nor #3s. Save me from realizing at 4 a.m. on the morning of the test that I have left my TI-83 calculator in the trunk of a friend's car. O College Board, provide me with the will to resist temptation if my classmates invite me to spend the night before the exam partying in a hot tub, as came to pass in an episode of *Gossip Girl. (Kaplan 119:9, 16)*

PRAYER FOR THE SAT SUBJECT TESTS

For those taking the U.S. History SAT II exam, add this silent meditation:

O College Board, reward me for staying home on Halloween Eve by allowing me to recall the content of the 10th, 19th, 25th, 22nd, and 18th Amendments. And because I have been a good customer who has paid to take your mandatory, monopolistic exams over and over again, may I forever comprehend the significance of the Taft-Hartley Act.

THE ESSAY

Let your "you" shine through, even if it's a you conjured up by your independent college counselor

THE MOST FAMOUS COLLEGE ESSAY ON THE INTERNET

The essay on the facing page, written by Hugh Gallagher, won a Scholastic Press writing contest in 1990. Gallagher subsequently sent the essay to NYU and was admitted. (It is not clear if he submitted the essay as a writing sample or, according to an internet rumor, as his actual personal statement.) After graduating, he released an album called *Bomb the Womb* and wrote a novel called *Teeth*. Reprinted with permission of the author; you can find out more about him at www.hughgallagher.net.

The Prompt:

In order for the admissions staff of our college to get to know you, the applicant, better, we ask that you answer the following question: Are there any significant experiences you have had, or accomplishments you have realized, that have helped to define you as a person?

THE SEDARIS FACTOR—DON'T DO IT, DADDY

Remember that admissions committees are experts in what the real 17-year-old voice sounds like: immature and overly verbose, with a tendency to use malapropisms and misspell "definitely." So your student should avoid writing that is too good. According to a (well-written) *Boston Globe* article, "If an essay is too polished, it could receive the dubious distinction of DDI, short for 'Daddy Did It.'" If a student's essay seems too polished, they'll check it against the kid's SAT or even hand it over to a professor for a second opinion. So parents, go ahead and correct the spelling and punctuation, but otherwise bite your tongue and make sure you don't edit your kids' tomes so they seem as if David Sedaris was the author.

The Essay:

I am a dynamic figure, often seen scaling walls and crushing ice. I have been known to remodel train stations on my lunch breaks, making them more efficient in the area of heat retention. I translate ethnic slurs for Cuban refugees, I write award-winning operas, I manage time efficiently.

Occasionally, I tread water for three days in a row. I woo women with my sensuous and godlike trombone playing, I can pilot bicycles up severe inclines with unflagging speed, and I cook Thirty-Minute Brownies in twenty minutes. I am an expert in stucco, a veteran in love, and an outlaw in Peru.

Using only a hoe and a large glass of water, I once single-handedly defended a small village in the Amazon Basin from a horde of ferocious army ants. I play bluegrass cello, I was scouted by the Mets, I am the subject of numerous documentaries. When I'm bored, I build suspension bridges in my yard. I enjoy urban hang gliding. On Wednesdays, after school, I repair electrical appliances free of charge.

I am an abstract artist, a concrete analyst, and a ruthless bookie. Critics worldwide swoon over my original line of corduroy evening wear. I don't perspire. I am a private citizen, yet I receive fan mail. I have been caller "number nine" and have won the weekend passes. Last summer I toured New Jersey with a traveling centrifugal-force demonstration. I bat .400.

My deft floral arrangements have earned me fame in international botany circles. Children trust me. I can hurl tennis rackets at small moving objects with deadly accuracy. I once read *Paradise Lost, Moby Dick*, and *David Copperfield* in one day and still had time to refurbish an entire dining room that evening. I know the exact location of every food item in the supermarket. I have performed several covert operations for the CIA. I sleep once a week; when I do sleep, I sleep in a chair. While on vacation in Canada, I successfully negotiated with a group of terrorists who had seized a small bakery. The laws of physics do not apply to me.

I balance, I weave, I dodge, I frolic, and my bills are all paid. On weekends, to let off steam, I participate in full-contact origami. Years ago I discovered the meaning of life but forgot to write it down. I have made extraordinary four-course meals using only a mouli and a toaster oven. I breed prizewinning clams. I have won bullfights in San Juan, cliff-diving competitions in Sri Lanka, and spelling bees at the Kremlin. I have played Hamlet, I have performed open-heart surgery, and I have spoken with Elvis.

But I have not yet gone to college.

UNIVERSITY OF CHICAGO ESSAY PROMPTS: SHALLOW THINKERS NEED NOT APPLY

If you can write a good essay about one of these topics, you probably don't need a college education.

Essay Option 1

"At present you need to live the question."
—Rainer Maria Rilke, translated from the German by Joan M. Burnham

Essay Option 2

The short film *Powers of Ten* begins with an aerial shot of a couple picnicking in a Chicago park. The camera zooms out ten meters. It then zooms out again, but the degree of the zoom has increased by a power of ten; the camera is now 100 meters away. It continues to 1,000 meters, then 10,000, and so on, traveling through the solar system, the galaxy, and eventually to the edge of the known universe. Here the camera rests, allowing us to examine the vast nothingness of the universe, black void punctuated sparsely by galaxies so far away they appear as small stars. The narrator comments, "This emptiness is normal. The richness of our own neighborhood is the exception." Then the camera reverses its journey, zooming in to the picnic and—in negative powers of ten— to the man's hand, the cells in his hand, the molecules of DNA within, their atoms, and then the nucleus both "so massive and so small" in the "vast inner space" of the atom.

Zoom in and out on a person, place, event, or subject of interest. What becomes clear from far away that you can't see up close? What intricate structures appear when you move closer? How is the big view related to the small, the emptiness to the richness?

Essay Option 4

Argonne National Laboratory and Fermilab (both national laboratories managed by the University of Chicago) have particle accelerators that smash bits of atoms together at very high energies, allowing particles to emerge that are otherwise not part of the everyday world. These odd beasts—Z bosons, pi mesons, strange quarks—populated the universe seconds after the Big Bang and allow their observers to glimpse the fabric of the universe.

Put two or three ideas or items in a particle accelerator thought experiment. Smash 'em up. What emerges? Let us glimpse the secrets of the universe newly revealed.

What About Essay Option 3?

The Neurotic Parent Institute has chosen not to disclose this prompt because it is just too good for prospective college students. It is clearly fodder for a novel.

EGREGIOUS TYPOS ON COLLEGE APPS

If it is August, or even worse, November, you must do everything in your power—including bribery—to make your seniors start working on their essays. Once they get them written, if you're still on speaking terms, make sure they proofread, and don't trust your computer to spell check. Just about every admissions person on just about every tour ends his or her presentation with a real example of a horrendous, humorous error sent in by a careless, bleary-eyed senior.

Here are some deal-breaking typos from college applications. Their authors are now working at Taco Bell because they never reread their work.

Vanderbilt:	"I can't wait to attend Emory."
Duke:	"I can't wait to attend UNC."
George Washington:	The essay writer recounted his experience volunteering in the "Big Bother" program.
NYU:	One applicant wrote his whole essay on his favorite book, *The Lord of the Files.* Another said he wanted to be a "Roads Scholar."
Georgetown:	"I can't wait to attend Emory." (Emory appears popular with sloppy proofreaders.)
Colgate:	After hating broccoli his entire life, the essay writer gathered up the courage to try broccoli casserole at his girlfriend's house. But he spelled *broccoli* incorrectly throughout the essay.
Northwestern:	One applicant recounted her experiences as a Candy Stripper. (We've heard at least four colleges claim this story as their own.) Another spoke about how much he was influenced by his basketball couch.

TOPICS/STYLES TO AVOID

Don't want the admissions people to find out that a grownup has assisted with your college essay? Here are topics, words, and punctuation symbols to stay away from:

▶▶	Acid reflux
▶▶	Ponzi schemes
▶▶	Backslashes/forward slashes
▶▶	Chemical peels
▶▶	Kale comparisons at farmers' markets
▶▶	Back trouble

▶▶	Pilates
▶▶	How your contractor ripped you off on your outdoor firepit
▶▶	The words "aforementioned" and "notwithstanding"—in fact, we advise thinking twice about any compound word other than "snowman."

WHAT ELSE NOT TO WRITE ABOUT

If you're planning on writing your own essay instead of getting professional help from an adult, here's the report on no-no essay topics from the admissions deans at some of the many schools the Neurotic Parent Institute has visited:

✖ The illness of a pet

✖ The illness of a grandparent

✖ The death of a pet

✖ The death of a grandparent

✖ I went to (fill in name of developing country) and learned that everyone there is just the same as the people in my hometown of Greenwich, Connecticut

✖ "Sports are a metaphor for life's more difficult lessons. Our team, faced with adversity, only triumphed when all the players realized that the whole is more than the sum of its parts"

✖ My Internship at Prada in Milano

✖ What I Think About When I Run Uphill

GUATEMALAN LATRINES

One of CJ's friends, Fanatical Planner, has already written a draft of her Common App essay. Yesterday she asked for feedback. FP thought I was qualified to read it because I was once a TA in freshman composition. That was during the last century, I reminded her, when there were completely different rules about comma usage. But she insisted, so I read her essay.

It was brilliant. FP's voice came through loud and clear. Her descriptions were vivid and memorable. By the time I finished reading, I was almost moved to tears. I waited a minute, composed myself, then called the poor girl and told her to throw the whole thing out and start over. The reason? She had chosen to write about the latrine she built during her community-service trip to Queztaltenango, Guatemala.

Unfortunately for FP (and her parents, who spent $6,000 for the experience), several admissions officers on our tour had singled out Guatemalan latrines as an essay topic to be avoided at all costs. One rep said they had received so many Central American latrine stories that he imagined there were now more outhouses than bananas on the isthmus.

So what *is* a good subject to write about? I did some research and discovered a book called *50 Successful Harvard Essays*. It's a great find because you can read the first one for free on Amazon.

And that essay is about, get this: *fixing a toilet in Costa Rica.* The author writes candidly that, on the first day of his summer program in San José, he ate black beans, then made his way into the ladies' room because he was desperate and couldn't find the men's.

"I sat down and did what generally one does after eating a lot of beans. I finished up (remembering to throw the toilet paper in the wastebasket, as is done in Costa Rica to keep the pipes from clogging) and pulled the gold-plated handle. Nothing happened. Huh, that's funny. Tried again. Nothing. **Sh*t.**"

The author goes on to describe how, thanks to innate plumbing skills he never knew he had, he was eventually able to fix the toilet. And that essay got him into Harvard. True, it was not this year, the most difficult year for college acceptances in the history of the world. But the applicant successfully wrote about sh*t (with an asterisk, no less), while thousands of dedicated latrine builders were rejected right and left from lower-tier schools.

What happened? One theory is that too many people read the Harvard essay book, triggering a flood of theses about *baños* in developing countries.

Or maybe merely building a latrine does not make you a compelling applicant, but stopping one up does.

15 REAL OPENING LINES FROM BENNINGTON ESSAYS

1	The day I told my mother I was a channel for John Lennon was the day my mother got her first gray hair.
2	When I was young, I was color blind.
3	If I am not constantly busy or trying new things, I feel moldy.
4	In my physics class last year, we performed an experiment with light.
5	I had three hundred and fifty eight secrets that were not mine.
6	Poverty afflicts billions of people worldwide, and I am one of those afflicted.
7	There are only three sections of the paper that I read on a daily basis: the comics, the weather, and the obituaries.
8	If I were to design a library, it would be in the shape of a sprawling flower whose skeletal structure would be made of steel encased by curvaceous colored Plexiglas.
9	The walk from my house to school has become slippery recently.
10	I believe in books the way some people believe in God.
11	When I was little I wanted to be a vampire.
12	In my sophomore year I became deeply involved in animal rights.
13	My friends usually cringe when I have them watch the film *Harold and Maude*.
14	The bus stops next to a small red and gray house.
15	A chair.

5 REAL OPENING LINES FROM TUFTS ESSAYS

1	For dinner last night, I had swordfish and parsnips.
2	My favorite book has no author.
3	We are alone in the realm of space-time.
4	I carefully placed her torso and legs in a black trash bag to bring her to the sanctuary.
5	I never planned on going to college.

10 OPENING LINES
FROM STANFORD ADMISSION ESSAYS

These come from actual students who were accepted to Stanford.

1	I change my name each time I place an order at Starbucks.
2	When I was in the eighth grade I couldn't read.
3	While traveling through the daily path of life, have you ever stumbled upon a hidden pocket of the universe?
4	I have old hands.
5	I was paralyzed from the waist down. I would try to move my leg or even shift an ankle but I never got a response. This was the first time thoughts of death ever crossed my mind.
6	I almost didn't live through September 11th, 2001.
7	The spaghetti burbled and slushed around the pan, and as I stirred it, the noises it gave off began to sound increasingly like bodily functions.
8	I have been surfing Lake Michigan since I was 3 years old.
9	I stand on the riverbank surveying this rippled range like some riparian cowboy—instead of chaps, I wear vinyl, thigh-high waders and a lasso of measuring tape and twine is slung over my arm.
10	I had never seen anyone get so excited about mitochondria.

7 SUGGESTED OPENING LINES FROM
THE NEUROTIC PARENT

These will work for students with writers' block or anyone who has severe nausea after reading some of the actual opening lines on these pages.

1	As we touched down in Guam, I remembered in horror that I had left the oven on.
2	No matter how hard I try, I cannot keep track of my socks.
3	When I'm bored, I Google myself.
4	As soon as I completed my first Lego, I knew that one day I would be designing luxury yachts.
5	If someone had told me, as I rode in my parents' Hummer to soccer tournaments, that my four favorite words would one day be Vegan, Sustainable, Organic, and Biodiesel, I never would have believed it.
6	A lawn gnome.
7	I have never owned the same mobile device for more than three weeks.

HELPFUL ADVICE FROM A COLLEGE COUNSELOR

Don't write the first line first.

THE UNCOMMON APP

OMG! I was supposed to get awards? And have activities? They're telling me that now?!?

THE COMMON APP

If your child hasn't participated in a five-figure application boot camp, please don't expect to us to share every secret with you. But we will give you a little snapshot, along with a few hints.

Only exceptional kids (females) will be able to figure out how to fill this thing out on their own, so if you're not paying a consultant, plan to have lots of free time available.

THE COMMON APPLICATION

For Undergraduate College Admission

Sadly, your children will have to consolidate all the fabulous things they've done and describe them in one or two lines. Sure, they can add a resume or "activity sheet," but on the actual app, less is more. They can create different versions for different schools—i.e. if your family is both Jewish and Catholic and your student is applying to Brandeis and Georgetown, he can say he's Jewish on the Brandeis app and Catholic on the Georgetown app. They can even say they want to study nursing on one and military science on another—but they should make sure not to mix these up. The bottom line: Unlike other forms your child fills out, someone is actually going to read this one.

SENIOR APPLICATION ANGST

Rising seniordom means rising anxiety. The NPI recently heard three angst-laden stories from reliable sources:

1

A rising senior flew 3,000 miles to spend a week living at a Vermont college counselor's home. She returned with completed drafts of her Common App, personal statement, and supplemental essays.

2

A rising senior's SAT tutor has moved into her family's guesthouse.

3

A concerned dad with business interests in Bangladesh is considering establishing residency there to increase his daughter's college chances. The caveat: He wants her to live there for a month before she attends her admissions interviews, so she will sound knowledgeable about Bangladeshi culture.

MARY ANN LEAVITT GOES TO COLLEGE

Tonight CJ and I attended College Case Study Night. High school juniors from four schools and their parents were given the chance to be college admissions officers for the evening. We met in groups, each with a real admissions dean (ours was from one of the most competitive liberal arts colleges in the country) and reviewed the Common Applications of four fictitious students. Then we had to come to a consensus about which of the four should be admitted to Fallbrook College, a mock liberal arts school with a new athletic facility and midrange Critical Reading SAT scores of 580-650.

The four candidates were:

- Kenneth Aldman, a dyslexic saxophone player from the under-represented state of North Dakota.
- Robert Brandeis, an intellectual, soft-spoken museum docent, applying early as a legacy.
- Makele Johnson, a charismatic African-American class president and newspaper editor-in-chief who had typos on her application and seemed to be using Fallbrook as a safety.
- Mary Ann Leavitt, a star soccer player and community-service leader who'd been abandoned by her father, with the impact of the loss captured nicely in her essay.

My group chose to offer a spot to Mary Ann (mainly because the soccer coach wanted her), although her grades had dipped the year her mom lost her job. We waitlisted Makele and Robert, the legacy kid who chose Fallbrook as his first choice and had practically straight As throughout high school, but ultimately was too boring to be admitted. I was heartbroken for poor Robert until I found out that most of the other groups accepted him. But mostly I was shocked that Kenneth was flat-out denied by our group, not even waitlisted. So much for my plan to move to North Dakota.

After we finished rejecting all those well-qualified kids, there was a giant college fair. The admissions people stood at tables, chatting and marketing their super-selective schools with slick brochures, as if getting into college in the early 21st century was like signing up for summer camp. To add to the surreal atmosphere of the evening, every few minutes we ran into people we hadn't seen since our kids were in preschool. Over and over we marveled at how the kids turned out to be so big (boys) or beautiful (girls). Can you believe we're here at *college* night, we asked each other. Just yesterday we were discussing potty training and Power Ranger obsessions. Our babies are leaving home. If they can only find a college that will let them in.

HOOKS

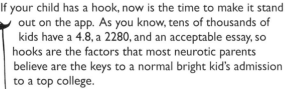

If your child has a hook, now is the time to make it stand out on the app. As you know, tens of thousands of kids have a 4.8, a 2280, and an acceptable essay, so hooks are the factors that most neurotic parents believe are the keys to a normal bright kid's admission to a top college.

Hooks include a lot of factors you cannot control: legacy, diversity, adversity, athletic talent, artistic/ musical/dramatic talent, and being related to the famous or the philanthropic. But if your kid is none of the above, have no fear. All you need to do is "hook" her up with an unusual passion—something that will impress a jaded admissions committee in time for her to become a specialist by the time she turns 16.

A respected guidance counselor recently told the NPI that she believes only 5% of unhooked applicants get into top schools. Here are her words:

"The admissions committees are not just about GPAs, test scores, and the rigor on your transcript—for each class of perfect kids academically who they accept, they reject another whole qualified group. What they want is for each applicant to find his or her hook...and we don't just mean passion."

Does your daughter love animals? That's a passion! Has she started a day care for parrots and toucans? That's a hook. But nowadays the hook needs to jump off the page. So how about teaching those tropical birds to speak their native languages? Spanish—that's a cliché. But Indonesian, Creole, Malay? Now that's a hook! And if you happen to have a smidge of Creole or Malay blood, all the better.

3 WAYS TO COMMUNICATE HOOKS ON THE COMMON APP

1 Essays.

2 Links to videos of symphonies your child has conducted.

3 Letters of recommendations. If your child has worked with political or spiritual world leaders, by all means get them to send in a letter. But don't flood the committee with correspondence from random members of Congress. Make sure the letters convey specific information about your student.

In the examples on the next page, you can see how the former does not hook the student, while the latter does.

Sample Recommendation Letter for an Unhooked Applicant

Dear Dartmouth,

It is my pleasure to recommend Jordan Silver for college. Jordan practices compassion, laying the foundation for a meaningful life, not only at the level of the individual, family, or community, but also for humanity as a whole.

Fondly,
Nelson Mandela

Sample Recommendation Letter for a Hooked Applicant

Dear Dartmouth,

Of all the young men whom I have had the pleasure to know, Kyle Bennett was the one who taught me about the different degrees of happiness. From him I learned that material objects give rise to physical happiness, while spiritual development gives rise to mental happiness. He will be an asset to your institution, especially if he decides to join a fraternity.

Namaste,
The Dalai Lama

THE RIGHT SPELLING ERRORS = ADMISSION TO HARVARD

We all know that China puts the U.S. to shame economically. But for some weird reason, Chinese parents want their kids to study at our brand-name universities.

As most of you know, this is not so easily accomplished. Even perfect students here find that Ivy admissions are a crapshoot. But the Chinese have managed to figure out exactly how to win the game. For fees starting at $15K, you can hire ThinkTank Learning to fill out your app, write your essay, help you come up with standout extracurriculars, tutor you until you get a 2250+ on the SAT, and even bribe your high school teachers to change some of your grades.

Best of all, according to the *New York Times*, you no longer have to live in China to benefit from these services. Six centers are now open in Northern California, with more to come.

ThinkTank says they are "able to distill the college admissions process into an exact science." That's according to founder Steven Ma, who compared his methods to genetic engineering. As he said in the *Times,* "We make unnatural stuff happen. There's a system built by colleges designed to pick out future stars, and we are here to crack that system."

Although many American colleges decry such practices, companies like ThinkTank—and there are others like it in China—are booming.

"Students, whose parents often pay tens or even hundreds of thousands of dollars, are molded by ThinkTank into well-rounded, socially conscious overachievers through a regimen often beginning as early as the year before entering high school," said Ma, a former investment banker, in the *Times.*

Because of the poor English skills of ThinkTank's Chinese clients, this can be a challenge. "We really have to hold their hand...including deliberately leaving spelling errors in their essays so they look authentic... and building extracurricular activities from the ground up." This means founding Model United Nations groups, building websites for student projects, and helping obtain funding to build a hydroelectric generator.

No, we did not make this up. We read it in the *New York Times.*

A bit incredulous that a company would brag to the press about its unethical practices, we checked out ThinkTank's dense, unstylish website, which looks as if it were designed by the guys who leave carpet-cleaning flyers on your windshield. You would think ThinkTank would be somewhat embarrassed (or concerned about litigation) about the questionable methods discussed in the article, but instead they proudly display a link to the *Times* piece. They even have lists of SAT scores and photos of smiling clients holding up their big envelopes from Stanford and Harvard.

We put in a call to ThinkTank to inquire about a position as a spelling-error consultant. Nobody is more adept at writing essays with the occasional typo than the Neurotic Parent Institute. For a massive fee, we would be willing share our vast knowledge of authentic teen mistakes, including "definately" and "existance." But so far we have not heard back.

Meanwhile, for the sake of our economy, let's hope that lots of these

ThinkTank kids fraudulently get into Harvard. Then, the first time they write an essay on their own, they will probably not include enough spelling errors to satisfy their professors, giving the competitive edge to the *American* kids who have beaten the system.

The NPI asked our intern, Gina, to contact ThinkTank to find out if they would accept her as a client. Here is the transcript of their conversation:

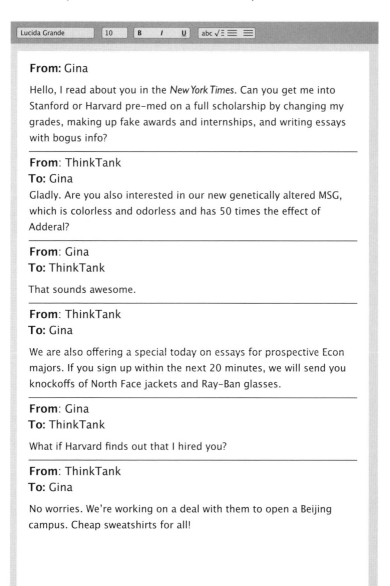

| Lucida Grande | 10 | **B** | *I* | <u>U</u> | abc √≡ ☰ ☰ |

From: Gina

Hello, I read about you in the *New York Times*. Can you get me into Stanford or Harvard pre-med on a full scholarship by changing my grades, making up fake awards and internships, and writing essays with bogus info?

From: ThinkTank
To: Gina

Gladly. Are you also interested in our new genetically altered MSG, which is colorless and odorless and has 50 times the effect of Adderal?

From: Gina
To: ThinkTank

That sounds awesome.

From: ThinkTank
To: Gina

We are also offering a special today on essays for prospective Econ majors. If you sign up within the next 20 minutes, we will send you knockoffs of North Face jackets and Ray-Ban glasses.

From: Gina
To: ThinkTank

What if Harvard finds out that I hired you?

From: ThinkTank
To: Gina

No worries. We're working on a deal with them to open a Beijing campus. Cheap sweatshirts for all!

From the annals of the Neurotic Parent blog

MY NEW EXTRACURRICULAR

I recently participated in a Japanese woodcarving class in a friend's courtyard. I signed up without knowing that this would be a spiritual, meditative activity rather than an art project. The point is to choose a piece of wood and whittle away, letting the object shape itself rather than planning what you want to create. There are a few unwritten rules: try not to cut yourself, don't keep dropping your sculpture, and, if possible, refrain from talking.

Halfway through the process, I began to relax and de-stress. I stopped worrying that everyone else's work looked like an egg, a whale, or a giant chopstick, while mine was "nothing." I didn't even care that the compliments I received were about the grain of my wood rather than what I had carved. For once I was free to enjoy the ride and not care about the outcome.

Ah, if only the college process could shape itself like this, I thought. Take a block of rough wood, focus on the journey rather than the destination, and poof! You end up with something smooth and functional, something that was meant to be.

My happy Zen ponderings dissipated when I broke rule #3 and began to chat with my carving buddy, a young woman who sipped green iced tea as she whittled. Although she was a first-timer like me, her piece of wood had transformed itself into the kind of pendant you could purchase at Barney's, while mine looked like a marked-down souvenir from the Maui airport. The small talk did, in fact, to turn out to be a huge mistake: My cool fellow carver was, I kid you not, an SAT tutor. And once she found out I was the Neurotic Parent, all she wanted to talk about was whether the UCs *really* do want subject tests this year, even though they say they don't.

So much for meditation and spirituality.

Chapter

ten

ADVANCED APPLICATION STRATEGIES

Organizational advice and obscure last-minute passions for teens & meddling parents

A MIDSUMMER'S REALITY CHECK

August is the time, according to all the specialists, to get a jump start on all the stressful tasks that define senior year.

After a major research study, the Neurotic Parent Institute has created checklists for rising seniors, one for each gender.

August To-Do List for Girls

❶ Finalize college list

❷ Download Common App

❸ Complete first drafts of the personal statement and three supplements

❹ Set up appointment with college counselor for essay feedback

❺ Contact teachers to ask for recommendations

❻ Write thank-you notes to above teachers

❼ Take weekly SAT subject test practice exams

❽ E-mail college admissions officers with well-researched questions about potential majors

❾ Organize fundraiser to benefit Tanzanian AIDS orphans

❿ Shop for college interview wardrobe

By Labor Day, most girls are well on their way to completing the tasks outlined on the above list, so they will be able to focus on their challenging senior year course loads and SAT retakes.

August To-Do List for Boys

❶ Turn on computer

❷ Download Common App

❸ Take a break and go to the beach. Why stress now?

SLACKER PATROL

What's to prevent you from exaggerating or overtly lying on your application? Nothing. Not even in the chill state of California. That's why the UCs randomly vet 5% to 6% of their 98,000+ freshman applications. If a student says she was the lead in the play, they want proof! Send in a video of your solo or at least a copy of the program. And if you can't get your coach to say you were really the captain of the wrestling team, you might as well withdraw your app.

According to the *Los Angeles Times*, "Each year, a small number of UC applicants…are caught fibbing about such claims as performing a lead role in a school play, volunteering as a tutor for poor children, or starring on the soccer field."

Those who are investigated are asked for concert programs, pay stubs from Jack in the Box, or letters from coaches, and some nervous applicants even submit videos of performances and sports trophies.

The stakes are high: One applicant who could not produce documentation that she was a volunteer coach for a young soccer team told the UC sleuths that she could not locate her supervisor. The officials said a letter from the parent of a team member would suffice. But the applicant never responded and her application was canceled.

Worried that your EC list is a bit suspect? Here are some ideas for supplemental material to *prove* you are telling the truth:

Glass from broken window when you hit a grand slam while pinch-hitting for the Red Sox

Melted glacial ice from your expedition to Antarctica

Split reeds from your performance at Tanglewood

Royalty statements from your off-Broadway musical

Leftover dehydrated food tubes from your journey on the space shuttle

Test tube of repaired cancer cells from your summer research experience

Thank-you e-mail from Nelson Mandela for speechwriting assistance

Photo of you fitting Kate Middleton for the hat you designed

ROUGH CUT

By now you get it: The latest trend in college admissions is that nobody is getting in. All that effort—working hard for good grades, paying tutors, devoting every spare moment to a bizarre passion—yet more and more kids are getting deferred or rejected, even though there are fewer kids applying. Add that to the many reports of unhappy freshmen who have transferred and of frustrated seniors who are unemployable. We cannot help but hypothesize that the whole admissions journey seems to be facing an existential crisis.

Thank goodness that technology has stepped in to make us feel better about the process. Student applications are no longer just for admissions committees—they have now hit YouTube big time. One new development, overshadowing the admissions videos produced by Yale and Macalester, is that Tufts now allows prospective students, in addition to the three required essays, to submit an optional video that "says something about you."

One applicant, a "dancing math girl," created and performed fifteen rhythmic algorithm movements and had her video go viral on YouTube with more than 127,000 hits. Her low-tech, intentionally cheesy dances included a line-graph electric slide and a memorable Sin and Cos interpretation, which she later performed on campus after she was accepted.

The Neurotic Parent applauds the optional video trend, and undoubtedly admissions officers will as well. Now applicants don't have to bore the committee with tales of Guatemalan latrine building. Instead they can just head off to the park with an iPhone camera and become famous overnight for reciting a brief *Macbeth* soliloquy. And watching a dumb one-minute video is infinitely less annoying than reading a lousy 250-word essay.

SABOTAGE KARMA

Some students and their parents are so desperate to get into college that they have taken drastic measures: sabotaging the competition.

The *Chicago Tribune* reported that admissions departments routinely receive anonymous letters about applicants, presumably from others who are competing for the same spots. Some of these notes are actually written in crayon and contain information about character flaws, racy Facebook pages, and minor drug busts. Stacey Kostell, director of undergraduate admission for the University of Illinois at Urbana-Champaign, told the *Tribune*, "People think if they disadvantage one student, it may advantage theirs," and she said her office routinely throws these missives away. But an admissions officer from Notre Dame reports that they do contact the applicant's high school to give students a chance to defend themselves.

The Neurotic Parent wonders why anyone would resort to sending an anonymous note to a college. Can't people just suck it up and accept that the world is unfair? Why would anyone want to live with this sort of karma? Your child might get into a great college but then you would probably be hit by a bus. Instead, we have a better strategy. Choose another college on your child's rival's list, and write a glowing recommendation for the dirty rotten scoundrel. For example, if your daughter has her heart set on Brown, and the mean girl who has made her life miserable since third grade is also applying there, send an effusive letter about the officious nemesis to Columbia. This process is a win-win: You can help give a ne'er-do-well a second chance while paving the way for your brilliant, flawless kid to get the break she deserves.

THE ALUMNI INTERVIEW: 7 ESSENTIAL HINTS

At some point during the admissions process, it's likely that your child will be contacted by a local alumnus or alumna for an interview. Here are some tips that will de-stress the process for your student:

1 You will definitely misplace the phone number and contact info of your interviewer. So prepare for the call by leaving Post-its all over the house. Once the interviewer gets in touch, store the number in your phone. The tricky thing will be not to lose the phone for two weeks. If you can accomplish this, you deserve to go to college.

2 When you get to Starbucks, do not order a Light Mocha Coconut Frappuccino No Whip, unless you are applying to a specialized program, like Cornell's School of Adjective Order.

3 Look the interviewer in the eye. Unless, of course, you are pretending to be blind, in which case you can wear cool Ray-Bans.

4 If you're lucky, your interviewer will be talkative, and you can just smile and nod. But some alums have gone to cocktail parties where they were trained to get you to ask questions. If so, you might have to hire a consultant to spend hours coaching you through mock interviews.

5 Do not ask questions that are answered on the college's website— and don't ask anything related to parking or partying.

Lame question: Do you validate?

Lame question: Are there subways near Kenyon?

Lame question: A girl in your brochure was carrying a Mulberry backpack. Which sorority is she in?

Lame question: Is your Guyana Studies program based in Africa or South America?

Good question: My passion is the prediction of the complex microbial communities and processes that underpin ecosystem properties. Can you describe the programs that would be available to me?

Good question: Is there a club I can join with the goal of mobilizing and educating to help foster a more peaceful campus and world, based not only on the absence of war but the presence of justice?

6 After the interview, ask one of your parent's colleagues, preferably a PR consultant, to write a brief thank-you note. Of course, sending something through the mail will be a new experience for you. Ask your parents to explain how to put a stamp on a letter and direct you to the nearest post office. You might also want to learn cursive for the occasion.

7 Don't forget that most interviewers are probably only taking the time to meet you because they want to stay active in the Alumni Association so they can eventually get *their* kids in.

From the annals of the Neurotic Parent blog

TEENS SUE AUTOCORRECT FOR SABOTAGING APPS

Recently, CJ mentioned (in a text) that he got an A on his Italian paper. Clearly I should have replied "Bravo!" But even the Neurotic Parent cannot always be clever, so I wrote back "YAY!" in caps.

Moments later, I received the following text from CJ: "Why is that gay?" Yes, in a dangers-of-artificial-intelligence moment of homophobic insanity, my Blackberry's spellcheck had changed "YAY!" to "GAY!"

Now, a sinister group of techno-nerds are casting their spell(check) on the college admissions level. It's even happening in Ivy admissions land. Thanks to MTER (Mom of Two Extraordinary Rowers) for this report:

At the Penn information session, the admissions rep mentioned that kids often forget to double-check their apps, and a disturbing trend has emerged, probably because of an evil programmer who was denied admission to Penn. A rash of applications have referred to the "Wharton School of Business" as the "Wharton School of Bunnies."

The Neurotic Parent Answers Your Questions

ALUM INTERVIEW FAQS

Q: What should I wear to my alum interview?

A: Whatever you like. All the interviewers we know have a story about the five terrific kids they recommended who were ultimately rejected. And the one weirdo they blackballed who was accepted.

Q: My favorite movie is The Hangover. If my interviewer asks me about my taste in film, should I be honest?

A: It doesn't matter. All the interviewers we know have a story about the five terrific kids they recommended who were ultimately rejected. And the one weirdo they blackballed who was accepted.

Q: My main extracurricular is that I run my school's Democratic Club. I just googled my alum interviewer and found out she donated $4,800 to the Tea Party. What should I tell her that I do in my spare time?

A: Genome research.

EARLY: WHERE THE ACTION IS

One of the most strategic—and confusing—aspects of the admissions process is figuring out whether to apply ED (Early Decision), EA (Early Action), or plain old RD (Regular Decision). Here are the basics:

ED PROS

❶ Greater chance of acceptance.

❷ If admitted in December, students get to have a life for the remainder of senior year, assuming they don't get a D—or get arrested.

❸ If denied or deferred, they'll learn a valuable lesson about dealing with rejection.

ED CONS

❶ A plan for the decisive—not the most teenlike character trait.

❷ If accepted, students must withdraw all other apps, so you'll never get to brag about all the schools they got into.

❸ ED is a sacred institution. You, your child, and the counselor must all sign a binding Early Decision Commitment, which, unlike marriage, you can't get out of.

EA/ROLLING

❶ EA is so phenomenal that we wonder what's in it for 'the colleges. Your kid can show the love *and* have a non-binding bird in hand by December.

❷ Rolling is even better—students get in commitment-free as early as October.

RD: OLD SCHOOL

Then there's RD, which lets you compare all financial aid offers. Also for those who can't resist taking the SATs one last time.

ADVANCED OPTIONS

In our advanced edition, we will cover ED2, SCEA (Single Choice Early Action), and DWTSRD, for students who missed their EA deadlines because they chose to watch the finale of *Dancing With the Stars*.

DO NOT USE YOUR IPHONE TO THANK YOUR INTERVIEWER

Just wanted to thank you for a great latte... and to let you know that I just found out I made the varsity cross-dressing team.

Well, good luck with that! I have some Manolos you can borrow.

Um...meant to say cross-country...this darn phone

The Neurotic Parent Answers Your Questions

URGENT QUERIES FROM READERS

September is the optimal time for college angst. Parents of high school juniors are debating when to begin testing and whether it's better to get a B- in an honors class or an A- in a dumbed-down class. And it goes without saying that parents of seniors are certified basket cases. So it comes as no surprise that the Neurotic Parent gets bombarded with questions in September. Here are two from senior parents from last fall.

Q: We summer with a member of Parliament, a tech CEO, and a supermodel. Should they write recommendations for our child?

A: Only if they enclose a check.

Q: My son is a legacy at (name of Ivy) and has almost all his ducks lined up. He has a GPA of 4.6. He has a letter of recommendation from Barbara Boxer. And he participated in a marathon while blindfolded so he could empathize with his sightless companions. The only piece missing is his SAT critical reading score, and he has already taken the exam three times. Should he take the ACT? And if so, can you recommend a good tutor?

A: No way! I'm saving the tutor for MY son (who did a blindfolded *triathlon*).

ATHLETIC RECRUITMENT MADE EASY

If your child is a talented athlete, he or she can get recruited to Division I (mascot, marching band, 100,000 people singing "Sweet Caroline" in the stands) or Division 3 (sleep later, shorter practices, but nobody attends the games) schools by following these super-easy steps:

- Attend three to four elite camps every summer
- Play with club and traveling teams in the right tournaments
- Bombard coaches with e-mails, videos, and updates about new records; wait until July before senior year to contact D3 coaches, but D1 coaches must be contacted by fifth grade
- Other stuff that will cost you an arm and a leg but could result in an amazing scholarship and primo seats for you

If all goes well, soon your athlete will have a likely letter in hand, which means it's likely your worries are over…until the first injury.

THE MAKINGS OF A TORTURED ARTIST: THE ARTS SUPPLEMENT

It's no secret that the Common Application is a challenge to fill out. It provides a mere ten lines to list extracurricular activities, so you'll need to find a top copywriter to adequately convey the fabulousness of your child's experiences within the designated number of characters. He or she can also attach a resumé, but there are mixed opinions about whether this is a good idea. Do admissions committees, who already have to read your students' heavily edited essays, really want to see pages of embellishments about their accomplishments? Of course they don't.

But for high school kids who have "made a substantial commitment of time and energy to one or more of the arts"—musicians, actors, dancers, singers, artists, photographers, filmmakers, or songwriters —there is a lot more work to do. First, your child must attach a form documenting the years studied, workshops attended, repertoires mastered, and awards and honors received. And, after slaving all fall on the personal statement and supplemental essays, your student will have no choice but to create a cutting-edge portfolio. This can be presented on a website or in a ten-minute CD or DVD that "demonstrates contrasting examples of expression and technique."

Once the portfolio is produced, photographed, videotaped, recorded, and/or otherwise packaged, you child will, of course, upload it or ship it to the 26 schools on your list. But you can also take it to a live cattle call of sorts, where hundreds of admissions reps gather to look at these portfolios in person. A parent who attended a portfolio review in Valencia, California said the line to see the RISD representatives was so long that it would have been faster to fly to Providence and meet on campus. And theatre, music, and dance kids must do just that: travel across the country for stressful auditions, all while taking five APs and volunteering fifteen hours a week at a pet adoption shelter.

The bottom line? If your children are talented, encourage them to give up their sculpture or music composition at a young age, before the arts supplement process completely ruins their senior year. A worthy substitute: Actuarial Science. It boasts a 0% unemployment rate...and no portfolio.

eleven

FINANCIAL AID

I learned law so well, the day I graduated I sued the college, won the case, and got my tuition back
— Fred Allen

BLING FOR BLINDNESS

Luckily, if you cannot afford to pay for college, many excellent schools claim to be "need-blind." This means that they will not consider your financial circumstances when deciding whether or not to accept your kid. This requires the admissions committee to put on blindfolds when sitting around and discussing your child, as well as promising not to peek at your zip code or the question on the first page of the Common App that asks if you are applying for financial aid.

If need-blind sounds too good to be true, it probably is. In fact, we've identified one particularly mysterious aspect to the concept: What if a college accepted an entire student body that needed aid? If the college were truly need-blind, this would happen all the time, because we know that admissions committees are averse to extracurricular activities that stink of privilege.

Because of the need-blind nature of many colleges, the parents who are paying full tuition are screwed. Not only do they have to fork over the price of a *pied à terre* in Santa Fe for their educations, but they are also constantly being hit up by the development office to pay for the tuition of their fellow classmates—the kids who will one day take away their jobs.

BEST MAJOR FOR THE TIMES

One of the happiest college students we know is at Lewis & Clark, studying evolutionary anthropology with a specialty in primatology. Unfortunately, even if he one day succeeds in finding a job, he will never be able to support himself. Neither will anybody in publishing, journalism, music, fine arts, education, drama, or social work, all dying fields. And although every three or four days the *Wall Street Journal* has a piece about how lawyers cannot find jobs, we're fairly certain that bankruptcy attorneys will continue to be in high demand. Unfortunately, few of their clients will be able to pay them.

PAYING SOMEONE TO MAKE YOU LOOK NEEDY

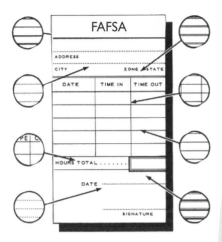

Many families have found that it is more difficult to fill out the FAFSA than to take the SAT. Ironically, a whole new lucrative industry has emerged, one that charges an arm and a leg to help prove you are poor enough to be aid-worthy.

Affluent families pay $1,500+ to "financial consultants" who solicit clients through presentations at top private schools. Other less expensive services like fafsa.com charge $80 to $100 to fill out the form, and they get thousands of calls a day from desperate families.

The government knows we all hate the tricky 100-question form and has proposed getting rid of it. Secretary of Education Arne Duncan said, "You basically have to have a Ph.D to figure that thing out."

The Neurotic Parent Institute wonders why this is a politically charged issue. Is it because the form is so difficult that fewer people will apply for aid? Or could it be that an easier form will harm the economy by putting all the friendly/fraudulent FAFSA helpers out of business?

CAN ANYONE SPARE 250K?

Unfortunately, we at the Neurotic Parent Institute are far from experts in financial aid. We're glad that paying full boat means that more truly needy kids can get aid, but we're not so happy about subsidizing kids whose well-off parents were foresighted enough to hide their funds in annuities. In fact, just about all the extra money we've earned as a result of our college degrees has gone to finance our kids' educations. But we know that for most families, paying for college is a much tougher nut to crack than getting into college. The only good news? If you can tolerate filling out a bunch of boring forms, you have a good chance of somebody throwing money your way.

NOSY FINANCIAL FORMS

Colleges are suddenly feeling guilty about the student loans that have ruined the lives of so many young people. No matter how much these graduates work, many simply cannot ever earn enough to repay the bank. So the new trend in humane college financing involves offering awesome financial aid packages to families who can manage to be organized enough to complete bureaucratic paperwork on time. These gifts usually come from private colleges and universities, and and schools also often give awards on the basis of merit. But if it slipped your mind to save half a million for your two kids, and you actually *need* the money, you must devote three 40-hour weeks to getting the paperwork done.

Here are the forms you need to know about:

The College Scholarship Services Profile

The College Board, the same folks who provide the dreaded SAT to your harried children, created the College Scholarship Services Profile (CSS), which is used primarily by private colleges. It involves a worksheet, a preliminary profile, and lots of other intimidating stuff. It's all guaranteed to be incomprehensible to your kids, so you can pretty much count on filling it out yourself, but only if you have a brother-in-law who is a CPA.

The CSS Profile asks applicants the purchase price of their parents' home, the amount of their parents' mortgage payment, the purchase price of their primary motor vehicle, and the total current value of each parent's tax-deferred retirement, pension, annuity, and savings plans. Include IRA, SRA Keogh, SEP, 401(a), 401(k), 403(b), 408, 457, and 501(c) plans, as well as the amount their siblings have in custodial accounts (in case you're thinking of hiding your college-age kid's money in their younger siblings' accounts).

Once the College Board collects all this personal data (and adds it to your SAT file, which they will have access to for the rest of your life), for a small fee they'll send it over to your college of choice. Then, once they determine that you are actually broke, your student will get a very nice check. Definitely worth it, but in order to complete the forms, you'll need to cancel your plans for the three months before the due date.

What are your alternatives? Pay someone to fill out your CSS Profile for you. Then you: a) will be in even greater financial need and b) the professional you hire can help you hide your more valuable assets, like your home, and you should wind up with a lower EFC (Expected Family Contribution) number.

With just some very quick random googling, we found *dozens* of sites that not only offer assistance in filling out your forms but will also help you hide some of your assets, such as your house. One, called "financial-aidsupersite.com," sounds like it has found a solid, presumably legal way to cheat the system. On its site, it proclaims:

"There are several ways to shelter your home equity from the CSS PROFILE to maximize your financial aid eligibility. One way to shelter your home equity from both the CSS PROFILE and the FAFSA is to move it inside a non-includable asset. If you move your home equity into a non-includable asset you do not have to report it on your CSS PROFILE. This one strategy has helped our clients receive tens of thousands more in financial aid." The amount they charge is not advertised on their site (and we were afraid we'd be sued if we contacted them), but we're sure it is quite reasonable, compared to legitimately spending all your savings on college.

The Famous FAFSA

According to our favorite research source, Wikipedia, the Free Application for Federal Student Aid (FAFSA) is a form prepared by current and prospective college students to determine their eligibility for student financial aid. You must check with each school to see whether it wants the CSS, the FAFSA, or its own form. The FAFSA is not only free and less probing than the CSS Profile, but it's better for procrastinators—the CSS is generally due in the fall, depending on the school, and the FAFSA is later. Just beware of fafsa.com, which is a scam site...and not free. Instead, look for the smiling kids on fafsa.ed.gov.

☞ *FUN FACT:* The CSS was formerly called the FAF. One can only imagine the confusion that caused.

The SHMAFSA

Thanks to the Neurotic Parent Institute, the CSS Profile and the FAFSA are not the only financial aid documents that you need to complete to be considered for aid. As of this year, most colleges will require the timely completion of the SHMAFSA, which stands for Significantly High Monetary Assets Financing SAT Assistance. This form attempts to recoup some of the exorbitant funds that many parents spend trying to get their kids into college. Sample questions include:

❻a. Itemize expenditures on prep materials, tutors, psychologists, educational specialists, medication, replacement calculators, and counselors. Include parking tickets issued on test day.

THE TIGER SCHOLARSHIP MOM

There is nothing like the lazy days of summer to prove that a college education is not worth it. Most of the kids we know spend their summers slaving away at internships, most earning nothing and some extremely lucky ones taking home $9 an hour. Meanwhile, recent grads are competing for barista positions all over the nation. One very bright and talented Barnard girl we know had to go through *four* interviews, including one with the owner, before she was finally hired to prepare coffee in Chelsea.

So if you're planning to send your kid to college, maybe you should force your student to apply for zillions of scholarships. Here's an informative College Confidential report by a woman we dubbed the Tiger Scholarship Mom, whose daughter received seven merit awards and whose scholarships now exceed her cost of attendance. We're imagining the lucky gal wearing an outfit from **KOHL'S**, enjoying a **BURRITO** dinner on her **LOFT BED** (just three scholarships on her enticing list—do you win goods/merchandise in addition to funds for schools?).

If you read the following College Confidential thread carefully, it sounds as if the poster's daughter also won some sort of lottery. We wish we could find out, and also report how many essays the girl was forced to write, but we're too lazy to do the research. Any (unpaid) interns out there willing to help?

☞ *NOTE: All of the following are real scholarships. My publisher has me on a ridiculous deadline—otherwise I would come up with parody names. But truth is stranger than fiction.*

🗐 05-07, 02:01 PM		#1
swicks2011 Junior Member Location: South Carolina Posts: 102	Hi, I was asked to share the list of scholarships my DD applied to, so here they are:	

All Media NY Writing Scholarship	**AXA Achievement Scholarship**
Alvin Cox Memorial Fund Scholarship	**Best Buy Scholarship**
American Fire & Sprinkler Association	**Brandon Goodman Scholarship**
American Public Health Association Get Ready	**Body by Milk Sammy Scholarship**
Ashley Marie Easterbrook Scholarship	**Burger King Scholarship**
Asian & Pacific Islander American	**C. G. Fuller Foundation Scholarship – SC Only**
	Charles L. Cummins/ Mae B. Wham – LOCAL

05-07, 02:01 PM

CIP Scholarship – Spring 2011
CIP Scholarship – Fall 2010
Federated Women's Club – LOCAL
Kiwanis Club – LOCAL
Coca-Cola Scholars Foundation
Doing Good Scholarship
Elks National Foundation MVS Award
ESA Foundation Scholarship
Freedom in Academia Scholarship
Gen and Kelly Tanabe Scholarship
GE-Reagan Foundation Scholarship Program
Horatio Alger Scholarship
ISSA Foundation Scholarship
Jane E. Hunter Scholarship – OHIO or SC
Janice M. Scott Memorial Fund
Jimmy Rane Foundation Scholarship – NC, SC, GA, AL, OK, MO, NE, AR, TN, LA, MS, FL, KY, TX
Kate Herzog Writing Awards
Kennedy Foundation
KFC Scholars Program
Kittie Moss Fairey Educational Fund Scholarship – Must Attend SC College
Kohl's Cares Scholarship Program
Leopold-Schepp Foundation Scholarship
Lowes Scholarship
M.A. Lee Foundation
McAlister Foundation Scholarship – LOCAL
Mercer Silas Bailey Memorial – LOCAL
OCA-AXA Asian Pacific American
OCA-UPS Gold Mountain Minority
OP Loftbed Scholarship
RMHC-ASIA Scholarship Program
Sam Walton Community Scholarship
Scottish Rite Masonic Shepherd Scholarship
Share Your Story Scholarship
Simon Youth Foundation Scholarship
South Carolina Sheriff's Association – SC
South Carolina State Fair Scholarship – SC
Strom Thurmond Foundation – SC
Sun Trust Off to College – Every Two Weeks
TG Charley Wootan Grant – Outside Texas
US Bank Internet Scholarship
USA Funds Access to Education Scholarship
Wendy's National Heisman Award Scholarship
William Orr Dingwall Asian Ancestry Grant
Winthrop University CLOSE Scholarship – College Based
Youth Foundation Hadden Scholarship
9 Beans and a Burrito Foundation Scholarship
Abbott and Fenner Scholarship
Big Sun 2011 Scholarship
Breylan Communications Scholarship
Directron.com Scholarship
Dowd and Guild Scholarship
ICBC Lawyers Scholarship

Hope that helps!
Take care,
Lisa

MORE ABOUT THE TIGER SCHOLARSHIP MOM

The Tiger Scholarship Mom's posting of the 67 scholarships her daughter applied to became a hot topic of conversation on College Confidential. Here's some of the exchange.

05-09, 07:53 PM   #2

bbarty

Junior Member
Posts: 82

Wow! Thank you very much! This was very helpful. I'm a soon-to-be senior and although I was aware of a decent number of these scholarships, there are so many on here that I didn't know existed. Any thoughts from the applying/awarding of the scholarship process as to which of the scholarships seemed to be the "favorites" (most amount of money awarded, easiest to complete application for, and most fun to apply for)?

05-09, 09:15 PM   #3

ivybound1

Junior Member
Posts: 149

Oh my... Is this a normal amount of scholarships to apply to? I've applied to one so far and that took me about a week to complete. How many did she get out of these?

05-10, 09:12 AM   #4

swicks2011
Junior Member
Posts: 102

She won 7 of them and 18 of them are still pending, but it doesn't really matter anymore because she exceeded her cost of attendance and now they are taking away from her SC Life scholarship (lottery money) & Federal SEOG. I have an appointment with one to see if they can wait and send the check next year when she would actually be able to benefit from it. We declined one because she no longer had a need for this school year and felt since the funds for it was limited that we'd rather someone else get it that still had need for this coming year.

She applied to 1 scholarship each week all of the past school year and 3 per week while school was out. I did all the searching and kept up with dates for her so literally just handed her which one to do next.

📄 **05-11, 04:10 PM**   **#5**

doublerainbow99	**Wow, thank you so much! Your daughter is very lucky to have you help her with scholarship searches! Can you share which numbers she used to win the lottery?**
New Member	

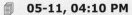

From the annals of the Neurotic Parent blog

A MISSIVE FROM THE TIGER SCHOLARSHIP MOM

One day after I posted about the mother who forced her daughter to write 67 essays, I received an earnest defense from the resourceful poster herself. The Tiger Scholarship Mom thought I was mocking her; in fact, I am envious of her abilities to get her child to raise enough money for college just by making her churn out a bunch of lame essays about sprinklers, loft beds, and Horatio Alger. What was I thinking? We could have used son's tuition money to purchase a vineyard in Tuscany.

This is the Tiger Scholarship Mom...I don't see what's wrong with letting others know if they are determined they can do it! My daughter would not be able to go to the college of her choice had she not done this. I did not force her but could only afford a lesser priced school and offered to help her find a way to go where she wanted if she was willing to do the work...It is the sad state of my finances and the economy that motivated her.

I then messaged the Tiger Scholarship Mom with the hope of finding out her financial aid strategies, not to mention her parenting techniques. Here is an excerpt from her reply.

She worked so hard because she knew it was the only way to go where she wanted to go....Honestly, once she wrote about three of them she really only had to tweak them to fit the others. While she was doing the one scholarship a week she was taking dual enrollment class (graduated HS with 34 college credits) & working 20-30 hours a week. She is very driven when it's something she wants. So far she has won twelve scholarships and $74,400 total...LOL ☺

I forgive the Tiger Scholarship Mom for the double-whammy LOL+emoticon. She is my hero.

SCHOLARSHIPS FOR DESCENDANTS OF THE ALMOST FAMOUS

CJ asked me to proofread his UC app yesterday, the day before Thanksgiving—what holiday fun! Even though he has already been accepted to a school he loves, he has to apply to our state schools in case we lose all of our savings before September.

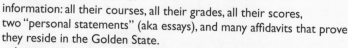

The UCs don't require teacher or counselor recs, or even a high school transcript, until you get accepted. Instead they expect the prospective students to enter a LOT of information: all their courses, all their grades, all their scores, two "personal statements" (aka essays), and many affidavits that prove they reside in the Golden State.

A mom whose son is now at NYU told me she filled out the UC app for her son last year because he refused to and she just wanted to see if he could get into Berkeley and UCLA. She said it took five hours, not including forcing him to write two essays.

The application is somewhat user friendly—it even "talks," giving you helpful hints if you get stuck—but considering it was probably produced by top engineering students, it's a technological nightmare. It repeatedly times out, and duplicate windows keep popping up, so if you change something, you never know whether it saved or not.

CJ's application was in pretty good shape, but he had neglected to fill in the most important section: Scholarship Eligibility.

Below are some of the grants listed on the app. Can these be for real? It doesn't matter. Even if they don't pay for your kid to go to college, they're so wacky that at least they provide a diversion for harried parents who have to spend the night before Thanksgiving proofreading, when they really should be roasting brussels sprouts.

A partial list:

❏ Descendant of a Confederate veteran of the Civil War
❏ Jewish orphan interested in studying aeronautics
❏ Descendant of a Mayflower passenger

❏ Descendant of Alice Mara Tibbits, Elede Prince Morris, or Rose Humann Rogers (and lots of other random names like these—can someone explain to me how these work? Do you have to know in advance that your great-uncle Bernie started a scholarship, or are you pleasantly surprised to find this out on the app?)

❏ Child or spouse of a member of the California League of Food Processors

❏ Chumash player on the Yuba City High School basketball team

Unfortunately, CJ does not qualify for any of these scholarships. In fact, he is probably the least likely kid in the state to be related to a Confederate soldier, a Mayflower passenger, or a Cuisinart.

But the Neurotic Parent Institute has discovered that the UCs will soon be offering the following awards to eligible students:

❏ New driver who was unfairly ticketed for rolling through a stop sign

❏ Student whose hamster perished after a fall down the stairs

❏ Facebook member with more than 1,200 friends

❏ Child of an early-model Prius owner

❏ Descendant of someone who believed Paul was dead and played Beatles albums backwards for their friends

❏ Child of a first-generation female blogger

For more eclectic scholarships, log onto the UC application website before the server gets clogged.

THANKSGIVING MESSAGE TO HIGH SCHOOL SENIORS AND THEIR PARENTS

If your greatest source of stress is that darn college admissions process, be thankful.

DESPERATE CRY FOR HELP

Dear Neurotic Parent,

I have enjoyed reading your blog for the last year, but it is not as fun for me any more because whenever I read it, all I can think about is how much we're spending for our daughter to study philosophy and Latin, two things she will never use in real life, at _____ (cool, prestigious liberal arts school).

Help! Please find us a grant or a scholarship. $15,000 a year will help, but more would be appreciated. This needs to be your new obsession. You need to find some crazy loophole for money. This is so you. You've got to focus on this one.

Everyone appreciates how funny and entertaining you are, but enough is enough. I can't believe you haven't found merit money for CJ yet. I bet you have, and you're keeping it from us. Please put your attentions to good use.

Your fan,
Desperate Parent

Dear Desperate Parent,
Thanks for your letter. Just when I was all relaxed about the college process, you've elevated my anxiety to a new level. I will get right on it.

Best regards,
The Neurotic Parent

DIVERSITY

At this point, I just want to say hi to Gina, my intern from Pitzer, Shelby, my intern from Skidmore, and Nancy the proofreader; I know nobody reads all the way through satiric guidebooks

LOST BOYS OF SUDAN

If you're a lost boy of Sudan, this chapter is for you. Other minorities beware, because although admissions committees are committed to diversity, you will only have an advantage if you're from an Under-Represented Minority (URM). Under-Represented Minorities, unfortunately, do not include Jews, Irish, Italians, Scandinavians, or Asians, although exceptions will be made if your parents were Boat People.

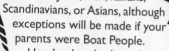

Here's who else has a leg up:
- Latin Americans, even the really wealthy ones who travel to Miami to do their Christmas shopping. So if you're expecting a baby, it is definitely to your advantage to give birth in Tijuana.
- People from the states "in the middle."
- The ambidextrous.
- Gypsies (those from the Budapest area have a slight edge over residents of the Czech Republic).
- Any aboriginal or indigenous peoples. It is worth investigating your great-great-grandma's ancestry if you think she might have had a fling while visiting Tonga.

TRANSGENDERISM: A HOOK TO BE RECKONED WITH

The University of South Florida has revised its housing applications so that students can now identify themselves as male, female, or transitioning. Those who check "transitioning" can choose to live with a random roommate or a friend, but can also snag a coveted single.

From the annals of the Neurotic Parent blog

NORTH DAKOTA

Many admissions officers are not only good speakers, but they're also quite witty. Several started their information sessions with icebreakers and some with clever jokes. At the George Washington University a presenter began by saying that admissions decisions had been sent out the day before. He was proud to say that the new class represented 48 states—and the admissions committee was still hoping to find students from the remaining two. He paused and then, with perfect timing, revealed that those two states were, in fact, Connecticut and New Jersey. This got a big laugh, because most of the people sitting in the room were from Connecticut or New Jersey. If you're from one of those two states, you're over-represented at GW.

So what were the two missing states? When the laughter subsided, he spilled: Montana and North Dakota. He told us that in case any of us were from either of those places, he would love to meet us after the session.

Yes, our whole college journey would be different if we lived in Big Sky Country or the Peace Garden State. So, after much thought, we are considering moving to North Dakota. (We actually prefer Montana, but it's on its way to becoming the new Colorado, which would be problematic admission-wise.)

So I dream of a new life in North Dakota, a life without college anxiety. As a North Dakota resident, CJ would have lots of choices. But what makes the move even more tempting is that once we sell our Southern California home, we would be in a better position to finance not just undergraduate school, but graduate school, business school, law school, medical school, a year abroad in Prague, and multiple community service summers in Malawi.

Best of all, CJ will have the perfect topic for his Common App essay: how he had to adjust to a place with tornadoes, blizzards, quail hunting, furry coon hats, and limited sushi. Plus, I've already checked and the SAT tutors charge less for a whole course of study than our guy does for one lesson.

Here's a West Fargo home we're thinking of buying: five bedrooms for $87,000, and I'm sure there's some flexibility in the price. Because I doubt we will be getting many visitors, CJ can have a whole room to store college brochures, and I will have a separate office for my blogging.

47 Farthing Way
West Fargo, ND

House for Sale: **$87,000**

Beds: 5
Baths: 3
Sqft: 2,636
Lot: 9,778

Would appreciate hearing from readers in West Fargo. Where's the closest Whole Foods? Are there mobile pet groomers? Is there a good Prius mechanic? Just let me know and we'll be on our way. But please don't tell anyone else about our strategy. It won't work if North Dakota becomes the new Illinois.

HOW ASIANS COMPETE, SINCE THEY ARE NOT THE "RIGHT" KIND OF MINORITIES: MINJOK LEADERSHIP ACADEMY

If moving to North Dakota isn't working out for you, you might be concerned that your child's college prospects are grim. We shared that fear until one Sunday, when we saw, right on the front page of the *New York Times*, the answer to our prayers. The headline read, "Elite Korean Schools, Forging Ivy League Skills."

The piece was about how going to brand-name American colleges has become a fad in South Korea. It was bad enough when our kids only had to compete with smart Americans. Now they have to contend with competition from students who attend the Minjok Leadership Academy near Seoul, where the average SAT score is 2203.

But there is hope on the horizon: Minjok accepts international students. If your child attends a place like Minjok as a high school senior, he could undo all the poor study habits he picked up in the U.S. during the previous twelve years.

At Minjok, the school day lasts fifteen hours. Teen romance is forbidden, and toothbrushing is mandatory before every class. Your child's classmates would be students like Kim Sooyeon. Ms. Kim, whose mother lashed her tongue if she scored lower than 100 on exams (even a 98 or 99), is bound for Princeton.

Once he saw the beauty of this plan, our son wasted no time in beginning the admissions process. At right is an e-mail exchange he had with Lee Won-hee, the founder of Minjok.

RUBBER SEOUL

High school juniors—are you contemplating getting a job at Jamba Juice this summer? Or maybe taking an art class at a local community college? How about working on a presidential campaign? Think again. Are those really the best choices for your future? Instead, for only 10 million won ($9,617 US, plus room and board), you can take a two-month, seven-day-a-week, ten-hour-a-day SAT prep course in Korea. (95% of the students are from overseas.) But you'd better sign up soon. Last year's classes sold out in April. And we're not making this up.

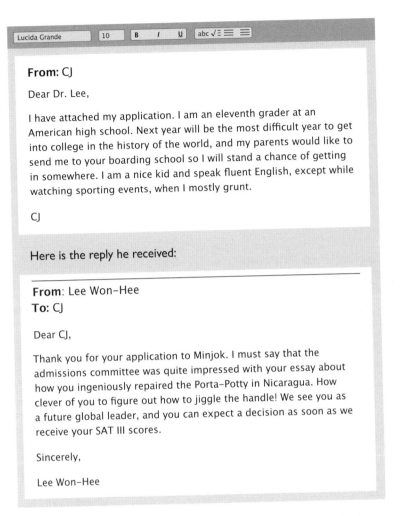

From: CJ

Dear Dr. Lee,

I have attached my application. I am an eleventh grader at an American high school. Next year will be the most difficult year to get into college in the history of the world, and my parents would like to send me to your boarding school so I will stand a chance of getting in somewhere. I am a nice kid and speak fluent English, except while watching sporting events, when I mostly grunt.

CJ

Here is the reply he received:

From: Lee Won-Hee
To: CJ

Dear CJ,

Thank you for your application to Minjok. I must say that the admissions committee was quite impressed with your essay about how you ingeniously repaired the Porta-Potty in Nicaragua. How clever of you to figure out how to jiggle the handle! We see you as a future global leader, and you can expect a decision as soon as we receive your SAT III scores.

Sincerely,

Lee Won-Hee

While we wait to hear if he is accepted, we bring you some inspiration via Minjok's motto:

> *Through education based on the deep awareness of the heritage of our people;*
> *Towards tomorrow's bright Fatherland;*
> *Let us study, not for the sake of personal gain, but for the sake of learning.*
> *Let us not choose a career in thoughts of personal gain,*
> *But choose a career based on our talents and aptitude.*
> *Such is my true fortune and tomorrow's bright Fatherland.*

Isn't a motto supposed to be just a short phrase? And isn't it passé to aspire to have a bright Fatherland? We could get critical, but what do we know about forging Ivy skills?

From the annals of the Neurotic Parent blog

MINJOK SIGHTING, PART I

Ah, June in New York: alfresco dining, long walks downtown, performances in the park. We considered all the possibilities, then planned the ideal activity for the day: an excursion to Philadelphia.

We had already toured the New York schools, and a visit to the East Coast would be incomplete without yet another college tour. So we awoke at 6:30 a.m. (3:30 a.m. PDT), cheerfully caught the 8:10 train, and set off to check out Penn.

Our rail journey was relatively relaxing until the engine died somewhere near Trenton. We ended up arriving at the information session with just moments to spare.

The room was packed, and we had to split up. I grabbed the last remaining seat—in the front row. It took a few moments before I realized I was sitting in the middle of a group of 44 students from...*drum roll*...the Minjok Leadership Academy in Korea.

MINJOK SIGHTING, PART II

I sat in the front row of the Penn information session, pondering the inspirational Ben Franklin quotes on the wall. The charismatic admissions dean explained the university's commitment to both the theoretical and the practical. He pointed out the many accomplishments of Penn students, including the recent success of a boy at Wharton who had invented ecological detergent pellets called Dropps, a sensation in the world of laundry.

But I could barely concentrate because of the presence of a large group of students from a world-renowned boarding school—the 44 Minjok kids, all taking copious notes in English. As I've said previously, their school had been featured on the front page of the *New York Times*. Minjok students achieve stellar test scores. Their secret? Fifteen hours of study a day, no dating, and berating from their parents if they score below 100% on quizzes.

The group was well behaved (although I did see a few yawns and squirms), but they could use some leadership training in the world of fashion. The boys, in head-to-toe light gray or brown polyester uniforms, looked as if they were wearing vintage Jetsons Halloween costumes. The girls wore collarless shirts with brass buttons tucked into floor-length dirndl skirts worn over baggy pants with bows at the ankles—like a *Sound of Music*–themed *Project Runway* challenge gone awry.

When the information session ended, we were split into groups. We followed our enthusiastic dual-major tour guide, and the Minjok students headed in the opposite direction. We caught up with the group at the athletic field, where I struck up a conversation with one of their chaperones.

I told the chaperone (who was dressed in Lacoste and khakis) that I'd read about Minjok in the *New York Times* and had even blogged about it. It soon became obvious that he didn't understand a word I was saying, so I let him do the talking. The group, he said, was on an American summer college tour for *freshmen*. This seemed a bit extreme to me, until I realized we had dragged our younger son, a rising freshman, along. (He seemed reasonably happy, even inspired, during the info session, but he later told us he was smiling because he was silently quizzing himself about baseball statistics.)

"So," I asked the Minjok chaperone, "How many kids are you sending to Penn in the fall?"

"Seven," he answered proudly.

"If our son attended your school, would that help his chances for college?" I asked.

"Thank you very much," he responded.

❋

After the tour, we headed to Pat's for cheese steaks. Then we visited the Liberty Bell and the interactive National Constitution Center, which must have been designed by Penn students, because it brilliantly integrates the theoretical and the practical, bringing history to life. Ah, if learning were always this entertaining and effortless! Unfortunately, this would be one of the last family vacations in which we could effectively drag our boys to a museum and have them enjoy it.

When we arrived back in New York, CJ seemed satisfied with the day and unfazed that the students of the Korean Minjok Leadership Academy have a better chance of getting into Penn than he does— unless he can come up with an improved laundry pellet by the end of the summer.

THE ULTIMATE DIVERSITY: HOME SCHOOLING

Do you want your kids to be in a demographic that represents just two percent of the nation? Do you own a kitchen table and a white board? Then the Neurotic Parent has a solution for you.

At just about every college information session, admissions officers stress that the transcript is the most important part of the application. By this, they mean not just GPA but also the rigor of curriculum. They want to know that your child has taken the hardest courses possible. How to ensure this? The best way, obviously, is to home school your children. Since you are in control, you can tell them that Remedial Bio will not be offered this semester, so they have to take AP Physics instead.

You can also guarantee that your student's grades show the kind of upward trend desired by admissions committees. It's simple: Just start out as a strict grader and segue to straight As by senior year. And your son or daughter can report a very high class rank, because even if you have seven children and your child is at the bottom of the class, a rank of seventh sounds pretty good.

Plus, your student will have the ability to pursue amazing extracurriculars, like gardening and hospitality management, and win numerous awards that schooled students do not have access to. One young home-schooled child we know, Olivia Bates, has already won first place in the ninth grade Bates Spelling Bee.

Another huge advantage of home schooling is that while your sons' and daughters' peers screw around during snack periods and dawdle on the way home, yours can take college-level online courses, learn languages, master instruments, earn money at part-time jobs, and do SAT prep during the school day. With all that extra time to excel, they should be able to gain admission into any school they want.

Best of all, your home-schooled kids will be so advanced academically by the time they get to the university of their choice that they can concentrate full-time on the top passions and pursuits of today's college students: alcohol, drugs, sex, loud music, and naked runs.

Chapter

thirteen

WAITING

At this point in the process, your teen is probably not talking to you, so you can think about relinquishing your controlling ways. Then, after you've taken some deep breaths, send a group e-mail to every connected alum who owes you a favor and hope for the best.

XANAX, PLEASE

If you're the parent of a senior, here is a list of
*people **not** to talk to until after April 1st:*

☑ Parents of kids who went to college three years ago, when everything was different.

☑ Parents of Intel Award winners, oboe soloists, and any sort of national semifinalists, especially if their kids are applying to the same schools as yours.

☑ Parents of recruited athletes, whose kids have already decided between three Ivies.

☑ Parents of relaxed, grounded kids who are only applying to two public schools, a match and a safety, and would be thrilled to go to either.

☑ Parents who use plural pronouns: "We got our Penn app in by the early deadline, and now we're working on the Brown supplement."

☑ Parents who say, "They all end up in the right place" and go on to tell you how much they themselves hated Princeton.

and, finally:

☑ English teachers who believe your child should not have used any forms of the verb "to be" in his/her essays.

WHAT TO DO WHILE YOUR CHILD IS WAITING

Before you know it, you'll find yourself in the midst of a "lull period," during which high school seniors experience an interminable limbo while still feeling pressure to keep up their grades. But that doesn't mean you must stop helicoptering. Here are some ideas to keep your skills sharp while you wait:

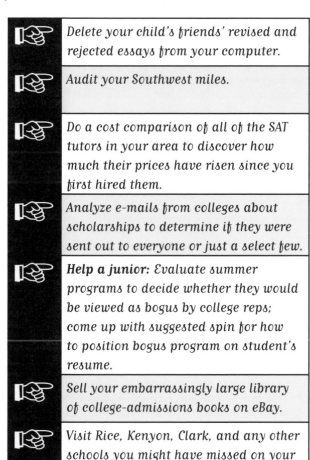

Delete your child's friends' revised and rejected essays from your computer.

Audit your Southwest miles.

Do a cost comparison of all of the SAT tutors in your area to discover how much their prices have risen since you first hired them.

Analyze e-mails from colleges about scholarships to determine if they were sent out to everyone or just a select few.

Help a junior: *Evaluate summer programs to decide whether they would be viewed as bogus by college reps; come up with suggested spin for how to position bogus program on student's resume.*

Sell your embarrassingly large library of college-admissions books on eBay.

Visit Rice, Kenyon, Clark, and any other schools you might have missed on your original tour.

HACKERS & SLACKERS

At the end of a recent early-admissions season, Columbia University sent out an e-mail informing its ED candidates that they would be receiving a decision by both e-mail and snail mail on a Thursday, rather than the Monday that was first promised.

Several students on College Confidential, the online forum for future CEOs (if accepted to the Ivies) and serial killers (if forced to attend their state Us), immediately figured out how to find out the decision a few days early.

By e-mail: Change the calendar on your computer, tricking it into thinking that it's Friday.

By snail mail: Call FedEx. Find out if Columbia has sent you a package (if they haven't, they probably sent a regular letter, which means you were denied or deferred).

The Neurotic Parent Institute believes that the student who figured out how to trick his or her computer into delivering an e-mail on an earlier date deserves to be admitted to Columbia. The student who came up with the much simpler plan of calling FedEx already knows how to work the system and doesn't need to attend college at all.

HACKERS & SLACKERS II: STANFORD EDITION

Prospective Columbia early-decision applicants are not the only ones who get impatient. Students waiting to hear from Stanford get anxious as well—and one seemed to figure out a way to find out his (or her, but we're assuming it's a boy) fate several days in advance. On angst-ridden College Confidential, an obsessed Stanford early-action hopeful theorized that if an applicant's admissions ID number gets him or her access to a welcome page on the regular Stanford students' site, it is very likely he or she has been accepted.

The thread that resulted was a collective panic attack. The method worked for some applicants but not for others. Those who were successful then worried that their admission would get rescinded. Others thought their numbers worked because they took a summer program at Stanford and still have access.

Update: Neither the Columbia nor the Stanford hacks turned out to have any validity. Moral: Get a life.

NEUROTIC SEPTEMBER SENIOR YEAR MUSINGS

❶ One app submitted. Two or three more to go, according to CJ. Is he a focused, Zen-like kid who knows what he wants—or is he just supplement-averse? I recently met a woman whose son applied to 29 schools. Surely CJ can come up with another 25.

❷ Booked a flight to Berkeley, a great, affordable school that's a one-hour flight away. Asked CJ if he wanted to visit Stanford as well. Before he could answer, the phone rang. The caller told me a story about this year's freshman orientation at Stanford. "Look around," the college president said. "Among you is a student who, when he was 8, discovered a new antibiotic that fights heart infections." Guess Stanford is off CJ's list. He didn't discover his antibiotic until he was 11.

❸ Separation anxiety. Everything that CJ does might be "the last time." Yesterday was the last trip to Bakersfield for soccer. Should I be happy or sad that I pawned him off on another mom? (A big shout-out to her!) And if I should be happy that I didn't have to drive five hours round-trip to see his team lose in 95-degree weather, how should I feel about him missing my birthday? Once I went off to college, did I ever again see my mother on her birthday?

REJECTED

Every year, all sorts of rumors float around our community about brilliant, qualified teens who did not get into college.

Heard that one girl showed up at her high school after spring break wearing a sweatshirt with the name of a college that did not accept her. She supposedly told her friends that she was offered a spot at that university but was taking a gap year instead.

Ran into someone in a restaurant who said the valedictorian of a top private school was admitted nowhere, not even into two of her safeties. The same anxious mom reported that a boy she knows was rejected from a school where a building is named after his uncle.

Driving around like traveling salesmen was the easy part of this process. Now the party's over and it's crunch time: SATs, SAT IIs, ACTs, APs, finals, summer job, start a foundation, invent a software program, write about it in an essay. And even kids with perfect resumes are in for disappointment.

But there's an alternative: For $40,000 you can hire Dr. H, the nation's premier college consultant, according to a profile of her in *Business Week*. She claims a 95% success rate for students getting into their top-choice schools—but she will rob you of those fun teen years, preventing you from being a camp counselor and forcing you to attend a nanotechnology program instead.

We read the whole article about Dr. H and learned that even though she attended Dartmouth (B.A.) and Columbia (M.A.), she got her Ph.D at Nova Southeastern University in Florida because she needed a "quickie doctorate" for credibility. But even more interesting is that she's "hoping to link up with a travel consultant, someone who could plan family trips to visit colleges."

That's where we come in: The Neurotic Parent's Exotic College Travel Tours. We will get you late checkouts at college-adjacent hotels, arrange for you to board your Southwest flights in Group I, and make sure your Garmin gets you onto Grand Central Parkway.

CARRYING A WAITLIST GRUDGE

*B*ecause the college admission process is now the most selective in the history of the world (regardless of the year you're reading this), people no longer just tell you where their children were accepted, but also where they were rejected, waitlisted, and deferred—all for no good reason other than that they were born in the baby boomlet.

In the past, if you asked someone where their son or daughter was going to college, they'd tell you the name of one school. But now, you'll get an answer like "She got into BU, and was waitlisted at Georgetown, Tufts, Wesleyan, Northwestern, and even GW." Or: "He's deciding between Emory and Wash U St. Louis, but still hoping to hear from Stanford." This is usually followed with a horror story about another child: "My niece, who was a congressional page, really wanted Penn but she was never able to get her SATs up over 2200, and she ended up being rejected everywhere except Indiana and Boulder." Or: "Our friend's son, who won all these trombone competitions, was waitlisted at Bard and Skidmore, and only got into SUNY Purchase as a February admit."

The Neurotic Parent is afraid that because our kids are not getting into their first, or second, or ninth choices, for their entire lives they will remember the list of all eighteen colleges to which they applied. When someone asks them where they attended college, they will rattle off the whole slew of places that turned them down, or even worse, kept them dangling. They might forever hold grudges against fine universities and not even want to take their own kids on college tours.

They could end up like our friend who, at age 52, is a top litigation attorney but is still mad at Columbia and Wesleyan because he never got off those darn waitlists. In fact, he wouldn't let his daughter (who ended up at Yale) even look at those two schools.

SCHADENFREUDE U

Sour Grapes Rationalizations About Why
Your Kid Is Better Off Not at an Ivy

Brown	flexible curriculum might encourage slacking
Columbia	anachronistic Core program; too far uptown
Cornell	freezing; bizarre majors; dangerous gorges
Dartmouth	too preppy; alcohol-promoting "Keggy" as unofficial mascot; middle of nowhere
Harvard	doesn't care about undergraduates
Penn	too pre-professional; Wharton envy by liberal arts students; cheese steaks cause indigestion
Princeton	too conservative; weird eating clubs
Yale	in New Haven; too much singing and dancing
All of them	too cutthroat; students too smug/nerdy/competitive; too difficult to get into grad/law/medical school. And did we mention *too hard*?

Chapter

fourteen

REJECTED/ DEFERRED

What to expect when they're rejecting

PRESTIGE: WHY BOTHER?

By early March, most college applicants have multiple excellent choices. But some are still waiting to hear from a dream school or two. One mom we know says her son really wants Brown, but then added that she herself really wants a pony. Another parent said her child had attended several accepted-student events but remained obsessed with Wesleyan, a super reach. And a couple we met at a party had driven down to San Diego to show their son San Diego State in case he didn't get accepted to USC, his dream school. But the tour guide used the word "conveniency" three times, and that turned the whole family off.

A REJECTION

After some digging, we got our hands on Steven Spielberg's rejection letter from the USC School of Cinematic Arts.

Dear Mr. Spielberg,
The admissions committee has reviewed your application and unfortunately cannot offer you a space in the class of 1965. Even though we agree that sharks and aliens could prove to be innovative themes for motion pictures, we just cannot let you in with your 2.0 GPA. We do wish you the best of luck and hope you won't hold a grudge if one day you become an icon in the film industry and decide to make a hefty donation to our film school.
  Sincerely, the Deans

The Neurotic Parent Institute was on the verge of funding a study to determine whether, in the case of college admissions, the desire for something better than the bird in hand is classic human nature. But after speaking to the parent of NPS (Nearly Perfect Student, with all As, two 800s on the SATs, and two more 800s on the subject tests), who was shockingly rejected from MIT, the Institute has formulated a different theory.

"He worked so hard," said the dad about his son, who had an internship in a biomedical ethics lab at UCLA and had won contests in fields I had never heard of and cannot pronounce. Another mom, whose daughter was waiting to hear whether her Penn deferral would be reversed, echoed this sentiment: "She deserves to get it because she had no life all through high school."

So it's not just prestige or "wanting something better" for our children that makes us crazed in this process. It's the idea that our kids spent hours studying for AP exam after AP exam, attending debate after debate, robotics competition after robotics competition, and then, for whatever lame, crapshooty reason, the "top" schools didn't want them.

The Neurotic Parent has a solution to He Worked So Hard and Sacrificed His Childhood Syndrome: encourage your children to slack off. Let them sleep late and have some other sucker be president of the chess club. Spend a weekend playing video games. That way, when your son or daughter gets rejected, you can say that at least she had fun in high school, and she can go off to a fine rah-rah school, maybe not top 20…but definitely top 200. She'll get a great education and get to have a life in college as well.

SIX DEGREES OF WAITLIST SEPARATION

Mr. NP and I are in Santa Barbara for a short, childless getaway. Before we left home, we heard about two kids we know who were just admitted from waitlists into the colleges of their dreams. One, a boy from CJ's school, was accepted at Georgetown after planning to go to Tufts. Another, our friend's niece, was all set to go to Syracuse until a week ago, when she was offered a spot at Skidmore.

Last night at dinner in a romantic garden patio, we were seated next to a table of loud talkers. Their conversation topic, of course, was colleges. The female loud talker mentioned that there would be a lot of waitlist activity this year. Harvard and Princeton had announced they would each accept 90 students from their waitlists, and this would cause a ripple effect, extending to all the universities in the world. Her cousin's son had just gotten into Princeton, she said, and he would now give up his spot at his second-choice school. Where had he planned on going before he had the good fortune to be un-waitlisted? Georgetown. Yes, without a doubt, he had opened a place for the boy from our school.

Then the male loud talker told the group, with authority, that although this was an extremely competitive year for college admissions, students from Santa Barbara public schools had done very well. In fact, he had just heard of a local girl who got into Vassar off the waitlist.

At this point, our waiter approached us to see if we wanted more wine, and we had to stop eavesdropping. But if we had continued to listen to the loud talkers, we're certain they would have revealed that the Vassar girl had provided the spot at Skidmore for our friend's niece.

HELP STOP TUFTS SYNDROME

CollegeConfidential.com is not a happy place for neurotic parents. Just about every student who posts on the site has perfect grades, exceptional scores, grew up in an igloo with Inuit relatives, and has sold a patent to Intel. These superhumans usually want to know their chances at top schools, but occasionally they ask others for nurturing and support.

Early on in our neurotic college quest we discovered a desperate CC post from a senior with the screen name of Weisenheimer2u. Weisenheimer had a 2340 SAT and a 3.9 unweighted and couldn't figure out why he or she was waitlisted at Bard. There was an immediate response from randomname25, whose theory was that Weisenheimer was the victim of Tufts Syndrome. Here is the exchange (and yes, it is real):

 03-29, 3:45 PM

Weisen-heimer2u:

Junior Member
Posts: 82

WAITLISTED with 2340 SAT, 3.9 GPA

**I just got waitlisted today! GPA UW: 3.9
GPA W: 5.2
SAT: 780 CR/800 M/760 W
SAT II: Math level 2 800/ French 760/
Chemistry 780/ Physics 800
Took the hardest course load at my HS:
APUSH (5), AP English Lang (5), AP Chemistry
(5), AP Calc BC (5), AP Computer Science
(5); captain of the math team, co-captain of
Science Olympiad, co-captain of the chess
team, volunteer tutor, started own web
design co. I know I must sound stuck-up but
WHY on earth did they reject me?**

 03-29, 05:10 PM

random-name25:

Junior Member
Posts: 102

Tufts Syndrome?

What exactly is Tufts Syndrome? According to Wikipedia, it is a synonym for "yield protection," the practice of turning down highly qualified students who seem to be using that school as a safety. Top colleges such as Tufts waitlist these students in order to keep their admissions yield high. They want to admit students who are actually likely to attend. Now, as evidenced by Weisenheimer's post, Tufts Syndrome has spread to Bard. I have also heard that UC Davis and Pitzer have been waitlisting valedictorians and dolphin trainers, assuming they will choose Stanford or Pomona instead.

The Neurotic Parent Institute predicts that Tufts Syndrome will reach epidemic proportions by the end of the decade. It will be impossible to find safeties, because if you're an outstanding candidate, colleges won't want you because they think you won't attend. And paradoxically, if you're a nice, normal kid who hasn't written an operetta, they won't want you because they think you actually *will* attend. The trick will be to find a college that isn't as sensitive as Tufts. There must be a school out there without an ego, one that won't have hurt feelings if smart kids turn it down.

Until a college like that surfaces, we ask all of you to take a moment to help stop this dreaded pandemic. You can make a profound difference in a most simple way. First, find a mediocre student. Then encourage this slacker to apply to Tufts...or Bard...or UC Davis. Once these institutions are flooded with applications from low-decile kids, their admissions people will begin to appreciate receiving apps from qualified candidates and maybe, together, we can get Weisenheimer2u off that waitlist.

The Neurotic Parent Answers Your Questions

TUFTS SYNDROME FAQS

Q: I wish to become active in the fight against Tufts Syndrome. What are some other universities it has affected?

A: Thanks so much to everyone who has cared enough to support the cause and stop Tufts Syndrome once and for all. We went back to College Confidential to see if there was a happy ending for the Tufts Syndrome victim who was waitlisted at Bard. No news, but we did find a comprehensive six-page thread listing other colleges that have exhibited symptoms of Tufts Syndrome: WashU, Lehigh, UC Davis, UCLA, Johns Hopkins, Northeastern, Kenyon, Grinnell, Rensselaer Polytechnic Institute, Swarthmore ("infamous for this"), and GW (by far the college mentioned the most). One student reported getting "tufted big time at Reed" and another said he "got the tufty at BC." Happily, however, one poster reported that Tufts Syndrome no longer exists at Tufts, so your efforts have met with preliminary success.

From the annals of the Neurotic Parent blog

SHOCKING WAITLIST NEWS

This is Waitlist Week on my blog, so I must extend a big thank you to the four readers who sent me the link to this piece from the *Wall Street Journal*: "Elite Colleges Reach Deeper into Wait Lists."

This article reiterates the "heightened wait list activity" theory discussed earlier, and I must confess that at first it did not seem blog-worthy. But after reading just a few sentences, I uncovered a truly surprising development: I've been spelling "waitlist" incorrectly for the entire history of this blog.

Here is the final paragraph of the article:

> To be sure, not all schools are seeing increases in their numbers of **wait-list** offers. Stanford University, for instance, has taken zero students from the **wait list** so far this year, the same as last year. "We are keeping a small number on the **wait list** just to respond to other **wait list** activity around the nation," says Rick Shaw, dean of undergraduate admission and financial aid.

As you can see, *wait list* as a noun is written as two words. (I had suspected this whenever I spell checked, but I assumed Typepad was not on the cutting edge of college vernacular.) And *wait-list* as an adjective is hyphenated. So what is the deal in the last sentence, where *wait list* is missing a hyphen before the word *activity*? Even a high school junior could tell you that it's an adjective there.

Did the WSJ spell waitlist incorrectly just to distract readers from the Stanford dean's weird logic—that they're maintaining a waitlist just to keep up with the activity back east? Do they really think that students who sent in their money to Stanford would give it up to spend four long, frigid winters at a university that kept them hanging? I don't think so.

I guess I should write an e-mail to the *Journal* to find out the answer to the wait list/wait-list mystery. But I'm afraid they'll think I'm one of those people who has too much time on her hands. I can imagine the editors laughing about my query: "That crazy neurotic parent! She should be reading about our hedge-fund picks instead of worrying about missing hyphens."

So if you are a copy editor, I'm waiting to hear from you.

And until I have definitive information, I will continue to spell "waitlist" as one anxiety-provoking, hyphenless word.

WAITLIST DONOR BANK

Recently, the Neurotic Parent received the following comments from readers:

"I have a niece who got into Middlebury off the waitlist and gave up her slot at Hamilton and her brother got into Emerson off the waitlist, which opens up a slot at Northeastern. How long do you think it will be before you learn who got those spots?"

"It was actually our Oberlin-bound DGC (Dylan-Ginsberg Clone) who happily gave up his Vassar space for the Santa Barbara girl."

These comments reflect a new trend that is unfolding for students who are admitted to their dream colleges from waitlists. Mere acceptance was once cause enough for celebration. But now many waitlist recipients feel a need to know the identity of the anonymous donors who made it possible for them to enroll at their reach schools.

With this in mind, the Neurotic Parent Institute has started a new foundation, Waitlist Donor Trace. Using cutting-edge research methods, we will locate the girl or boy who gave your child the gift of matriculation. And for a nominal fee, you can receive periodic updates about how your donor is faring at the better school that let him or her in at the last moment.

We are also starting a Waitlist Donor Bank. Top students can now be proactive in giving a lucky girl or boy their hand-me-down acceptances.

So if you are someone like Mr. 2400, CJ's friend who achieved a perfect score on the SAT, here's a simple strategy that could potentially touch the lives of thousands of students all over the world: Apply to eighteen colleges. You will probably be accepted at sixteen. Send in deposits to every college that accepts you. Then, when you get the call from Harvard or Princeton, you can provide places to sixteen lucky waitlist recipients. Not only do you get to go to a prestigious school, but you can also help other human beings in limbo, like the Middlebury and Emerson kids mentioned above.

This act of selflessness will take much less effort than going to Namibia to work with the baboons, and it will give you the incomparable satisfaction of having made a difference in the life of an eleventh grader who has had to overcome the misfortune of having been born at the peak of the baby boomlet.

ADMISSIONS ENVY & COMMON APP REMORSE

At the end of every early-decision and early-action season, parents all over the country try to unravel the mystery of why certain kids got in to certain schools and others were left by the wayside. The most common discussions:

➡	Figuring out why eleven students from a prestigious school in the area were all rejected or deferred from Stanford or Brown. And why a legacy kid/inventor was deferred from Yale when he didn't just *do* model UN—he gave a speech at the *real* UN.
➡	Dissecting why some apps were successful and others weren't. An essay about Katrina aid = REJECTED! An essay about gathering up the nerve to sky dive = DEFERRED! An essay with clever musings about getting lost in Boston = ACCEPTED! We will never know why but we can theorize forever.
➡	Agonizing about mistakes on an already-submitted Common App. Once you click, you cannot fix typos or add omitted ECs or that Junior Statesman award. The Common App asks for a list of extracurriculars, which you must rate in order of importance to you. Should your son have said that working in the aquarium meant more to him than playing baseball on a traveling team? Should your daughter have mentioned the archery award she received in ninth grade? Once you click you can never go back.
➡	Rehashing the mantra that the deans and guidance counselors and parents of older kids repeat over and over again: *They all end up where they're supposed to. . . They all end up where they're supposed to. . . .* Fine—but does that apply to the Most Difficult Year for College Admissions in the History of the World? And what about the six graduates from our school who are thinking of transferring or "taking a year off" to become organic farmers?
➡	Getting angry at your high school's competent, hard-working, well-meaning college counselor. Or, even worse, at the ridiculously expensive independent counselor you've hired because you didn't trust the free counselor at the school.

WE REGRET TO INFORM YOU THAT YOU'RE A PATHETIC LOSER

The Ivies, in a time-honored tradition, have chosen April Fools' Day to inform students whether they are accepted or whether they'll have to endure four years of mediocrity at somewhere like...UC Berkeley.

Yes, what an appropriate date this is to open a double-password-protected e-mail and see the following message on the screen:

You had straight As, got 2360 on your SATs, and built an orphanage for AIDS babies? You expect that to impress us? Waitlist for you!

If you're lucky, you won't have to spend any more time in limbo and will get a straight rejection. You can count your lucky stars if you get a truly final decision: "You're just as qualified as tons of other kids who applied, but we had to screw up someone's life, and that someone just happens to be you. Trust us, you'll get over it someday, even if your parents won't."

LAST-MINUTE APPLICATION HYSTERIA: WHICH VACATION TO RUIN?

If your student applied Early Decision, November 1st and/or 15th were days for celebration. By then the Common App had to be completed, ending procrastination and endless essay revisions.

After that, what psychology should early applicants employ for completing their remaining seventeen applications? Some students finish it all before early results come out in mid-December. They believe that if deferred or rejected, they'll be too depressed to do a good job on their remaining RD apps. These students play it safe but risk having to write dozens of essays for naught—and they forgo a relaxing Thanksgiving.

Others believe they shouldn't spend one moment on any essay or application they won't need if they get accepted early. These gamblers say it's bad karma to answer the prompt "Why Johns Hopkins?" when they've applied early to Northwestern. They live dangerously, turning the process into a nailbiter and ruining their family's last winter vacation as they desperately work on apps until the moment the ball falls at Times Square.

Therefore, we propose a new anti-festival: **Winter Hellday**. Falling on December 16th, before the other holidays, this is a 24-hour period during which rejected and deferred early applicants must stay up all night with their bleary-eyed parents. At the stroke of midnight on December 17th, all RD apps must be turned in. This way, applicants and their families can spend the rest of their winter vacation worrying, rather than writing.

APRIL FOOLS

You're in! Oops—just kidding!

In one of the worst admissions boo-boos ever, UCSD recently sent an e-mail to all of its 28,000 rejected students congratulating them and inviting them to an event for accepted students.

The *Los Angeles Times* reported that one high school senior, Cole Bettles, was elated to receive a congratulatory e-mail from UC San Diego inviting him to tour the campus, particularly because he had been rejected from many other schools on his list. His mom called the relatives in San Diego and planned a large celebration for right after the orientation.

"They were like, 'Oh, my God, that's so awesome'," Bettles said. Then he checked his e-mail again and found another message saying the school had sent the e-mail in error and, in fact, his application had been denied.

Turns out that everyone who had applied to UCSD, whether they'd been accepted or rejected, had received an e-mail saying, "We're thrilled that you've been admitted to UC San Diego, and we're showcasing our beautiful campus on Admit Day."

Other schools have screwed up, but this was by far the worst snafu in admissions history. "It was really thrilling for a few hours; now he's crushed," said the young man's mother, Tracy Bettles. "Unless you have a high school senior, or remember what it's like, you don't know. It's really tough on them."

And it was even tougher on the mother, who had to call all the relatives and explain this new option in the admissions game. Now, in addition to admit, defer, deny, and waitlist, colleges have a new choice: renege.

INDIGESTION = REJECTION: WAS IT THE BUFFALO WINGS?

Curious about why certain students are accepted to highly selective institutions while thousands of equally qualified applicants get rejected?

We now know the answer: The students who enjoy the highest acceptance rates hail from locations where admissions reps have enjoyed delicious meals without suffering unpleasant gastrointestinal consequences.

In a Daily Beast post, an admissions officer from a large public university was honest about the random and arbitrary nature of the process. She admitted that her rejections are not always determined by the most academic of reasons. Here's the quote:

All in all, we're less selective than some of the elite schools or the Ivy League. But there are still some factors out of an applicant's hands. One night, I got food poisoning at a restaurant in Buffalo. The next day, I rejected all the Buffalo applications. I couldn't stomach reading them.

REJECTION REHAB FOR PARENTS

The Neurotic Parent Institute is in the process of purchasing land in Utah to establish a supportive environment where parents can recover from the devastation caused by Early Action and Early Decision deferrals and rejections. Called Early Visions (because all rehab places contain the word "Visions"), the facility will provide a holistic, healing program that will include:

- techniques to prevent whining and hyperventilating in front of your kids
- seminars by financial advisors who will assure you legacy parents that you would have lost all your alumni donation money anyway in today's volatile market, or at least in a Ponzi scheme
- daily inspirational councils with successful graduates of schools that kids can actually get into, like Wisconsin and Tulane
- spiritual voodoo-based ceremonies for burning college sweatshirts, destroying car decals, and breaking mugs

We'll be offering discounts for parents of kids who scored over 2250 on the SAT, or for any alum whose child was rejected after donating $500,000 or more. The first client to sign up has already posted on College Confidential:

12-12, 01:32 PM	#107
WordWorld Junior Member Location: Bay Area, CA Posts: 64	**DS was rejected from Stanford's SCEA on Friday. He was a very strong contender and we are rethinking and mourning. He's white but also has Hispanic ancestry on DH's side. >2200 SAT, multiple 5 APs, Math II 800 and other subject tests >750. UW GPA around 3.9, weighted around 4.3. Multiple legacy and we have donated a fair amount every single year since S was born. Biggest weakness was less than stellar ECs. His essays were pretty darn good.**
	I actually think H is taking it worse than S—when I called to tell H, he went down and ripped the Stanford license-plate holder off his car and threw it away (at work, not in front of son!). He then came home early to pack up every piece of Stanford clothing and memorabilia (including two of my favorite wine glasses) and put them in the attic.

Early Visions is filling up fast—we just received five new reservations from parents of gifted, qualified kids who were rejected from Penn, Northwestern, WashU, and Cornell. Hurry and reserve your space before Yale and Princeton announce their EA results.

REJECTION LETTERS FROM THE HEART

Lately everyone is too depressed to read news about financial matters, so the *Wall Street Journal* has been reinventing itself as the ultimate source of information about college admissions. A recent piece was about rejection letters, both really mean and really nice.

1. THE CRUELEST: BATES

Surprisingly, the meanest rejection came from sweet little Bates in Maine:
"The deans were obliged to select from among candidates who clearly could do sound work at Bates."

2. THE MOST FINAL: STANFORD

The Stanford deans were afraid that kids would try to beg for a second chance, the way you can for the UCs.
"We are humbled by your talents and achievements…and although you are…a fine student…we are not able to consider appeals."

3. THE MOST HUMANE: DUKE

Duke hired a team of Buddhists to pen its rejection letter:
"I know you will find an institution at which you will be happy; I know, too, that the school you choose will benefit from your presence."

4. THE MOST EXISTENTIAL: HARVARD

Of all places, Harvard lets the rejectees know the truth—after you've wasted your youth on APs and SAT IIs, it turns out that it really doesn't matter where you go to college.
"Past experience suggests that the particular college a student attends is far less important than what the student does to develop his or her strengths and talents over the next four years."

Finally, here's a quote from the Neurotic Parent's favorite rejection letter. It arrived in the mail of a friend one April 1st:

5. THE MOST SHOCKING: POMONA

"As you know, your daughter Olivia was denied admission to Pomona College. We feel compelled to inform you that this was due to information that her guidance counselor provided to our admissions department. We are concerned about Olivia's recent vandalism spree in a place of worship, and therefore cannot offer her a place in the class of 2013."

This turned out to be an April Fools' joke written by Olivia herself on "Pomona" stationery, which she created by scanning the font from her actual rejection letter. After her poor parents recovered, they framed the letter and came to the realization that the kindly Harvard admissions guy was right: Their daughter will go on to be a superstar, even though she didn't get into Pomona.

ACCEPTED

What a relief! Now your child can forget about changing the world and get back to his video games

From the annals of the Neurotic Parent blog

SOMEBODY WANTS HIM

As if the world hadn't changed enough in the course of the last fortnight, CJ received two life-changing e-mails yesterday. The first was from a college that was not on his radar but made him an offer too good to refuse: a short, no-fee "personal app," a four-week turnaround for a non-binding decision, and automatic consideration for a scholarship.

Congratulations!

You have been admitted, and we welcome you to the XX University family. You will soon receive a formal admission letter and invitations to special programs for admitted students.

EMBARRASSMENT OF RICHES

Shopping list for the lucky ED applicant

- 2 college-logo T-shirts
- 1 sweatshirt
- 1 mug
- 2 car decals
- 1 doormat
- 24 sessions with a therapist who specializes in senioritis

Then, twelve hours later, CJ checked his application status for the very first university we had visited (pre-blog), a school that he'd fallen in love with instantly.

There, on the screen, was a new link, "View Decision":

CONGRATULATIONS—You're IN!

The brief acceptance message included a link to a welcome video, with stately halls of learning, charismatic professors, and a diverse group of smart-looking students frolicking together in the autumn splendor.

It's only November and we are pinching ourselves: Can this be real? Can our lucky senior be "done" before most of his apps are even filled out? No need for safeties! Should he just throw together essays for a few reaches and call it a day? In short, hooray for non-binding, rolling, and early action schools!

And what do I panic about now? It's a good thing that the economy sucks, because I barely qualify for Neurotic Parent status anymore. I guess I can spend the next seven months finding things wrong with the institution that wants my son, but it's all uncharted territory from here.

The Neurotic Parent Answers Your Questions

EARLY DECISION ETIQUETTE: IT'S BINDING

Q: My son/daughter was accepted early at his/her dream school. Should I tell my friends, whose kids might have been deferred or rejected?

A: No. Wait for them to find out through the grapevine, which takes about five minutes these days. But do tell all your relatives, and expect them to ask why you would commit to paying $50,000 a year before hearing from your state flagship.

Q: Theoretically, if you have a satirical blog about the college admissions process and your son or daughter gets accepted early to his or her absolute dream school, how do you continue to come up with material for the blog?

A: Consider writing about premature separation issues, how to pay for college in this economy and other kids' admissions dramas.

Q: Theoretically, if you have a satirical blog about the college admissions process and your son or daughter gets accepted early to his or her absolute dream school, should you reveal the name of that school to your readers?

A: No. But you should give your readers subtle hints (such as "Southwest flies there" or "they have seven a cappella groups") so they will keep reading.

From the annals of the Neurotic Parent blog

NUESTRA SEÑORA DE LA DECISIÓN ANTICIPADA

Why did CJ get into his Early Decision dream school? Was it his Math SAT score? His leadership experience? His tenth-grade scholar-athlete award?

In fact, it was probably none of the above—it must have been divine intervention. Here's the story:

Just before Thanksgiving, a friend from graduate-school days, BL (Brilliant Linguist), stayed with us while he was lecturing at UCLA. He lives in Darwin, Australia and is considered the world's foremost authority on aboriginal languages. While visiting, he transferred some data to my computer so he could print out a fascinating doctrine about indigenous knowledge, digital technologies, and remote community capacity.

The next day BL e-mailed from the airport to tell me that he'd left his flash drive in my computer. I asked if he wanted me to FedEx it to him, and he answered that snail mail was fine. He had another copy of the file, but he did need the keychain it was attached to. The keychain, which he called Nuestra Señora and which had an image of Mother Mary on one side and Jesus on the other, is a souvenir from the Sanctuario del Milagroso de Buga in Colombia. It is also clearly a powerful good-luck object, even for those of us who are as un-Catholic as they come.

Here is our e-mail exchange:

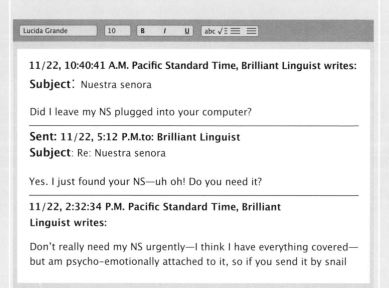

11/22, 10:40:41 A.M. Pacific Standard Time, Brilliant Linguist writes:

Subject: Nuestra senora

Did I leave my NS plugged into your computer?

Sent: 11/22, 5:12 P.M.to: Brilliant Linguist
Subject: Re: Nuestra senora

Yes. I just found your NS—uh oh! Do you need it?

11/22, 2:32:34 P.M. Pacific Standard Time, Brilliant
Linguist writes:

Don't really need my NS urgently—I think I have everything covered—
but am psycho–emotionally attached to it, so if you send it by snail

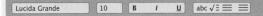

| Lucida Grande | 10 | **B** | *I* | U | abc √ ≡ ≡ ≡ |

mail I'd be grateful.

Sent: 11/22, 9:06 A.M. to: Brilliant Linguist

Subject: Re: Nuestra senora

Maybe I should hold onto NS until CJ is supposed to hear from X University (12/15), then send it to you for Xmas. How does that sound?

12/15, 4:52:46 P.M. Pacific Standard Time, Brilliant Linguist writes:

Okay, how did NS do with her intercessions on behalf of CJ? Did he make it to X University? Sorry you missed our party—it poured with monsoonal rain and has continued to do so all week—in fact there's a cyclone warning out. Hope you have happy hols. Pls forward NS to me soon as she is of no further use to you.

Sent: 12/15, 5:12 P.M.to: Brilliant Linguist

Subject: Re: Nuestra senora

It worked!!! He got into X University...a true miracle. He's over the moon.

Will send her back to you to prevent you from being swept away by the cyclone, but will have to borrow her when we start the college process again.

12/15, 7:22:08 P.M. Pacific Standard Time, Brilliant Linguist writes:

Wow congrats to CJ (and to NS)
Meanwhile the cyclone is about to hit.
More if we survive.

Sent: 12/15, 10:45 A.M.to: Brilliant Linguist
Subject: Re: Nuestra senora

Whoa, that's really scary. I hope this wasn't my fault for hanging onto NS.

So it seems as if CJ's college acceptance success can be traced to a spiritual turn of events that eventually caused a storm of biblical proportions. I sent Nuestra Señora back to BL, but I'm still not sure if she arrived in time to prevent major devastation to his city.

MAJOR OPPORTUNITY: A FAUSTIAN SCHOLARSHIP

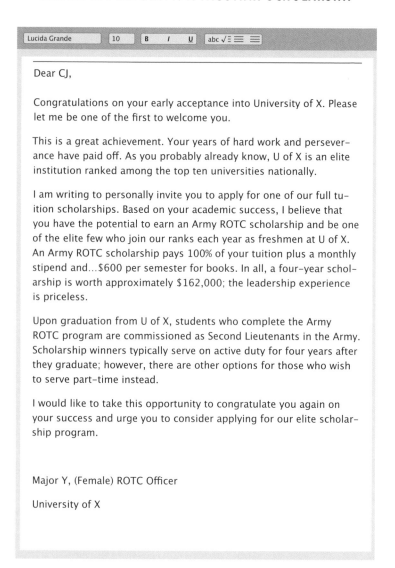

| Lucida Grande | 10 | **B** | *I* | U | abc √≡ ≡ ≡ |

Dear CJ,

Congratulations on your early acceptance into University of X. Please let me be one of the first to welcome you.

This is a great achievement. Your years of hard work and perseverance have paid off. As you probably already know, U of X is an elite institution ranked among the top ten universities nationally.

I am writing to personally invite you to apply for one of our full tuition scholarships. Based on your academic success, I believe that you have the potential to earn an Army ROTC scholarship and be one of the elite few who join our ranks each year as freshmen at U of X. An Army ROTC scholarship pays 100% of your tuition plus a monthly stipend and...$600 per semester for books. In all, a four-year scholarship is worth approximately $162,000; the leadership experience is priceless.

Upon graduation from U of X, students who complete the Army ROTC program are commissioned as Second Lieutenants in the Army. Scholarship winners typically serve on active duty for four years after they graduate; however, there are other options for those who wish to serve part-time instead.

I would like to take this opportunity to congratulate you again on your success and urge you to consider applying for our elite scholarship program.

Major Y, (Female) ROTC Officer

University of X

Yes, CJ really received this e-mail—and not long after a reader asked me to uncover ways to get money to pay for college. This might be the answer to everyone's tuition nightmares, while at the same time creating an opportunity to remake *Private Benjamin* for the 21st century.

EARLY DECISION ETIQUETTE: BLISSFULLY BINDING

The tables have turned. Those who were admitted recently to Stanford Early Action, which is not binding, received handwritten notes from their regional admissions reps. Some of these notes, which are really kind enticements designed to protect Stanford's yield, were posted by proud admittees on College Confidential.

> *I admire your hard work in the classroom, with your community, and your family. I am confident you will continue to excel in the remainder of your senior year and I look forward to seeing the contributions you will make at Stanford. ¡Nos vemos pronto!*

> *I really enjoyed reading your answers to the supplement, particularly the one about a 'library superhero.' We need more people like you. Good luck!*

> *You are a brilliant writer. I loved your piece on creationism and evolution. I can tell that you are a deep thinker, and Stanford will be lucky to have you.*

Thanks to expert fieldwork, the Neurotic Parent Institute has uncovered another batch of notes, straight from the Stanford admissions reps for the New Economy:

> *Your essay about how difficult it is to be the only young prince in your Swiss boarding school class was riveting—exactly the sort of diversity we're looking for at Stanford.*

> *I enjoyed reading the annual report from your grandparents' foundation. Thank goodness they were not affected by the Madoff situation. And what a thrill to discover that you are their only grandchild!*

JUNK MAIL—NOT

One of CJ's preschool buddies, MH (Musical Hippie), was fortunate to receive acceptances to several of his top-choice colleges. After much deliberation, he narrowed his list down to two schools, Oberlin and Middlebury, then spent the next fifteen days vacillating. Finally, on the evening of April 31st, the night before deposits were due, MH called his parents from a rehearsal and told them that he'd made up his mind. He would be attending Oberlin.

Thrilled that he'd decided (and worried that he'd change his mind), his parents volunteered to send in the acceptance card right then and there. MH agreed and told his dad where to find the Big Envelope from Oberlin. The father located the card in a pile of acceptances in MH's room. Underneath the pile was a small, unopened envelope, also from Oberlin. The dad tore it open and found that his son was the recipient of a $50,000 scholarship— an unexpected award that proved that there really is a higher being making sure that "they all end up in the right place"—and reminding us all to periodically rifle through the piles in our teens' rooms.

PATM: POST-ACCEPTANCE TEMPORARY MATURITY

We recently attended Senior Talk at our children's school, an annual event when seniors reflect on their high school experience and give advice to younger students and anxious parents. (Ironically, although much of the imparted wisdom was directed at juniors, there was not a single one in attendance—they were all home studying.)

The panel, eight articulate kids who had just completed the college application process, would soon be attending an impressive range of schools: Wesleyan, NYU, Tufts, Northwestern, Duke, Lewis & Clark, Stanford, and Tulane.

Surprisingly, the panel's suggestions proved to be a combination of Buddhist philosophy and advice our grandmothers gave us:

1 Enjoy your senior year.

2 Become friends with your teachers.

3 Take advantage of your free periods to get your homework done.

4 Take physiology, even if you suck at science.

5 There isn't just one right college; you can be happy in many places.

6 Sign up to do things you love rather than activities you think will look good on your resume.

7 Read a lot—not SparkNotes, but actual books.

8 Be a good person.

9 Live in the moment.

10 Get enough sleep (honest—we actually witnessed teens earnestly advising other teens to get enough sleep).

What made these seniors so wise and rational? Not the presence of their college counselors—they'd already hit them up for recommendations. The Neurotic Parent Institute has categorized this as PATM: Post-Acceptance Temporary Maturity, a phenomenon that occurs during the four months between the arrival of the first fat envelope and matriculation into college. This is the only period in their lives when teenagers seem sane and capable of doling out conventional wisdom.

Mark our words: As soon as they get to college, no more PATM. By the end of the summer, these grounded, Zen-like kids will be napping during free periods, reading SparkNotes, pulling all-nighters, and living in the future once again.

SEPARATION ANXIETY

If you're the emotional type,
you can skip this chapter

Welcome to the blow-by-blow account of the end of the Neurotic Parent's eldest son's run at home as a minor, written three years ago.

UPDATE: *It's all good. As I write this, rising college junior CJ is almost 21, and he's outside shooting hoops with his best friend from kindergarten, just as if he never left home.*

SEASON FINALE

So, after an 18-year run, it's time for the finale of our children's childhoods.

If you have a high school senior, I hope you don't have a time-consuming job, because there's an event practically every day and every night, all leading up to the end of parenting as you know it.

Here's the schedule we're facing while CJ wraps up his senior year, rated by quantity of Kleenex, on the K-KKKK scale:

> Senior Parent Separation Night - KK

> Last Meal at In 'n Out Following the Quarterfinals in the Inland Empire - K

> Final Club Soccer National Cup Semifinals - KK

> Varsity Soccer Play-offs/Awards Party - KK

> "Lifers" Assembly: Graduating seniors share memories and impart wisdom to tiny kids from the neighboring elementary school...it truly was just yesterday that our seniors were so little - KKKK

> Senior Dog Day (bring your best friend to school—our genius canine stayed awake through AP Calc BC) - KK

> Final MRI/ER visit of regular season volleyball - KK

> Club Soccer Awards Dinner - KK (CJ had to miss this because of above injury, but I attend alone and, after thirteen years of soccer, it was a real tearjerker)

> Senior Show - KKKK (and I don't even have a kid in theater)

> Last Taco Dinner Delivered by the Neurotic Parent to Journalism Class during Newspaper Production - K

> Last Trip to Tux Rental Place (the salesman asked CJ what color his prom date's dress was, and he found out by text that it was...turquoise) - K

> Final Grad Night Committee Meeting (I am part of a secret society planning a sober all-night activity to follow graduation) - K

> Senior Boys' Day (this was an event at another school, but I cried just hearing about it) — KKKK

UPCOMING (all in a period of eight days): Volleyball Award Night, Prom Photo Op, Preschool Moms' Coffee, Pre-K BBQ Reunion/Grad Party, Parent Association Thank-you Breakfast, Senior Breakfast/Awards, Lifers Cocktail Party, Senior Dinner at the Principal's House, Graduation, Grad Night, Post-Grad Night Breakfast, Summer of Deep Breathing, and then we'll move on to that life-changing mid-August weekend called Move-In, which thankfully they don't call Move-Out—but isn't that what it really is?

From the annals of the Neurotic Parent blog

POTLUCK/CRYFEST

Last Friday my friend IOMOHR (Incredibly Organized Mother of Handsome Rower) hosted the most appropriate gathering imaginable, a transformative evening with such fantastic opportunities for female bonding and introspection that it almost provided a rationale for all of our suffering of the last few months.

Here is an excerpt from the invitation:

Has one or all of your pups left the den in the recent past? Can you weep at the drop of the hat or are you available to assure the rest of us that there is a silver lining to their departure and/or that they will be living with us again in no time? If so, this potluck/cryfest is for you! Please let us know what you'll be bringing. I'll supply a big green salad and drinks—and lots of Kleenex.

Almost 30 attended, most of us more adept at preparing a frittata than dealing with our feelings of separation, anger, and loneliness, not to mention the compulsion to "have work done" so we won't look as old as we feel.

Because we shared our feelings in council format, I am bound to secrecy, but I can mention a few of the standout potluck dishes: chicken marsala, potatoes fontecchio, cauliflower soufflé, cranberry pudding, apricot galette, and two very comforting pasta dishes.

Despite the secrecy, I will share one common theme, which seemed to affect at least half of the group. Here's the pattern that emerged: With our newly found free time, many of us have taken to sitting and reflecting in the unusually clean rooms of our sons and daughters who have gone off to college. I was thrilled to hear that I was not the only one who has adopted this emotional habit. In my case, the experience is even more painful—not only am I surrounded with the poignant souvenirs of CJ's fleeting childhood, but there is still a pile of items that need to be returned to Target and Ikea, and I don't know what I did with the receipts.

THE KIDS ARE ALL RIGHT—BUT THE MOMS ARE NOT

It's fall, and moms of new college students are not doing well. Many aren't sleeping. One has stayed in bed for several days eating tapioca. Others are spending most of their time discussing their fears about bed bugs with their manicurists. But the smart ones got right on a plane after move-in and headed to Tuscany.

Dads are deeply invested in their midlife crises. Lots of surfing, running, tennis, motorcycle riding, yoga, Facebooking, and/or purchasing expensive barbecue equipment.

Boys, at least those affiliated with the Neurotic Parent Institute, are hopeless at communication. They will answer texts, usually within 36 hours, but mostly with one-word, misspelled responses, with extra letters for emphasis. Occasionally they'll say they're tired, especially the day after tailgates. Frustratingly, they are rumored to have been participating in frequent and lengthy iChats with their high school friends.

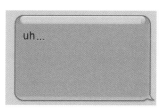

uh...

Girls call and text to complain nonstop during the first two weeks about (among other things):
➤➤ too much reading
➤➤ art history is not challenging enough
➤➤ messy roommate
➤➤ partying roommate
➤➤ food not as good as when she toured the school last year
➤➤ dorm room too hot
➤➤ missing their friends

Then, after two weeks, they all seem to be fine.

Parents of older kids confirm over and over again that no news is good news. Three veteran moms report that the only time they heard from their sons and daughters during freshman year was when they were in police custody.

From the annals of the Neurotic Parent blog

SCHOOL'S OUT...FOREVER

Yesterday at 3 p.m. the bell rang and the entire senior class squeezed onto an outdoor stage for a group hug. Then they lit up cigars—not a very PC tradition, but symbolic nonetheless. They may have had seniori- tis for the last three months, but now they can slack off as much as they want. They're done.

CJ didn't come straight home because he had also graduated from traffic school this weekend and had to deliver his certificate to the courthouse. But my younger son GC (who experienced his own mile- stone yesterday—no more braces) brought home the yearbook, the best I have ever seen—so cool, with such cutting-edge design, impres- sive illustrations, and such clever copy that I want to send CJ back for another four years to experience the studio art and creative writing classes he never took.

Laughing and crying as I went through the pages, I decided that we had indeed made an excellent choice in sending our kids to a quirky progressive school rather than to a more cookie-cutter institution. After all, it's the journey, not the destination. I felt proud of my own son but was mostly in awe of the class as a whole. So many of them are al- ready producing collectible art, important music, and readable prose. And those who are just normal kids still came up with entertaining, in- sightful, and self-effacing "most likely to's" for themselves.

➤➤ Most likely to spike the punch with lemonade

➤➤ Most likely to survive because of what he learned on the Discovery Channel

➤➤ Most likely to become Japanese

➤➤ Most likely to have gone through a phase of being your friend

➤➤ Most likely to beat up his opponent after losing in the semifinals at the ping-pong world championships

➤➤ Most likely to quote from *Friends* in her wedding vows

➤➤ Most likely to have a font named after him

▶▶ Most likely to have an overly suggestive senior page (photo shows
student proposing to his history teacher)

▶▶ Most likely to owe more in alimony than student loans

▶▶ Most likely to teach her children the wrong colors

These kids may not have memorized the preamble to the Constitution, but they are *all* ready to work for Jon Stewart. If CJ stays in touch with just a fraction of his class, he won't need to make any connections in college, because of the incredible creative energy in his high school class.

My one disappointment with the yearbook? CJ's senior photo is ridiculous. Another tradition in our progressive school—on par with the cigars—is to pose for a silly photo, the kind you would take in a photo booth. (Somehow I never knew about this custom or saw the embarrassingly juvenile portrait of my son until yesterday, even though it's also on his student ID.) So his main yearbook photo shows him wearing a too-small baseball cap and holding a large wooden fish. Seven or eight of his close friends are also photographed with the same nautical artifact, making funny faces. This was their first stab at performance art, which has a time and a place, but in this case was unfortunately captured for posterity. The Neurotic Parent fears that CJ's grandchildren will see the random fish and dumb baseball cap and come to the conclusion that their grandfather was a nutcase—or else just a really happy teen with many Friends for Life.

COUNTDOWN TO COMMENCEMENT

Tomorrow at 4:30. Can it really be?

Survived the Senior Breakfast, the Prom Photo Op, and the Pre-K Reunion. Now it's the night before graduation—and the Neurotic Parent Institute has definitive proof that even the least anxious parents have become basket cases.

Some ubiquitous parental developmental stages:

- Spending hours going through photos, posting them on Facebook, e-mailing them back and forth, and choking up about not just how cute your grad was, but what a young-looking mom you once were.

- Agonizing over whether to give the grad a gift (in addition to the requisite laptop...and the outrageously expensive college education).

- Discovering in horror that the prom photos are blurry and you need a new camera.

- Doing hours of online research about which camera to get.

- Deciding at the last moment to self-publish a book for your grad because you're not the scrapbooking type and you have eighteen years of memorabilia dumped in large plastic boxes. So you spend hours selecting precious art works and research papers to include in a gift from the heart—but then you realize that it's a whole lot easier to do a simple photo montage.

- Abandoning the montage idea because choosing the music is too much to handle emotionally.

- Deciding at the last moment to write a poem for your grad but getting stuck when it comes to the tone. Should it be comedic (for him) or poignant (for you)?

- Being interrupted from your poetry writing by a group of eighteen hungry Lakers fans who have stopped by unannounced to watch Game 5.

- Realizing suddenly you have nothing to wear to graduation, especially nothing that looks good with flats (no heels allowed on the turf).

- Calling various parents for advice about what time to arrive and where to park.

- Developing what you think is stress-related carpal tunnel syndrome and finding out it's stress-related pre-arthritis.

- Accepting that not only has your baby grown up, but that suddenly you are the mother of...an adult.

8 SURVIVAL TIPS FOR ABANDONED PARENTS

Once you finish shopping for slim hangers and bed risers, you will realize that the whole experience is just a pricey time killer designed to distract you from that surreal moment when you give up your child and head back home a confused, teary, empty old person facing a long, sad existential crisis.

Yes, this is the emotional abyss you will soon share with your child's classmates' moms and dads. With that in mind, the Neurotic Parent is proud to offer emergency survival tips for those who just cannot cope with the loss of their older, younger, or (gulp) only child.

1 Pretend that your son or daughter has gone to camp. For four years.

2 Get a dog. Name it after your son or daughter. How cute it will be when Virgil comes home for Thanksgiving and finds a furry little Virgil in the house, one that not only obeys curfew but is always fast asleep by 9 p.m.

3 Remember, they're not sad. They're tailgating and reading Sartre and running the Naked Mile. They're FREE—and they might even learn to think on a higher level and unlock the secrets of a new field, like neuroeconomics.

4 Plan a business meeting 300 miles from your child's college and use it as an excuse to pop in and take him or her (with new friends) out to dinner. Blame it on JetBlue's schedules. (Seriously, we were heartbroken until we did this.)

5 If applicable, begin helicoptering and micromanaging your younger child. If you don't have one, try a niece or nephew.

6 Send care packages and cheery notes to all your child's high school friends at their various colleges.

7 Become addicted to Facebook. Spy on your kid's new friends. Play Scrabble with your former attorney. Find comfort in the Facebook posts of other parents. Here is one mom's status:
Kleenex, 1 trip to Duane Reade, 2 trips to Staples, 3 trips to Bed Bath & Beyond, more Kleenex, and a boy in college.

8 And the best suggestion of all: Look for the silver lining. One intuitive friend with impeccable taste cried for several days until she realized she now could delete her son's season passes on TiVo. Although a seemingly learned Dartmouth man, his list of TV shows included *SuperJail, Nitro Circus*, and *ManAnswers*. She chose to keep *Top Gear*, a show about macho British race-car drivers, to watch on those lonely nights when she really misses her boy. We followed her lead and deleted our son's four nights of weekly football recordings, but kept his ten seasons of *Friends*. We'd thought of turning our attention to studying Italian or designing an outdoor living room, but now we have a way to keep nostalgically busy—and to be reminded of our son's shallow taste in entertainment—every night until Thanksgiving.

From the annals of the Neurotic Parent blog

THE POWER OF BUNNIES

Mr. NP and I had dinner tonight with four other couples. Three out of the four are about to send their youngest children off to college. The moms, who all seem to be dealing with the transition relatively well, are nonetheless forming a support group. I can see how they will need it with the stress of their babies moving out. Just trying to get Son #2 to begin to think about his essays is stressful enough.

I wanted to find some words of wisdom for my friends who are about to become empty nesters, so I scoured the web for some sensible advice.

And I found it on College Confidential.

🗐 **09-04, 01:24 PM**	**#1**

marnik **Junior Member** **Join Date: Nov 2007** **Posts: 71**	**As I begin reviewing "Parent Orientation" schedules and "Student Orientation" schedules, the reality that my only daughter will be moving 2.5-3 hours away has me in the beginnings of a panic state. I do not let on to her, but gosh, this is way more difficult than I could**

RE-NESTING

The NPI has been approached to provide tips for empty nesters who wish to re-ignite the relationship with their spouses. We're commissioning a study on the subject, but while we wait for the results to

have imagined. All the worries about getting in to college are now worries about how will she "do" college (probably very well without me nagging). I am so proud of her, and I know she will be fine. I think the worries are about how I will do.

09-05, 01:24 PM   #2

Northstarmom
Senior Member

Join Date: Aug 2004
Posts: 11,427

Before my last kid at home left for college, I found it very helpful to get a couple of pets so that I would not have to come home to an empty house. The pets I got are rabbits. They are quiet and cute, and stand on their hind legs to welcome me home (because they know I'll give them treats).

I have no doubt that Northstarmom knows what she's talking about. Surely she is an expert parent, because she has 11,427 posts on College Confidential. It is a great relief to know that there will be a simple solution to the inevitable trauma I will be facing in four years, when Son #2 leaves the nest. Thank goodness for the internet—and for furry little creatures everywhere.

---

come in, maybe you could see a movie together. Or, for coziness, perhaps the two of you could spend a night in your son or daughter's empty bed.

SEPARATION NIGHT

Last Thursday our school sponsored an evening for parents of seniors to prepare us for that day next August when we have to drop off our babies. Thirty people showed up. We sat in a circle with three school psychologists and had a council. I can't tell you anything that was said (would have to kill you), but you can imagine. There was laughter. There were tears. And there were funny, poignant stories about when we went off to college a generation ago, when the world was completely different...or was it?

Until a few moments ago, I was feeling pretty good about the outcome of the evening. What I gleaned was that it will be incredible for CJ and not so bad for me, because I had such a positive experience going off to college in the aforementioned world of yesteryear.

But I just read the first few lines of the handout we were given, and now I'm wondering just how easy this process will be:

"Tonight we are going to talk about what it means to say goodbye to a relationship that has sustained you for over seventeen years. For most of you, this has been the most incredible relationship you have ever experienced."

I defy you to show me a school handout that is more of a tearjerker.

PASSAGES

I vowed I would not turn this into a teary Emptying Nest blog. But I must mention that last Friday CJ "graduated" from varsity soccer. As I watched the highlight reel of his team's miraculous winning season (his school has more of a reputation for animal rights activism and sweat-lodge rituals than for strong athletics), images of my fourteen years as a soccer mom flashed before me—the drives to Victorville in bumper-to-bumper traffic, the heat, the cold, the mud, the rain, the nerve-wracking penalty kicks, the emergency visits to the orthopedist. The nostalgia was overwhelming as the team hugged their coaches goodbye—but then CJ reminded me that he still has a whole club tournament season ahead of him. In fact, he has to be in the far reaches of the OC this very Saturday morning at 7 a.m.

And with our younger son GC semi-committed to JV soccer, I can look forward to three more years of forgotten cleats and unfair refs.

ALL GROWN UP

CJ voted today, proudly and enthusiastically. Neighbors who have known him since he was 3 years old saw him in line and marveled at the milestone.

It's hitting me: Good thing he's going to college, because he's now old enough to go to war.

seventeen

BED BATH & BYE-BYE

Empty nests on sale — 20% off

IF YOU CAN'T LEAVE 'EM, JOIN 'EM

The college-obsessed editors at the *New York Times* recently published a piece about a popular new real estate trend. All over the country, from South Bend, Indiana to Knoxville, Tennessee, parents are purchasing second homes in college towns. Why? Primarily to attend hockey games and do their kids' laundry. However, the NPI suspects that they actually want to save on the rising cost of empty-nester support groups.

The *Times* reports, "Many…want front-row seats to watch their family athletes perform. Some seek a gathering place for football games or family holidays." And others want to retire in a place with college-town amenities, so it makes perfect sense to go where their offspring are attending.

The article quotes a researcher who wrote a dissertation about parent-student relationships during the transition to college (not surprisingly, an increasingly popular area of study). "Boundary-setting is important," the researcher concluded. "Research has found that the parent-child relationship grows better once the child has left the house. Parents should be careful not to interrupt that process."

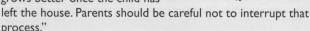

The Neurotic Parent Institute supports this study. Our suggestion is to forget about moving to the town where your kids live—instead, go where they'll want to visit *you*. And then please invite us for a visit in Aspen, St. Barth, or Barcelona.

LINENS ANONYMOUS

My name is Neurotic Parent and I am a bedaholic. Perhaps you are, too. Here are the warning signs:

❶ Visiting Bed Bath & Beyond alone; staying until closing time.

❷ Ordering high-count bed linens online, hiding them in your car, then sending them back.

❸ Daily or frequent trips to Ikea, even if it's 30-plus miles away.

❹ Inability to stop surfing Overstock.com; viewing all 1,543 search results for gray towels.

❺ Opening sealed memory-foam mattress toppers at bedding stores to assess the odors.

❻ Secretly checking out mattress toppers at friends' homes.

❼ Becoming angry when confronted by spouse about how ridiculous your conversations have become.

❽ Neglecting care and maintenance of your OWN bedding, while stockpiling for child.

❾ Contacting friend in Amsterdam about where she purchased a twin XL non-ruffled bedskirt.

❿ Poor sleep habits due to nightmares about foam vs. fiberbed and top sheet vs. duvet cover.

The saddest, most ironic part about this new obsession is that my children have attended soccer camps for years, where they routinely stayed in run-down dorms or cabins. They always took our oldest, torn, stained bedding, which they never even unpacked—they just slept in a ratty sleeping bag on the bunks, with no top sheet. And they always came home happy and well rested.

Perhaps this developmental abnormality happens because this is the last time we have any control as parents, even if it is only control over a mattress topper. Or it could be that our troubling behavior stems from a last-minute intrinsic compulsion to protect our kids by helping them be more comfortable.

Intervention

Many thanks to SDM (Stylish Designer Mom) for conducting an intervention to help me deal with this addiction. I can assure you: You will move on from your bedding obsession, partly because eventually you will have to do some real work, and partly because it is terrifically boring, even though you can learn a lot about innovative fibers, particularly modal.

Here's how SDM got me to go cold turkey: She pointed out that everything you buy gets trashed immediately anyway.

IMPORTANT BEDDING WARNING

After your child gets into college, don't think for a minute that the anxiety will end. There are more significant decisions to be made…and many mistakes to be avoided. Most of these mistakes involve bedding. Even if your kid can sleep anywhere and is used to threadbare linens with stretched-out elastic, you will find yourself spending hours making decisions about bedding options.

Before you head to Bed Bath & Beyond or Target, you must take heed of a potentially perilous situation, which will be emphasized by notices you'll receive in the mail that will try to gently prepare you for an awful situation. These missives might even come from your child's university.

"Warning!" they will say. "You **CANNOT** use regular twin sheets on a twin XL bed! They won't fit—they're too small. You'll need to get a bed set especially made for long twin beds." Or, "Buying the wrong size bedding for your dorm room can be a disaster."

We checked out these alerts on Snopes.com, and they are *not* urban legends: Although many college students are under 5'7", their beds are all 80" long. And this means not a single sheet you have in your linen closet will work.

But you do not need to succumb to the widespread freshman linen panic, a situation so desperate that it has spawned harsh comments on the bedding site dormbuys.com:

"Universities…have the audacity to send 'fear' letters to incoming freshmen homes, **BUT THEIR SCARE TACTICS WILL BE MADE KNOWN**." The blogger goes on to write that certain manufacturers bully consumers into making them feel "as if only their sheets will work on your college's beds," when you can actually procure them at many places.

BOTTOM LINE

Now is the time to take all the anger and anxiety you have left over from tutors, essays, GPAs, college visits, SAT subject tests, etc. and transfer it all to worry about sheet length.

To complicate matters, all twin XLs are not created equal. There's the percale vs. sateen vs. flannel dilemma. And it is worth pondering whether your child will even use a top sheet, and if not, what will happen to a duvet cover that is not laundered for four years?

Once your future freshman has actually selected sheets, underbed storage bins, and hand towels, many other critical decisions loom.

For example, should you get:

➡ *A "memory foam" pad? (cons: retains heat, has chemical odor, expensive)*

➡ *An eggshell pad? (cons: falls apart, outdated, now replaced by memory foam)*

➡ *A zoned Isotonic mattress enhancer or a 400-thread-count Egyptian cotton "overstuffed" mattress pad—or both?*

➡ *A feather bed or hypoallergenic fiber bed?*

➡ *A bed bug protector?*

The most challenging part of this decision-making process is that these items are not mutually exclusive. For example, if you get the memory foam, you still need the mattress cover—and how can the foam remember anything if it's squished by a quilted, overstuffed cover by Laura Ashley?

The Neurotic Parent Institute has come to the conclusion that the solution is to purchase a brand-new, comfortable mattress rather than try to enhance a 50-year-old sucky one. Mattresses are readily available in most college towns for $79, a lot less than the cost of an elaborate layered system.

BEDDING TRANSFERENCE

In June, like clockwork, parents on College Confidential begin to obsess about whether to get an eggshell mattress topper or a Tempurpedic one. This is just transference: You're actually either upset that your kid is leaving or you're still freaking out about that B+ in Algebra I that kept him out of Columbia.

To qualify the extent of parents' bedding concerns are numerous threads on College Confidential about the twin XL sheet situation—including this query from a mom who insisted on empirical research rather than speculation:

🗐   **07-15, 03:02 PM**   **#1**

Got2BeGreen
Member

Join Date: Jan 2011
Posts: 372

Have you put a standard twin fitted sheet on an XL mattress?

I'm looking for advice from people who have actually tried putting a standard twin fitted sheet on a twin XL mattress. How well did it work? Would you do it again?

I know that the standard twin fitted sheet is 75" long, and the standard twin XL mattress is 80" long. (The mattresses at my daughter's college are 78"). I also know that the college mattresses tend to be thinner than mattresses at home. Please don't speculate in this thread about how well you THINK it would work. I'm really looking for empirical evidence.

Thanks!

🗐   **07-15, 03:22 PM**   **#2**

Mom22039
Junior Member

Join Date: Oct 2009
Posts: 96

Our D had two sets of sheets. One set was XL purchased at Target and the other was from Lands End. The Lands End flannels worked very well. The deep pockets compensated for the fact that they were not XL.

🗐   **07-15, 03:41 PM**   **#3**

lookingforward
Senior Member

Join Date: Dec 2006
Posts: 1,098

My kid found the XL sheets a bit loose, took twins back to school—and they didn't reach. (i.e., the top of the corner seam doesn't reach the top corner of the

🗐 **continued**

bed. Deep pockets "may" compensate. Or may not.) Trick to get a good deal is shop now—Target and Walmart.

🗐 **07-15, 04:22 PM**   **#4**

sunnyflorida
Senior Member

Join Date: Jun 2006
Posts: 2,915

If they are for DEEP mattresses and especially if they have elastic all the way around and not just at the corners, they work. A twin XL is longer but narrower. And our experience is they are likely NOT DEEP.

Lots of new XL sets and sheets at Bed Bath & Beyond. And lots of 20% off coupons.

🗐 **07-15, 04:23 PM**   **#5**

jym626
Senior Member

Join Date: Oct 2004
Posts: 8,273

The regular twin jersey sheets fit fine. But they get all stretched out weird.

🗐 **07-15, 04:29 PM**   **#6**

college_ruled
Senior Member

Join Date: Sep 2008
Posts: 1,087

Yes, I have gotten old, stretched-out jersey sheets (twin-sized) to fit a twin xl bed. However, the fitted sheet did not work with a mattress topper. (The pockets on the fitted sheet weren't particularly deep.) I have had twin xl sheets that wouldn't stay on the bed, because the pockets were too deep. Go figure.

🗐 **07-15, 08:46 PM**   **#7**

spdf
Member

Join Date: Aug 2008
Posts: 453

I showed up to college with my standard twin sheets, never having heard of an XL twin. There was no hope of getting the fitted sheet to stay on, so I ended up tucking the top sheet around the mattress.

🗐 **07-15, 08:52 PM**   **#8**

Lauren2299
Junior Member

Join Date: Apr 2011
Posts: 261

My best friend tried to use twin sheets her freshman year and it didn't work out for her. She is now, however, on medication, and she's sleeping much better.

From the annals of the Neurotic Parent blog

FRESHMEN/GENDER STUDIES

CJ found out his housing assignment last week. The dorm, although not ideally located, has a common room with ping-pong, foosball, billiards, and video games, so he's all set there. And the roommate sounds great—a smart team captain from a mid-Atlantic state who, like CJ, attended a small, progressive independent high school. A computer randomly assigned them to each other, and unlike other universities that require students to fill out elaborate forms for roommate matching, their school asked just these four questions (with CJ's answers in parentheses):

Q: Do you smoke? (A: No)

Q: What time do you go to sleep? (A: Varies)

Q: What time do you get up? (A: Varies)

Q: Do you listen to music when studying (A: Yes)—(Does this mean they BOTH will listen to different music at the same time, or that his roommate doesn't listen to music, but doesn't care if his partner is noisy?)

Congrats to the computer program for what seems to have been a stellar job of matchmaking, considering the minimalist nature of the above questions. Other colleges ask if you hang up your clothes, whether you've shared a room before, if you prefer classical to hip-hop, and to identify your favorite flavor of ramen noodles. Although I secretly hoped CJ would be matched with an African prince, it won't be such a bad thing for him to live with someone from a similar background.

But although this seems to be a match made in heaven, CJ has been reluctant to communicate with his new roommate. While girls we know have been planning color schemes, exchanging long lists of favorite films, and sharing class schedules, CJ and his roomie sent each other just one two-line private message on Facebook. When I suggested that he find out his new pal's phone number, my son looked at me as if I were insane. Okay then, how about finding out where he lives, his summer plans, or whether he's bringing the fridge or the microwave?

Mortally embarrassed to use any method of communication other than instant messaging, CJ said he will wait until they both happen to be on Facebook and then possibly initiate a chat. Apparently his college asked a fifth question, which I did not see:

Q: Would you ever consider using any technology other than random Facebook messaging (such as e-mail, cell phone, BBM, iChat, AIM, texting, snail mail, or even a land line) to contact your new roommate?

A: I couldn't possibly be compatible with anyone who actually makes an effort to communicate.

PACKING WISDOM
FOR PARENTS OF BOYS

❶ Do everything in your power to rid yourself of the mindset that he's going to the tundra, where nothing will be available.

❷ In fact, if you forget to pack or buy something, and you have a boy, he will never notice. That is a good thing, because you'll never have to pay for it, and it won't clutter up his room. For example, if you forget to pack a soap dish, he won't buy any soap for the three to four years he is in the dorms.

❸ Your son will suddenly develop a preference for Axe.

❹ All that is really necessary is his cell, a laptop, and an ATM card. And maybe a mattress topper.

PACKING WISDOM FOR PARENTS OF GIRLS

❶ Your daughter will start perusing the Ikea catalog on the day she submits her Common App. Even for the level-headed, nonmaterialistic girls, it's never too soon to start collecting suitable flip flops and sweatpants.

❷ No matter how many felt-clad flat hangers you buy, you will need 50 more.

❸ She will refuse to leave a single pair of shoes at home, so start collecting shoe-storage contraptions now.

❹ Those stylish shower totes are designed for boys, who don't use them anyway, so don't waste your money. Girls need something much larger to haul their shampoo, conditioner, body wash, shaving gel, razors, skin toner, pore tightener, firming lotion, hair products, scents, loofahs, and extra towels down the hall. We suggest a rolling duffel.

From the annals of the Neurotic Parent blog

REGISTRATION & GLOBALIZATION

Preparing for college has changed since the
days when you:

→ applied to just three schools

→ got into all three

→ spent $3K tops per year
     on tuition

→ enrolled in psychology,
     philosophy, and a course about
     Malcolm X

→ took over the library

→ after graduation, providing you could type, found an entry-level
     job in the field of your choice without anyone ever asking where
     you attended college, what you studied, what your GPA was, or
     how many years it took you to graduate

Now, of course, everything is different—and the registration process
has changed as much as the admissions process. One inevitable earth-
friendly innovation is that there is no longer a printed course catalog.
Course descriptions are now listed online, but not in a readable way.
(Imagine the Manhattan phone book—you'd never read it on the
internet the way you'd flip through the pages of the real thing.)

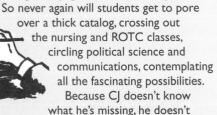

So never again will students get to pore
over a thick catalog, crossing out
the nursing and ROTC classes,
circling political science and
communications, contemplating
all the fascinating possibilities.
Because CJ doesn't know
what he's missing, he doesn't
really care that his school only provides a virtual schedule. In fact,
he barely glanced at the offerings and instead chose his classes with
the help of his three upperclass friends by text messages, a phone
conversation (!), and even a lunch (!!).

They gave him advice like, "Don't take calculus, chemistry, or
Spanish—they're all too hard." (Too bad those happen to be his
strongest subjects.) Other suggestions involved not signing up for
anything before 11 a.m., checking out teachers on ratemyprofessor.com,
and a big hint about an entire department known for its easy As.

The three upperclassmen didn't completely neglect "love of learning" courses. They each suggested two to three life-changing professors, but, alas, their classes all had long waiting lists.

So the Neurotic Parent, who never once helped choose a class for CJ in high school, felt compelled to step in and find some interesting options.

In no time I discovered the REAL reason why colleges have stopped printing catalogs: Today's classes all deal with the same common theme: globalization. In just a quick look-see, I found 72 classes that point out that It's a Globalized World After All. For instance:

→ Globalization and Domestic Politics

→ Labor, Gender, and Globalization

→ Globalization and Public Health Discourse

→ India in a Global Age

→ Even a capstone seminar in Canadian globalization (hmm... are the rest of you as surprised as I am that our neighbor to the north has become globalized?)

The Neurotic Parent Institute has determined that CJ's school is not the only institution that has become obsessed with the "G" word. Also, a newly funded NPI study has shown that colleges EVERYWHERE have abandoned their catalogs for supposed ecological reasons. But this is actually a massive international cover-up designed to prevent students from realizing that the majority of college classes are now globalization-related.

Even universities in China and India and Iceland and Ghana and Dubai and Brazil have jumped on the bandwagon.

Wow—I wonder how all those countries all decided to do the same thing at the same time? Maybe there's a course I could take that will explain this unprecedented phenomenon.

NUMBER ONE, COED STYLE

You're approaching the final countdown. But though the shopping is almost completed, every BB&B purchase creates anxiety and leads to hours of additional research. Window fan or Vornado? Will the sticky hooks work, or is it better to purchase the over-the-door ones, even if you don't know whether there IS a suitable door? What kind of rain boots would a teen actually wear, especially a teen who has never used outerwear? Are bed risers as treacherous as they look in the package?

This whole process reminds us of the daunting task of outfitting the nursery before the baby arrived. Suddenly there were essential consumer decisions to be made about bouncy seats, toilet locks, onesies, splat mats, and especially strollers, all products that new parents barely knew existed before landing in Babyland. You would think that items for an 18-year-old would not feel so unfamiliar, but they are equally as alien: egg-crate foam, microfridges, shower buckets. How can you make responsible choices about these essentials if you've never before encountered them?

The wise SDM (Stylish Designer Mom), a consultant to the Neurotic Parent Institute who has sent two kids off to college, insists that on move-in day, Bed/Bath/Buyer's Remorse will be the least of your worries. And the event of saying goodbye to your baby will also be not such a big deal, she promises, because you will no longer have to be mad at him or her every night for missing dinner and coming home late.

But according to SDM, there is one inevitable move-in situation that will wreak havoc on your psyche: Using the bathroom in the dorm on move-in day. SDM broke it to us gently, but the vivid details of her shocking story remain: When she moved her son into a top liberal arts college in Connecticut, she visited his dorm bathroom, and there at the sink was a dad, washing his hands. My friend nodded politely to him, then entered a stall. As she sat on the lavatory several feet away, the friendly father continued to engage her in small talk. "Where are you from?" "Has your son decided on a major?" "Did you fly to Hartford or New York?" and so forth.

The emotional impact of dropping off your child is one thing, but having to chat with male strangers while peeing is enough to push any mother over the edge.

TARGET THERAPY

Deep down I feel I must be loyal to Bed Bath & Beyond. After all, it is the only store that lets you reserve dozens of items at your local branch, then edit your order when you get to your college town, without paying in advance. And they allow you to use coupons that expired in 2004.

But today I found myself in Target, BB&B's principal dorm-supply competitor. I was there on a mission to find an essential collegiate item that I'd never heard of until last week: 3M Command Strips, which are used to hang up posters in dorm rooms without damaging the walls. The entire westside of Los Angeles is out of this miracle substance because there are an awful lot of Bob Marley posters waiting to be hung at UCLA and USC.

I scored big time, Command Strip–wise, then wandered the aisles, remembering when I used to go there for T-ball equipment and Power Ranger underwear. I ended up buying a microplush blanket for CJ, another newish comfort-bedding item—sort of like a stuffed animal hide. I also checked out the underbed storage drawers offered for three days only as a College Prep Special and became depressed when I saw that they were hipper and cheaper than the ones we registered for at BB&B.

I returned home, vowing never to go back to Target—unless, of course, I need to return something I bought today. It was just too intense reliving all my child-oriented bargain purchases of the last 18 years and seeing all the better deals we could get if we were driving to CJ's school rather than flying.

Then I glanced at the parents' forum on College Confidential and discovered that I am in the minority. Other senior moms go to Target for an uplifting experience, not a melancholy one. One frequent contributor, named lindz126, confessed:

> "*Oh and the Target thing...it was my therapy last yr after my s left for college—whenever I felt sad I'd go to Target, wander around, you know like you can only do at Target, and fill a basket to send him as a care package. Always worked to make me feel better, feel connected to him.*"

Darn! On top of everything else, I have developed Target Aversion Syndrome. No care packages for my son—unless I can bring myself to find solace at Ikea.

MOVE-IN TIPS

What to pack:

1 A **TOOL KIT** to keep your husband occupied and out of your hair. And make sure you pick something up at Target that will take a lot of time to put together. (This is akin to packing Legos for your toddler.)

2 Even if it's 90+ degrees outside, don't forget a **PASHMINA**, a **CARDIGAN**, and a **FLEECE JACKET** to wear indoors. Most hotels in college towns outside of the Sunbelt haven't heard of carbon footprints and set their AC at 58 degrees.

3 **PREPPY SHORTS** with whales on them. People really wear these in certain parts of the country.

4 A **SPY CAMERA**, because your son or daughter will be embarrassed if you try to take photos publicly.

5 Hundreds of **BB&B COUPONS**. If you have a sister-in-law who lives in the suburbs, chances are she and all her friends have been hoarding these for years. Even if you have never used coupons in your life, you will feel so good about saving $2.18 on a bath towel that you won't mind losing your son or daughter.

COLLEGE LIFE

"If you want to get laid, go to college. If you want to get an education, go to the library." —Frank Zappa

From the annals of the Neurotic Parent blog

PARENTS' WEEKEND

We're on our way to reconnect with our wayward eldest for a weekend of campus fun, athletics, and stimulating lectures like "Global Opportunities in Places like Ghana that Cost Twice as Much as Regular Tuition." The consummate host, CJ seems to actually be looking forward to our arrival and is taking an active role in ensuring a fun visit for the entire family.

We land at 11:45 p.m. and will arrive at our hotel at 12:30 a.m. But the late hour will not stop him from providing his younger brother, GC (Good Conversationalist), with an immediate glimpse of college life. Here is a snippet of our latest text communication:

Mom: We're on the plane, about to take off. Is it true you invited GC to sleep in your dorm? Where and when should he meet you?

CJ: I will let u know when it gets closer to the time. And give him cash.

PARENTS' WEEKEND, PART II

I'm very pleased to report that we survived parents' weekend. In fact the visit was a smashing success, other than a torrential downpour during the football game, a fourteen-hour journey home involving a missed connecting flight, and our younger son's permanent corruption after spending three nights with his brother in his dorm.

CJ is incredibly happy and reasonably healthy (after recuperating from H1N1), and he actually managed to get excellent mid-semester grades without missing a tailgate.

One minor disappointment: We barely were able to have a conversation with our son because most of our time together involved loud sporting events, crowded restaurants with his friends' families— and watching him nap in our hotel room. Every night at 9:30 he would politely bid us goodnight and head off to a vibrant social occasion that lasted until 3 a.m. And each morning, while waiting for him to wake up, Mr. NP and I enjoyed a speech by the president, a cappella performances, economics lectures, and spirited brunches, all the while commiserating with other parents about how education is wasted on the young.

Later in the week, the parents of CJ's high school class had a reunion coffee, and the themes seemed to be the same: many undeclared majors, minimal homesickness, phone calls home mostly to ask for something—and how to deal with our college students when they come home for Thanksgiving and expect us to be supportive of their girls-and-boys-gone-crazy good life while under our roofs.

BREAKING NEWS ON THE A CAPPELLA FRONT

To get our minds off certain deferrals and rejections of loved ones (plus stressful sophomore PSAT scores), we have two major announcements:

1 We received a call from Proud Mother of a Future Congressman, who let us know that the Tufts Beelzebubs have made it to the finals of "The Sing Off," an NBC reality show that features a cappella groups competing à la *American Idol*. If you're so inclined, you can go to the show's website and vote for the Bubs...or for Voices of Lee (Lee University, Ohio) or Nota (University of San Juan, PR). We cast our votes for the Bubs, but we also listened to Voices and Nota, and they're all dynamite.

2 In a super-coincidental development, just hours later we received an e-mail from PMOFUSP (Proud Mother of a Future U.S. President) inviting us to hear America's oldest underclassmen a cappella group, the Yale Spizzwinks(?) during their world tour, which includes Ecuador, Brazil, Paraguay, Hong Kong, Thailand, Singapore, Burma, Malaysia, and Sherman Oaks, California, where we will have the pleasure of seeing them. "In the past," the invitation stated, "the Spizzwinks(?) have received raving reviews for performances at the White House and Carnegie Hall."

The Neurotic Parent Institute did some research, and it turns out that the parentheses and question mark are cleverly(?) an official part of the Spizzwinks(?) name. The Neurotic Parent has volunteered to accompany them on their world tour to translate this essential punctuation into Malaysian and Portuguese. And we could also clean up the grammar in their brag sheet. Shouldn't it be "rave reviews," rather than "raving"? Any Yale scholars out there who can help us out on this?

From the annals of the Neurotic Parent blog

YAAA

Below is the extent of our son's communication (by text) since we dropped him off at college. Our A/A-student seems to have picked up a multiple-letter texting disability, making him sound like a preteen Jonas Brothers fan.

And the only information he's actually volunteered:

(Finally—no immature multiple letters. But he did add a "ha ha.")

BLAME VERIZON

We have reached a new level of frustration in our ongoing mission to converse with our son. Even Mr. Neurotic Parent, who previously advocated waiting until CJ called us, finally caved after a few weeks of very limited communication and ordered me to contact our MIA offspring.

Success! Moments later, I heard his collegiate voice—along with a cacophony of ambient background sound effects that sounded like a combination of a rock festival, a space shuttle landing, and a Black Friday sale at a New Jersey mall. CJ seemed amenable to speak with me, but it was impossible to decipher his words. "I can't talk now," he finally said. "I get terrible reception all over campus." "Maybe you could answer my Blackberry messages once in a while," I screamed. "The Blackberry doesn't work in, like, half of the dorms," he answered. He then said, "Listen, it's my turn in a Madden tournament...Love you!" and hung up.

Our next attempt to reach him resulted in an even more garbled dialogue. This time it sounded as if he were at a tailgate party, although he said he was working on a project in his dorm room "with a partner." "I CAN'T TALK NOW...LOVE YOU," he let me know, sweetly but firmly.

Disheartened, I waited until 11:01 p.m. his time on a Sunday night, the hour I always called my parents from college, because 8 p.m. was when long-distance rates went down. Obviously there's no such thing as long-distance rates any more, but I thought the Sunday evening timing might result in some nostalgic good karma—and maybe a regression to the technological conditions of the '70s, when you could actually hear people on the phone. Presumably CJ would be winding down from the weekend, finishing up his homework for a Monday class. Instead, I got no answer. I tried sending a text, but although a "D" appeared, letting us know my message was delivered, there was no "R," indicating that it had been read.

"Stop bothering CJ," said GC, his younger brother. "It's Sunday night, so he's probably watching football, or he could be at a frat party or at a club. And besides, *nobody* gets service on campus."

Nobody, that is, besides the girls, who dutifully call home three times a day with crystal-clear coverage. They must all have enhanced fiber-optic network plans that are unavailable to members of the male gender.

REASONS TO FINALLY CALL HOME

A) Wallet stolen
B) Received first exam grade, a 94 (after incorrectly being recorded as an 82)
C) Nasty virus
D) All of the above

From the annals of the Neurotic Parent blog

MOM FOR A DAY

Just a few days ago, I was sitting at home with a box of tissues, desperately missing my firstborn. Now everything has changed. I managed to finagle a free 24-hour stopover at his campus during a massive business trip. And I am thrilled to report that, other than some disturbing laundry issues, CJ has actually morphed into....a college student. The highlights:

▶ **THE EXTRA-CURRICULARS:** Our emotional reunion started off with a passionate request: "Mom, can you take me and two of my friends to Goodwill to get outfits for tailgate? I *think* we know how to get there." We never did locate the Goodwill, but the boys put together the perfect fashion statement at Ross Dress for Less: matching silk autumn-motif caftans, beanies, hot-pink sunglasses, and coordinating belts.

▶ **THE FRIENDS:** CJ seemed to know just about everyone on campus, and 100% of those who he introduced me to were smart, funny, polite, and diverse. Having just read the *New York Times* piece about how your friends' behavior influences who you become, I felt relieved. He has chosen the nicest group to misbehave with.

▶ **THE FOOD:** We had lunch in the dining hall, which was really more of an upscale food court, offering Asian, Mexican, Italian, BBQ, vegetarian, and salad bar selections. I was about to go for the salad bar, but I could practically see viruses lurking on the tongs. Fortunately there was another soup and salad station, where I found a mushroom barley soup that truly would have been excellent had it been warm.

▶ **THE ROOM/ROOMMATE:** Yes, his room could have used a thorough vacuuming, but it wasn't nearly as smelly and disgusting as many of the dorms we'd seen on our college tour. CJ and his roommate have not become inseparable buddies, but they seemed content to be in the same space—and the two even took on a redecorating project together in my presence. Plus they share a fascinating passion: intramural flag football.

▶ **THE POSTERS:** My boy, on his own, shopped for art! Above his desk was a cool wanna-be lithograph featuring multiple Warhol-style images of a 20th-century turntable—the kind that dominated my own college experience. And the second work he purchased also conveyed a powerful retro statement: Directly above his bed is a giant rendering of the mighty Teenage Mutant Ninja Turtles.

THE TECHNOLOGY: Unlike some loving parents we know, we are very mean and thus far have not provided our son with a giant flat-screen television. But his strong survival skills led him to befriend roomies down the hall who have THREE giant flat-screen televisions. (Both students received full scholarships with allowances for purchasing electronics, so they have set up what is, in essence, a sports bar, and the TV-less CJ is a regular.)

THE DINNER: It might have been nice to have some alone time with my son, but the conversation probably would have focused exclusively on why he hadn't changed his sheets in over a month, which would have caused our relationship to deteriorate. So, to find out a few details about his new life, I invited FCT (Former Compulsive Texter—remember her from the college tour? She and CJ have been together since kindergarten and the adventure continues). Unlike CJ, FCT actually enjoys informing adults about what's happening in her life. She had just finished a five-page essay, and in a celebratory mood, was willing to provide anecdotes about everything— except the women in CJ's life (she obviously had been warned).

THE CLASSES: Mysteriously, although CJ has had a few quizzes and handed in several assignments, NOTHING has yet been graded. But if there were a grade for tailgate attire, my well-adjusted freshman would be #1 on the dean's list.

"AT MY GATE"

See above for the most wonderful text message a mother can possibly receive. The concise, impactful words choked me up. Hard to believe that three months have passed (let alone 19 years) and he's actually on his way home for Thanksgiving! Wish I could report that I'm preparing all his favorite foods and that I cleaned his room—but better yet, I managed to get him a DMV appointment tomorrow to replace his driver's license, which was stolen at a club, along with the rest of his wallet.

Yes, we sent him his passport so he can travel. And so far it is still in his possession.

From the annals of the Neurotic Parent blog

5 THINGS I'M THANKFUL FOR

1 CJ made it home without losing his passport, which he needed for ID because of the stolen license.

2 He didn't come back a new kid—he's our same old immature, slothful teenager! He wore the same clothes, watched the same sports, played the same video games with his brother, and hung out with the same friends until 3 a.m. He also practices the same annoying habits, such as texting 24/7, even during Thanksgiving dinner.

3 He wasn't braggy or pompous about the knowledge he has acquired at college. In fact, he made it a point not to recount any of the great ideas he has been exposed to from his distinguished professors. He can, however, discuss the intricacies of the fraternity rush process.

4 He didn't gain the freshman 15 (like the girls), or lose the freshman 7 (like the other boys).

5 He's happy. Very happy. He is not the subject of nasty "transfer" rumors, such as: "Spike is so-o-o *unhappy* with the weather in Boston. I heard he was going to *transfer* to Santa Barbara." Or "Natasha really should have gone to a school in the city. I heard she's trying to *transfer* to NYU."

Adults discuss these potential transfers the way they whisper about impending divorces. This amuses me: I can't help but think back to the days when transferring was the norm, when 78% of my friends jumped around from college to college and it wasn't such a scandalous event if you moved on after a year or two. Of course, in those days you didn't have to write three new essays and conjure up honors, awards, and quirky extracurriculars to make the move.

HOT TIMES IN BOSTON

Thanks to a reader for the following submission:

My sister knows some people with a son who goes to college in Boston. They were having a heat wave there, and instead of telling their son to buy a fan, they set him up in a hotel for a week. And it was not just any hotel—it's where they stay when they're in town.

ICHAT ETIQUETTE

The Neurotic Parent is pleased to report that it has been a pleasure having our son home for the winter holidays, even though when here, he is usually asleep. In the spirit of forgiveness, and because we are so proud of his first-semester grades, we have excused him for forgetting to stay in touch for the last five months. That hasn't stopped us from imposing firm restrictions for the new semester: Henceforth, he will be required to iChat with us for three to five minutes every Sunday night. Apparently this is a common practice, adhered to by most college students.

But one mom, whose son attends a top New England LAC (liberal arts college), has warned us that iChats are not always as satisfying as one would think. Yes, her son dutifully video-called home every week, but there on the bookshelf behind him during the most recent call was a half-empty two-liter bottle of vodka.

COURSE SELECTION GUIDE FOR FRESHMEN

 No classes that meet before 11:40 a.m.

 No classes that meet after 4:40 p.m.

 Friday classes? Forget it!

 Try to find seminars that meet just once a week and require only two quizzes and an in-class PowerPoint presentation, even if the subject is of no interest to you.

 Check the online catalog for courses that sound exactly like what you have already studied in high school, assuming you have held onto your old essays and papers.

 Three times a week? Lab or discussion session? No way!

 Enroll in intriguing classes with Fulbright professors that require two fifteen-page papers? Not a chance!

 Interested in Hip-Hop Globalization, Entrepreneurship, or Abnormal Sexual Behavior? Don't even bother checking—those classes are full.

From the annals of the Neurotic Parent blog

I HAD A DREAM

I dreamt that CJ was home for an entire month, yet we only shared 3.6 hours of quality time:

- ➡ Beach vacation (with three other families): 33 minutes doing a jigsaw puzzle together in the early mornings.

- ➡ Screening of our old video montages after a cousins' dinner: eighteen minutes of togetherness on the couch.

- ➡ Shopping trip for hoodies: 23 minutes in the car and at the mall, broken up by marathon texting sessions and encounters with high school classmates.

- ➡ Orthodontist visit with adult-braces guy (yes, CJ could have gotten there by himself, but I went along and read magazines in the waiting room, as if he were in middle school): 29 minutes.

- ➡ Dinner at Thai restaurant, with conversation centering around an analysis of Mr. NP's obsession with *Top Chef* and the origins of boba: 38 minutes.

- ➡ Packing for the two road trips he took: seven minutes.

- ➡ Field trip to the Verizon store when his cell phone broke hours before he was due back at school: 43 minutes.

- ➡ Ride to airport (does it count if he was sleeping?): 26 minutes.

Since he might not come home for spring break, I'm looking forward to the summer, when I should be able to clock five to nine hours of quality time in four months.

THUS FAR

He's back...no longer a college freshman. He is still clad in his hoodie and baseball cap. He continues to text incessantly, including with several high school pals who are now college dropouts. He doesn't look or act more mature, but there have been glimmers of erudition. Above all, I was shocked to witness him using the phrase "thus far" in conversation. I guess every penny we spent on freshman-year tuition was worth it.

ROOMMATE UPDATE/SITCOM PITCH

Here's a text from one of our readers, who just took her son to a top liberal arts college in the northwest:

"All is good. Met 2/3 roommates. The queen and the hick. Will meet prom king tomorrow, and my son the stoner should round out the mix."

BETTER THAN OLD-FASHIONED PLAGIARISM

Now there is relief for college students whose homework helpers wrote all of their high school essays for them: They can hire the Shadow Scholar, who earns $66,000 a year writing papers for college students. He even does 75-page assignments for kids who are barely literate enough to send a legible text and have been known to send such profound messages as "thanx so much for uhelp ican going to graduate to now."

As we learned in a recent article in *The Chronicle of Higher Education*, the Shadow Scholar can stretch a 40-word paragraph into four pages. His biggest customer bases are nursing students and "lazy rich kids." And he has perfected the use of stock academic phrases like the following (fill in the blanks):

"A close consideration of the events which occurred in _____ during the _____ demonstrate that _____ had entered into a phase of widespread cultural, social, and economic change that would define _____ for decades to come."

If we were professors, we would not be thrilled to have to read hundreds of 75-page papers. In fact, at our age we can barely get through one book club book a month. So if we were professors, we might be tempted to hire somebody to read the 75-page papers written by random ghostwriters who never attended class. With this in mind, the Neurotic Parent Institute has commissioned a study to find out whether a new crop of Shadow Professors has emerged.

In the meantime, the Institute is also pondering why any professor in his or her right mind would assign a 75-page paper. Why would anyone possibly want to encourage kids, who lack clarity of thought to begin with, to ramble on forever? We suspect kickbacks from Shadow Scholars.

TEXTERS ANONYMOUS

In my lifetime, phone technology has gone from party lines to busy signals to long-distance operators to area codes to princess phones to calling cards to answering machines to wireless phones to call waiting to voicemail to mobile phones to cells to texting to Skype...and the advances are not ending any time soon. We have produced so many great telephonic ways to stay in touch that we barely have time to communicate in person.

All of us know adults with Crackberry and iPhone issues, those rude people who check their chats and peek at sports scores during meetings and in the movies. But according to a recent Neurotic Parent study, the highest percentage of smart phone addicts are now college students.

Statistics reveal that text addictions begin in high school but escalate the minute one arrives at college. Back in the day, when your parents drove off, you'd celebrate your independence by lighting up a cigarette. Now, teens suddenly find themselves with nobody to tell them to stop texting, so they send messages during meals, classes, and parties—and some even sleep with their mobile devices so they can text throughout the night.

I observed this out-of-control texting last week when I visited CJ. His new fraternity brothers were not as ROTC-ish as I feared, and some actually looked as if they were on their way to MTV internships. They were exceedingly polite and good conversationalists who could discuss anything from bioethics to Arizona's immigration policies.

But even the smartest, funniest guys had more than their napkins in their laps. My son was one of these offenders. He already had a borderline addiction when he left for college; now he is so dependent on his handheld device that I fear he will not be able to resist as he drives around this summer.

The obvious remedy is to take away his smart phone, but since that's the only way CJ communicates with us, that would be like cutting off our thumbs to spite our hands (poor metaphor attempt).

Instead, I've contacted Verizon about offering a new Neurotic Parents' College Plan, which I hope will soon be available in our area:

⟶ Limits contacts to those over 45 years old.

⟶ Bans "Lost My Phone" messages on Facebook.

⟶ No connectivity in restaurants, classrooms, movie theaters, or moving vehicles.

➠ Keyboard locks after 2 a.m., except for texts to home.

➠ Free satellite tracking and password-change updates for account holders.

So readers, if you would like to sign up for this limited-availability package, just sign the e-mail petition I plan to send around. And, in the meantime, make sure to bore your kids with lots of stories about the days when we actually had to memorize phone numbers.

PLEASE LEAVE—BUT FIRST, COULD YOU GET ME A FLAT-SCREEN TV?

Somehow the four-month summer has vanished in a surreal flash, and in three days, CJ is scheduled to return to college for his second year. This time I am accompanying him without Mr. Neurotic Parent or GC. Many of CJ's friends are already back at school, and now that they're big sophomores, many have set up their rooms without their parents. With this in mind, I asked CJ whether he really wanted me to go with him and was thrilled to find out that he did.

"I think you should come," he said, "because if you don't, I'll probably go the whole year without unpacking." But he warned me that he would not be available for lunches or dinners, and other than for runs to Super Target, he would not pay any attention to me at all.

I do not like to think of myself as a Velcro parent, who are presumably even more involved than the helicopter parents of the '00s. According to a piece in the New York Times called "Students, Welcome to College; Mom and Dad, Go Home," many schools are now instituting "parting ceremonies" to prevent mothers and fathers from attending classes with their kids or going to the registrar to change their classes.

I actually see myself as a mom who CAN separate (I was the first to make it to Starbucks after preschool drop-off), but when I glanced at my Southwest itinerary, I was horrified to find out that I had scheduled THREE nights to help CJ move in to his new dorm. And changing my ticket at this point is a lose-lose scenario because the "web only" fares are long gone.

So if you're near CJ's college this weekend, and you want to have breakfast, lunch, dinner, coffee, and/or drinks, you can find me hiding out in my hotel room, un-Velcroing myself.

From the annals of the Neurotic Parent blog

BEYOND BED & BATH

What a surprise to find out on Facebook that parents of sophomores are once again spending hours at Bed Bath & Beyond! For my son this year, five minutes there was enough—his only purchases were a multi-shade tree lamp and a replacement charger for his Shark handheld cordless vac (which meant buying a whole new one).

In fact, CJ's things held up exceptionally well during the summer. Once the stuff came out of storage, we discovered that, although he was missing his speakers and tennis racket, most of his other possessions, including his shower caddy and memory-foam pad, were still in one piece and not too stinky. And he was now the proud owner of many more items than he started out with last year:

➡	an Aerobed
➡	a king-size navy fleece blanket
➡	two "Shaker Heights Chess Club" T-shirts
➡	a little boy's SpongeBob tank, size M
➡	a professional tape measure, the kind that contractors use
➡	Ray-Bans
➡	an orange plaid sports jacket
➡	a Wayland High (MA) lacrosse sweatshirt
➡	bowling shoes (yes, rented)

Second-year students, at least at CJ's school, are *so* over Bed Bath & Beyond. The last thing they want their dorm room to look like is a dorm room. Instead they try to replicate the ambience of a club—from the '80s. So they have moved on to the Salvation Army, which presents a challenge because the Salvation Army doesn't offer "pack and hold" options. And they don't send you 20% off coupons.

In an incredible stroke of good luck, CJ's roommate LG (Lead Guitarist) arrived 36 hours before us with his mom, DG (Design Genius). Before we even boarded our plane, DG and LG had rented a Suburban and checked out every thrift shop in a 25-mile radius. But first they picked up the massage chair that they'd shipped from New Jersey (a retired bar mitzvah present that begged to go to college).

By the end of the day, a bold red cotton duck sofa and a clean-lined black hardwood coffee table were positioned under the stone Gothic window. Both were in such good shape and so classic that they could have come from Crate & Barrel. Even the artwork was in its place: Fourteen eclectic posters adorned the walls, and a row of baseball hats hung above one of the lofted beds. On either side of the sofa were high plywood end tables that looked like something Frank Gehry had designed—and they were, in fact, the standard-issue desks brilliantly positioned vertically.

"Nobody uses their desk for studying sophomore year," CJ told me, as his frat brothers waited their turn for a chair massage. And after we (actually, he) put together the tree lamp, there was nothing for me to do but check out of my hotel early and drive four hours to see *my* college friends. Not that CJ didn't want to be with me. But this year he could wash his own mattress pad. And he had a definite opinion about the location for the hook for his bathrobe. So I bought him two giant bottles of the Axe revitalizing shower gel he wanted. And then it was time for me to go.

The Neurotic Parent Answers Your Questions

URGENT QUERIES FROM READERS

In the fall, while the over-involved parents of high school seniors are struggling with their own angst, new sorts of worries consume the parents of first-year college students. (That's right, they're called first-years now—"freshmen" is sexist.) These parents worry about kids who are either not communicating at all (boys) or texting/Skyping 25 times a day about the untidy habits of their roommates (girls). They send us questions:

Q: I had a fight with a member of the staff of Bed Bath & Beyond in Walnut Creek. Will they take it out on me and put aside the wrong items for my daughter in the Somerville, MA store?

A: Worse than that. They will send part of your daughter's order to two different stores in Boston, 45 minutes away. (True story.)

Q: Our son is off to a well-known hipster school. But hard as we've tried, we cannot interest him in indie music or marijuana. Will he fit in?

A: Good question. Have you thought about packing a giant bong to use as a pencil holder? Special order at BB&B.

Q: My daughter has changed my level of friendship on Facebook. I am now just a "limited friend," which means I can no longer see photos in which she's been tagged. But she has awarded "full friend status" to our housekeeper, Imelda. It's not fair!

A: This has become such a common issue that the Neurotic Parent Institute has started a new service. For a small fee, we will get our housekeeper to friend Imelda and report back.

ONE BOY'S BURSAR ACCOUNT:
A DUBIOUS ACHIEVEMENT

Date / Description	Amount
05/11 (spring semester, freshman year) Replacement ID Card	10.00
06/14 (spring semester, freshman year) Housing-Key Replacement Charges Res. Halls	65.00 22.17
09/09 (fall semester, sophomore year) Replacement ID Card	10.00
09/09 (fall semester, sophomore year—yes, two in one day!) Replacement ID Card	10.00
09/14 (fall semester, sophomore year—yes, three in one week!) Replacement ID Card	10.00
11/01 (fall semester, sophomore year) Replacement ID Card	10.00
11/05 (fall semester, sophomore year) Mailbox Key Replacement	16.16
12/06 (fall semester, sophomore year) Replacement ID Card	10.00
12/13 (fall semester, sophomore year, again two in one week) Replacement ID Card	5.00
01/10 (spring semester, sophomore year) Housing Damages	5.00
01/18 (spring semester, sophomore year) Replacement ID Card	10.00
01/24 (spring semester, sophomore year, lower rate for turning in previously reported lost card) Replacement ID Card	5.00
01/31 (repeat business discount) Replacement ID Card (volume discount)	5.00
03/01 Replacement ID Card	5.00
03/08 Replacement ID Card	5.00
05/02 Replacement ID Card	5.00
05/23 Housing Damages	9.88
06/16 Housing Damages	93.00

When CJ came home for the summer, we complimented him on his stellar GPA, then had a frank family discussion about how he would have to spend most of his summer earnings on paying us back for his lost cards. We also commended him for the drop in his lost cards (from March 8th to May 2nd). But he told us that, in fact, he had still lost multiple cards during that period. He'd just discovered he could pay the fines with cash.

nineteen

ROUND TWO

*Having a second child gives you a chance to
make the same lame mistakes
all over again, as well as many new ones*

ON THE ROAD AGAIN

When my first son, CJ, was applying to colleges, everyone said the process would be easier the second time around. Instead, everything is much worse. Although there are now fewer 17-year-olds in the world, application rates are soaring, admissions rates are plummeting, and issues about testing, essays, rigor, and suddenly viewing your friends as competition have not gone away. Even though at press time, we don't know where our second son GC (Good Conversationalist), is headed, we are taking the bold step of publishing blog entries from his college tour. Of course, since he does not yet have an admission in hand, this section will not win any awards for candidness—for the juicier stories, you'll have to purchase the next edition.

HYPER SKYPERS

Much has changed in the three short years between our two college-application journeys. One of the newest trends: interviews by Skype. Great schools such as Wake Forest, Penn, Whitman, Pitzer, and Bard now offer applicants the chance to dress nicely from the waist up and meet an alum or admissions official on a Macbook Air.

Parents of Skypers on College Confidential suggest conducting the interview in front of a "neutral, uncluttered background," but one girl we knew took the opportunity to the next level by prepping her room. She removed her Marilyn Manson poster, strategically placed her bassoon and mandolin on a shelf behind her, and stacked such works as *The Portable Nietzsche* and *Absalom, Absalom!* on her desk.

Sure enough, the admissions rep asked about the instruments, and, before they finished, the girl had a chance to impress her Skype-mate with a few bars from Stravinsky's *Rite of Spring*.

This trend has inspired the Neurotic Parent Institute to offer a new service: Skype Staging, which will include wardrobe consultation and bong removal. For desperate applicants we'll have the upgraded Gold Package, with tips from a hair stylist, lighting director, and sound guy. We'll also provide an IT expert to coach nervous interviewees in how to cause glitches and temporary breakdowns of their computers—so when they're asked difficult questions, they can realistically freeze their screens, cut off their callers, and even cause power outages.

MOST IMPORTANT YEAR OF THEIR LIVES THUS FAR

Just when I thought I could spend my time worrying about CJ's dorm refrigerator (missing parts—has to be sent back to Target), I went to the 11th grade back-to-school night for GC, my high school junior son, who has now officially started the college search process. I heard all sorts of great advice from the wise deans, including:

"It's all going to be great."

"Don't worry if they are not yet intellectually mature or haven't yet discovered their authentic selves."

"Now is when they need to learn time management."

"They should get to know their teachers" (for future recs)

and of course, the ubiquitous:

"They will all end up where they're supposed to be."

But one of the calm administrators let it slip that this is the "most important year in their lives thus far," and everybody began to sweat. Soon the entire room was secretly texting Tutor Tom, the top SAT guy in town, who has doubled his rates since CJ used him three years ago.

OOPS...I DID IT AGAIN!

CJ has had an emotional growth spurt. He has declared a major. His laundry is not scattered all over the floor. He has a planner. He knows the bus system. He has procured silent auction items for campus fundraisers. He has invited me to an a cappella concert. He even has a job on campus (okay, it's as a flag football ref, but his earnings will pay for his over-the-top Halloween costume). And most importantly, he has friends who are already looking for angel investors for their startups. So you might well think it's time for me to relax.

And yet.... GC has only JUST signed up for the SAT question of the day, 2.5 full months later than most of his friends. That means they have completed 75 additional practice questions, enough to boost their final scores by at least 50 points. And as much as I nag GC, he has not yet come close to finding a cure for malaria, and so far he has no plans to shoot a documentary about the homeless kids he works with.

Even worse, the parents in his grade all attended a college coffee while I was dining in farm-to-table restaurants with my college sophomore. They undoubtedly picked up some helpful hints that they will not share with me, because who would? It's now each neurotic parent for him or herself—hogging tutors, finding unusual activities, and hiring all sorts of waitlist counselors and interview coaches.

DEJA U

I am pleased to report that after three straight weeks of 24/7 planning, I have finalized arrangements to embark on a whole new spring break college tour, this time with our younger son.

Figuring out the logistics was a full-time job: There was laughter as we read between the lines of the Fiske Guide. There were tears of frustration when GC announced that he had a commitment at home on the day I'd reserved our first visit. There was anxiety when I looked up the schools on his list on Naviance—although he has a balance of urban, rural, D1, D3, public, and private, he is visiting mostly reaches, super-reaches, and crapshoots. There were angry phone calls to Thrifty Car Rental, with pleas for reduced drop-off fees. Then, finally, after a meeting with the dean, we utilized two Delta mileage awards, purchased four changeable Southwest "wanna-get-away" fares, booked several hotels with Hilton Honors points, and memorized countless Amtrak and Bolt Bus schedules.

Have I ever mentioned that our two sons are very different? CJ, the elder, is a gifted mathematician/sports fanatic/fratstar who probably could not name the governor of the state where he goes to school. GC, the younger, is a compulsive newshound/indie rock fan/quasi-intellectual who brings up issues at the dinner table like, "Do you think ten years from now there will still be such a thing as countries?"

One would imagine that the two would have completely different college lists. One would expect that GC would want to check out schools like Reed or the University of Chicago. But somehow, because of his desire for a classic college experience, we have ended up with a shockingly similar itinerary for Child #2. Other than the omission of the four schools we saw (in one day) in upstate New York, we are going to many of the same institutions of higher learning that I visited with CJ three years ago. During our ten-day expedition, I will be a repeat visitor at all but two universities.

But there are other significant changes. Because GC hates to get up early (especially in EST), we "only" have eight schools on our itinerary this time, compared with the fourteen we saw on CJ's tour.

And once again, we are not concentrating on one geographic area the way you're supposed to. That's right, the eight colleges are in eight different states. To avoid too much bonding time, we will be traveling with another family for half the trip, and also meeting up with random classmates in other locations. We'll move at a more mellow pace, sticking to just one tour per day, and will spend full weekends in two locations. And this time, our son is actually attending classes. He checked ahead and booked a concert in New York. And, of course, being the good conversationalist, he even scheduled an interview or two.

THE COLLEGE-OBSESSED CAB DRIVER
& OTHER BELIEVE-IT-OR-NOT OCCURRENCES

➺ A Russian cab driver, when dropping us off at NYU, asked GC's friend what he'd scored on the SAT.

➺ A student presenter at the Wesleyan info session shared that she is a double major in Public Health and Gender Studies, plays varsity volleyball, works as an assistant midwife, teaches salsa dancing to 6-year-olds, and is co-writing a paper with her professor about alternative birthing in Chile. It reminded all of us of our own extracurriculars in college.

➺ A friend of a friend in New York spent $40,000 in tutoring just for **one** SAT subject test (U.S. History). Her tutor, presumably a Supreme Court Justice, charged $2,400 per hour. Sadly, the student was denied admission to Dartmouth but is attending Middlebury.

➺ We've heard of three or four Stanford alumni who donated generously to their alma mater only to find out, in horror, that their qualified kids were rejected. So save your money and invest in Kirkland Signature vodka instead, the beverage of choice on every campus in the nation.

➺ The opening of the NYU info session included exotic views of a new campus in Abu Dhabi. Unlike NYU in New York, which costs $55K and had 42,000 applicants in 2011 (up 11% from '10), NYU Abu Dhabi has only 150 students and offers students 100% merit scholarships. The presenter compared life in the two cities and encouraged all to apply. A caveat to freshmen: It's difficult to get a parking permit for your camel.

➺ We have now twice heard the following anecdote with the motto, "Proofread rather than spellcheck." On two different campuses, admissions officers told us about an applicant who, when describing his tutoring experience, repeatedly wrote that he enjoys "torturing" children.

MOST OBNOXIOUS QUESTION BY
A PARENT ON **THIS** COLLEGE TOUR

Q: *What percentage of professors during a given semester are actually teaching?*

A: All professors teach undergraduate courses.

Q: *Yes, I know that, BUT, I asked SPECIFICALLY how many teach during a given semester. Suppose there are 50 professors. What percentage of them are actually teaching in a given semester?*

A: Well, you can ask the Dean of Admissions about that.

(This transpired at Brown, a school with academic awesomeness; why would anyone care if every professor doesn't teach every semester? Why not badger the admissions reps about an important issue, like why freshmen everywhere have to buy a $6,800 meal plan that never gets used?)

THE COLLEGE TOUR DIET

Shockingly, the trustees of the Neurotic Parent Institute have discovered that they consistently lose a couple of pounds on each college-tour trip. We are pleased to share our cutting-edge nutritional program with interested readers. In a nutshell, the secret is to eat like a college student and indulge in fatty and/or fried foods, candy, and desserts all day long. Food choices should be items that you haven't eaten in 35 years and would never consider indulging in at home. It also helps to travel with friends who start the day with waffles or three-egg omelets. Immediately after eating, go to your hotel room and take a nap, or get into a minivan for a sedentary four-hour ride across several states.

Here are the essentials of the program:

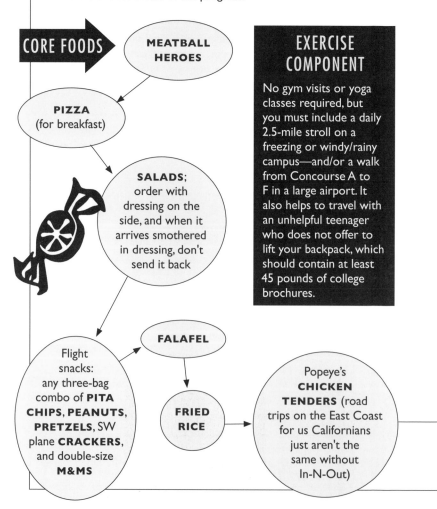

CORE FOODS

MEATBALL HEROES

PIZZA (for breakfast)

SALADS; order with dressing on the side, and when it arrives smothered in dressing, don't send it back

Flight snacks: any three-bag combo of **PITA CHIPS, PEANUTS, PRETZELS,** SW plane **CRACKERS,** and double-size **M&MS**

FALAFEL

FRIED RICE

Popeye's **CHICKEN TENDERS** (road trips on the East Coast for us Californians just aren't the same without In-N-Out)

EXERCISE COMPONENT

No gym visits or yoga classes required, but you must include a daily 2.5-mile stroll on a freezing or windy/rainy campus—and/or a walk from Concourse A to F in a large airport. It also helps to travel with an unhelpful teenager who does not offer to lift your backpack, which should contain at least 45 pounds of college brochures.

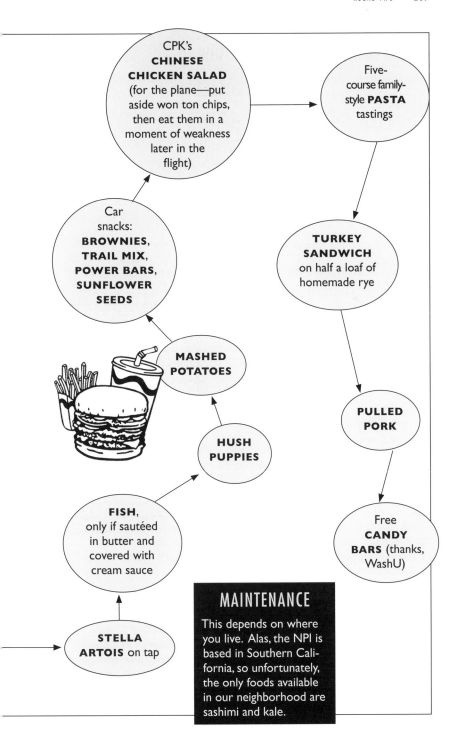

CPK's **CHINESE CHICKEN SALAD** (for the plane—put aside won ton chips, then eat them in a moment of weakness later in the flight)

Five-course family-style **PASTA** tastings

Car snacks: **BROWNIES**, **TRAIL MIX**, **POWER BARS**, **SUNFLOWER SEEDS**

TURKEY SANDWICH on half a loaf of homemade rye

MASHED POTATOES

HUSH PUPPIES

PULLED PORK

FISH, only if sautéed in butter and covered with cream sauce

Free **CANDY BARS** (thanks, WashU)

STELLA ARTOIS on tap

MAINTENANCE

This depends on where you live. Alas, the NPI is based in Southern California, so unfortunately, the only foods available in our neighborhood are sashimi and kale.

From the annals of the Neurotic Parent blog

BAD NEWS/GOOD NEWS

As I post from Ann Arbor, one of the greatest college towns in the universe, I am faced with a major dilemma. Almost every school on GC's preliminary list has just released statistics that show this was the year with the highest amount of applicants and the lowest acceptance rate ever. So if I post something positive about our experience at a college, I could screw things up for GC and his travel buddy, MM (Mr. Mellow). Or if I say anything negative, admissions officers might read this and decide not to admit a kid whose parent badmouths their school on the internet. This means that throughout the trip my posts will be full of benign anecdotes, like a list of the following bad news/good news situations:

Situation #1: NCAA Tournament

Bad News: I created a bracket so I could bond with my son during this trip. This was a very time-consuming task for somebody who knows virtually nothing about college basketball.

Good News: Three of my teams lost one day after I predicted the outcome of the tournament, so I no longer feel obligated to watch the games.

Situation #2: Emergency Landing

Bad News: Our plane developed a hydraulic leak. We sped up, landed in Detroit early, and found ourselves surrounded by dozens of fire engines.

Good News: We weren't informed about the "issue" until after we landed. And we could continue to play Sporcle while truck fans cooled our brakes for 90 minutes.

Situation #3: Misplaced Jacket

Bad News: It was seventeen degrees last night, twelve with the wind chill. But GC still somehow managed to leave his jacket at the $A\Sigma\Pi$ fraternity house, where he visited one of his brother's friends. He returned to the hotel with just a fleece.

Good News: The weather here is clearly not a major deterrent for GC.

Situation #4: Zingerman's Waitlist

Bad News: We were deferred, then waitlisted, at Zingerman's, the best deli in the Midwest. However, if we take a gap year, there is hope for admission next fall.

Good News: Instead, we had lunch at a Korean place in the very cool

Kerrytown market, which gave us time to see my cousin EE (Equestrian Extraordinaire) in the closing ceremony of the UM marathon, in which she had danced for 30 hours straight to raise money for a pediatric hospital. She said on Monday we might be able to get into Zingerman's for lunch.

❋

SACRIFICING

We have entered another dimension of time and space: CJ is a college junior. And GC is a high school senior...and we are officially old people.

It's too bad we cannot relax and enjoy one more year of pre-empty-nest quality time with our teen, but instead we have to deal with Early vs. Regular strategies, biting nails over test scores, proofreading activity lists, and agonizing over whether it was a mistake to omit Bowdoin, Colby, and Bates from our tour. But at least we haven't blown all our retirement money on remedial help for our kids. In yet another *New York Times* piece about the outrageous level of educational spending in New York, we read an account of a Riverdale Country School family that paid **$35,000** in one year to **one tutor** from Ivy Consulting. (This did not include the $100K+ they spent the previous year on SAT prep.) The $35,000 accounted for preparation for **one oral exam**, the culmination of **one high school course.** That's $750 to $1,500 a week for the year.

The Neurotic Parent Institute has done preliminary research about the class in question, and we discovered that it is a course called Integrated Liberal Studies. According to Wikipedia, there are "readings and assignments covering Western culture, surveying classical philosophy as well as the history of science, and featuring literature, religion, and arts components." The reason the class is so notorious is because it uses "source material" (real books) rather than textbooks.

I started this post depressed about the melancholy fleeting moments of youth, the circle game cliché that has taken over my life. But now I have something to look forward to. As soon as my youngest leaves the house, I can move to a Hudson-view townhouse in Riverdale and become a Liberal Studies tutor. As a source-material aficionado who's as liberal as they come, I am super-qualified to prepare kids for oral presentations. Just ten students at $1,500 each a week comes to $780,000 a year—considerably more than I earn as a blogger.

I had planned to use this post to rant about how Bs, once defined as "good," are now the end of the world. But it is the pressure of those potential Bs that makes parents spend more on a tutor than on tuition at an Ivy.

What joy it is to have found my cause! As soon as I brush up on my classical philosophy, I am prepared to devote the next stage of my life to wiping out Bs at Riverdale.

COMPARATIVE EDUCATION

Yes, folks, we are *still* on our college tour. We have now been on the road for ten days. We have visited seven schools in seven states, plus one federal district. We have rented four cars, taken three flights, one train, and one bus. And at the moment, we are currently at Logan International Airport (with free WiFi and rocking chairs), happily waiting for a Southwest flight to Chicago (which we hope won't have holes in the fuselage), where we will connect to St. Louis (which GC hopes won't be a "lame" city) for our visit to the fabled WashU.

We have met up with five of our older son CJ's childhood friends, all now young adults, who have shown GC the real side of college life at their universities. And we have run into countless other kids from the SoCal area. At Wesleyan, GC attended the information session with five fellow students from his chem class. And at Penn, GC hugged and/or fist-pumped a tour bus of students from our rival high school.

This morning, GC *almost* attended a Comparative Education class at Brown with CJ's soccer buddy CE (Crossword Expert, whose many accomplishments include writing Monday and Friday puzzles for the *New York Times* and being a reader of this blog). But the class met at 9 a.m., which is not in the cards for GC. A pity, because our trip has been a living comparative-ed lab. Here are some of the superlatives:

MOST OUTSTANDING TOUR GUIDE — MIDWEST:

A smart, funny Atlanta native at Northwestern, who put a positive spin on the winters ("we all bond by huddling together") and is double majoring in Public Health and Communications.

MOST OUTSTANDING TOUR GUIDE — NORTHEAST:

Mr. Diction, a Brown junior from the suburbs of Boston. As our umbrellas were turned inside out by gusty winds, Mr. D, a campus DJ and varsity rower, convinced us all that Brown was heaven with "the happiest students on earth." And he clearly had taken a creative nonfiction course: Instead of instructing us to notify him if he was about to "hit something" while walking backwards (like the tour guides everywhere else say), he told us to let him know if he was about to "fall off a cliff."

BUSIEST STUDENT:

Another one of the Brown tour guides, originally from Cincinnati. She recently petitioned the administration and instituted a subsection of a department, focusing on developing regions of the world. A four-year varsity volleyball player, she also builds houses for Habitat for Humanity in Uganda and has overseen research in Ecuador. And she is a Peer Advisor and a tour guide. (All this at a school that, like the others, advises prospective high school students to stick to one or two extracurriculars.)

BEST MEAL:

Most were decent, good, or great, except the fast food in Midway. Standouts include the Q Shack in Durham, Zingerman's Deli in Ann Arbor (we got in!), Red Stripe Brasserie in Providence, and Eataly in New York.

BEST FOOD ON CAMPUS:

Penn, by far. The freshly prepared sushi in the student union may not be quite on the level of Nobu, but it is a cut above Whole Foods. And the stir-fry looked just as tasty. Plus we saw food trucks lining the perimeter of the campus.

LEAST CALORIC MEAL:

N/A.

MOST EMBARRASSING MOMENT:

Mr. NP (who met us in Durham) has a phone app that made a slot-machine sound during an info session.

MOST ACRONYMS:

Georgetown (a few of the many examples: GERMS, Georgetown Emergency Response Medical Service; GULC, Georgetown University Law Center; CHARMS, Campus Housing Roommate Matching System).

MESSIEST LIVING SITUATION:

That would be our older son CJ's dorm.

MOST TEDIOUS EXPLANATION:

A detailed description about the difference between varsity, club, and intramural sports. We usually endured this lesson twice at each college, once by the admissions dean and once by the tour guides.

NEWEST TREND ON CAMPUS:

Quidditch, a cappella groups, and neuroscience are so 2009. Nowadays you hear more about sustainable dorms, robots who have heart attacks, and Ultimate (Frisbee, that is—this has become such a popular sport that enthusiasts have dropped the name of the disc). But Michigan still brags about its squirrel club.

MOST DIVERSITY:

One of our student info-session leaders was named *Hamlet*. What's in a name? Clearly, his parents knew this would help get him into a top school.

The Neurotic Parent Answers Your Questions

QUESTIONS FROM READERS

Q: Our Harvard tour guide compared Harvard to Hogwarts five times during our tour. Is this a trend?

A: Yes. It is replacing excessive mentioning of a cappella groups.

Q: Should my eighth grader begin tutoring for the new PPSAT?

A: Sorry—it's too late. She should have started in fifth grade.

Q: It seems as if the Wall Street Journal and the New York Times each have an article every day about how difficult the college admissions process is this year. Or am I just hyper-aware because I have a rising senior?

A: This is NOT your imagination—76% of the reporters for the Journal and the Times also have rising seniors who will be competing with your child.

Q: Will you help my son with his essay?

A: I would love to, especially because my own son won't let me. Please e-mail it to me. But keep in mind that I overuse parentheses and the verb "to be."

Q: I have heard that admissions officers look down on high school community-service trips to exotic impoverished places. Yet just about every college website shows a photo of students surrounded by orphans in Swaziland or Bolivia. Why is it okay to go on these trips in college, but not in high school?

A: Hmm. That's a good one. The Neurotic Parent Institute has commissioned an emergency study and has come up with these preliminary results: They're hypocrites.

BARISTA READINESS

A college degree is fine, but at the end of the day, they'd better know how to prepare a venti, sugar-free, nonfat, vanilla soy, double-shot, decaf, no foam, extra-hot, peppermint white chocolate mocha

I WANT MY MTV INTERNSHIP

A friend's daughter recently graduated from Rice, one of the finest universities in the nation (despite a name that's a little too heavy in carbs). This cum laude student, who studied English Literature, is thrilled with her new job as a casting assistant on an MTV reality show in New York.

Another friend's son, a rising sophomore at Brown, is home in Los Angeles for the summer. He is one of those talented, charismatic kids who could get a job anywhere. His summer internship? A gofer on an MTV reality show. And yesterday I heard about the brilliant sister of one of CJ's friends, who is undecided about her undergraduate major at Penn but is fairly certain she wants to be a physician. She had the opportunity to do autism research at UCLA this summer. Instead, guess where she's working?

Yes, college kids across the nation are shunning community service trips to Burundi and apprenticeships at law firms, opting to prepare coffee for the crews of *Pimp My Ride* and *Punk'd*.

(**Disclaimer:** I have not actually seen these shows, because I cannot find MTV among the 587 channels we subscribe to, but I'm sure they are of the highest quality. I do remember the *Addicted to Love* video, though, and it was awesome.)

This MTV career trend should come as a great relief to neurotic parents everywhere. Surely it should not matter which college your son or daughter attends if his or her ambition is to end up as a P.A. on *Jackass*. But according to the Neurotic Parent Institute, that is not the case. The surprising results of our study indicated that 93% of the support staff on *The Real World* attended Harvard, Princeton, or Yale. That means students from less-prestigious colleges have been forced to seek work in the real real world instead.

How should a student prepare for one of these 21st-century dream jobs? According to Dr. Gordon A. Power, academic dean at Stanford, the best choice of majors would vary from show to show. He suggested the following:

Pimp My Ride – Mechanical Engineering
Jackass – Trauma Psychology (M.S. preferred)
Punk'd – Cultural Anthropology
Celebrity Rap Star – Musicology

Dr. Power also advised not limiting one's options to MTV. He encouraged recent grads to explore related opportunities on programs such as *Pussycat Dolls' Girlicious* on CW, an appropriate choice for those pursuing Women's Studies.

But the true victims of the MTV job glut are those students who slacked off watching MTV reality shows while in high school. These kids, unlike their Ivy League counterparts, stand little or no chance of ever working on *Viva la Bam*. Sadly, disillusioned students from second- and third-tier schools will now be forced to find employment at less desirable places like Google or Goldman Sachs.

BARISTAS

Once your students graduate from college, they will spend many months looking for a job before signing up for an incredible (but unpaid) service opportunity in Africa. Once they return, they will think about graduate school but will find out that:

A) Because they took hard classes at a great college, their GPA is less than stellar and they can't get in anywhere decent

OR

B) Because they were slackers at an easy college, they can't pass the GRE.

At this point, there is only one road worth taking—head to the nearest Starbucks, pass four interviews, and give it your all. We have just received access to the resumes of the guys and gals who are preparing our lattes…and boy, are they impressive. These kids could soon be running the world, if only there were an economy to afford them.

KYLIE	JACK	JOAQUIN
Kylie graduated cum laude from Princeton, where she majored in Urban Studies and received a grant to travel to Uganda. Here she studied the public transportation infrastructure and implemented offshore wind farms. She is interested in microfinance, public health, and urbanization. Kylie is currently a barista at Starbucks.	Jack graduated magna cum laude from Dartmouth. He spent his junior year abroad in Tanzania, where he taught biomedical engineering while living in an ostrich sanctuary. After returning to the U.S., he founded a legal aid clinic in Mississippi, while he also played trombone in a jazz band. Jack is currently a barista at Peets.	Joaquin has a BA in International Relations from Pomona. He founded the Poverty Collective (PC) as a freshman and worked on assignments with the Ethiopian Mutual Foundation (EMF), Concern Guyana, and the United Nations Orphan Relief Fund in Addis Ababa. Joaquin is currently a barista at Coffee Bean & Tea Leaf.

IN A NUTSHELL: HAIKUS FOR THE NEUROTIC PARENT

COMMON APP HAIKU

As the clock strikes twelve
The freaking server is down
What now? A gap year

ESSAY HAIKU

I soared 'round the world
In a hot-air balloon, so
I'd get into Brown

EXTRACURRICULAR HAIKU

An orphan delights
In the large bungalow that
I built in Haiti

NAVIANCE HAIKU

My scattergram graph
Features diamonds and "x's"
No happy green squares

COLLEGE TOUR HAIKU

The brick walls greet us
After miles on the long road
She won't leave the car

RECOMMENDATION HAIKU

I once failed a quiz
Will a gift card from Nordstrom
Cause you to forget?

ACT HAIKU

After four sittings
Finally, a 33
ED, here I come

U.S. NEWS & WORLD REPORT HAIKU

Third-tier magazine
In a stack at the dentist's
Determines hot schools

INTERNSHIP HAIKU

Piping hot coffee
Prepared by pre-med students
Tweeting all summer

From the annals of the Neurotic Parent blog

PRELUDE TO EMPTY NESTING

A fter we put GC on a plane to his summer program, Mr. NP and I set off on one of our first childless vacations ever—a summer respite at a spa in the mountains. Which mountains? The ones in the state where our older son, CJ, attends college, of course. That way, after three days of restorative romantic alone time, we could return to the joys of parental meddling. So here we are at our favorite hotel in CJ's college town, waiting for our son to wake up so we can help him put his belongings in storage after his stint at summer school, because he's going abroad for the fall semester.

We thought we could make ourselves useful doing laundry and taping boxes. But because he is a junior and has lost most of his possessions, it seems we only need to wash two towels (the other four are missing), one twin XL sheet, and one duvet cover. And the schlepping will involve just a few books, a micro-fridge (the mash-up appliance with the most toxic emissions on the planet), a flat-screen television (which he somehow acquired without purchasing), and his tree lamp.

Everything else is already packed in two medium-size duffels. In fact, it was never *unpacked* after spring semester. CJ has survived the summer session in an apartment on campus with no Tempurpedic pad ("it fell apart"), no clip-on reading light, no message board, no shower caddy, no pop-up hamper, no tool kit. Virtually all of the supposedly essential items that we enthusiastically purchased for him when he started on this journey two years ago have disappeared, and our son has embraced the Simple Life.

Parents of rising freshmen take note: Donate your BB&B coupons to a homeless shelter, pack two old towels, give your kid a hug, and head to the mountains. Forget about colleges and pat yourself on the back if your son or daughter has turned out to be a kind and happy person.

Then, when you regain your senses, you can start pulling strings so your child will get a barista position in a desirable location. And, of course, it's never too soon to start worrying about graduate school.

THE
NEUROTIC
PARENT
GLOSSARY

A selective list of terms to master for the NPAPs
(Neurotic Parent Advanced Placement exams)

THE NEUROTIC PARENT GLOSSARY

Alumni interviews: Meetings in Starbucks with thirty-something investment bankers who give money to their alma maters to make sure their own kids will get in some day.

APs: Stressful, boring classes taken in high school, designed to prepare kids for the stressful, boring classes they will take in college.

BWRK: Bright, well-rounded kid. Just what the top colleges aren't looking for.

Club Sports Wake-up Call Syndrome (CSWCS): The realization that your kids have wasted 10,000-plus hours on a super-time-consuming extracurricular that will not help them get into college.

College Confidential: An internet forum frequented by neurotic parents and their even more neurotic kids.

Common App: An online college application shared by 450-plus universities, making it possible to apply to 450-plus schools with just a click.

Crew: If you are strong, muscular, and like getting splashed by freezing water before dawn, this could be your ticket to a great college.

Demonstrated interest: Certain colleges not only want you to spend hours on their applications, they also want to make sure you like them by making the effort to visit the campus, attend a class, engage your local admissions rep in clever e-mail repartee, purchase the most expensive sweatshirt and banner at the bookstore, and memorize the college's website so you can ask informed questions during your alumni interview.

Division sports: D1 stands for Division 1 sports, played at rah-rah universities and the Ivies; only world-class athletes need apply. D3 means Division 3 sports, played at smaller schools, where mortals might actually get some playing time. And R2D2 sports is the division for robotics champs; participation will lead to a much better job than D1 or D3.

Early action (EA): A win-win if you get in; you find out early, but you don't have to go.

Early decision (ED): The odds of getting in are usually greater, but it's a binding decision. No turning back now.

ECs: Extracurricular activity undertaken by students, often in the hopes of improving admissions chances. JV volleyball, secretary of multicultural club, and babysitting job = weak ECs. State record-holder in the butterfly, founder of iPads for the Indigent, and summer job as Congressional Page = acceptable ECs.

Engineering: A discipline whose students have so much work that they can't play video games during

U.S. News & World Report: A failed news magazine. Now, instead of reporting news, it bullies colleges into spending money on getting more students to apply so they can turn more down and artificially gain prestige in their ratings.

Ultra-early decision: A cutting-edge process being pioneered at MIT—embryonic fluid analysis will result in in-utero acceptance; multiple ultrasounds required.

Valedictorian: The student with the best GPA in his or her class. Also the favorite kind of student the top colleges like to deny, so they can brag about how many valedictorians they've rejected.

Viewbooks: What colleges call their brochures. Many have dedicated forests to keep up production of these slick, 40-page pamphlets that entice kids to apply, even though they will be rejected.

Yield: The percentage of students who actually matriculate at a school that accepts them. As Common App applications have skyrocketed, yield has plummeted, so colleges are scrambling to "protect" their yield.

Zinc: If your daughter worked on a research study focusing on dynamic shear deformation in zinc crystals, she's a good bet for HYPSM.

Acknowledgments

Thanks to the inspirational Mia Silverman, for encouraging me to blog.

Thanks to the influential Nicole Foos, for helping the blog go viral.

Thanks to Colleen Bates, my brilliant and extraordinary editor and publisher. I promise that I am not kissing up to her so she will let me write another book; she truly is the greatest.

Thanks to Joseph Shuldiner, our genius designer, for creating a look that makes the college application process seem cool. And to the rest of the team at Prospect Park Media, who helped shape and market this book: Caroline Purvis, Patty O'Sullivan, proofreader Nancy Ransohoff, blog designer Kate Hillseth, publicist Deb Shapiro, and distributor Aaron Silverman.

Thanks to my partners in neurosis and loyal blog fans for the support…and for the material: Melissa Bachrach, Laura Baker, Wendi Bahrynian, Roopa Bhalla, Anna Boorstin, Steve Byrnes, Debra Brunsten, Jane Bryson, Laura Chavez, Patty Cohen, Priscilla Cohen, Tamar Dames, Chuck Davis, Jan Davis, Lisa Ellenberg, Barbara Fisher, Laurie Freedman, Garson Foos, Jeff Fried, Judy Gambee, Mady Goldberg, Fred Goldring, Gale Goldring, Debra Greenfield, Seth Greenland, Mary Gwynn, Dale Hernsdorf, Miranda Heller, Kristie Hubbard, Sharon Jachter, Rob Keilson, Nancy Klein, Eric Kleinman, Phyllis Levine, Laurie Levit, Diana Lyne, Susan Murphy, Donna Nadel, Rick Nowels, Barbara Katz, Vicki Kennedy, Susan Kaiser Greenland, Nancy Klein, Wendy Levin, Tracy Lincenberg, Anna MacDonnell, Louise Nicholson, Emilyn Page, Jenny Pascal, Sari Polinger, Cheryl Raiss, Susan Rabb, Judy Ranan, Alex Rockwell, Cinda Rosenberg, Andrea Rosenthal, Janet Roston, Eric Roth, Philippa Rubell, Paul Ryan, Jane Salonen, Diane Shader Smith, Susan Smahl, Neysa Stone, Cathy Tauber, Henry Ullman, Leslie Ullman, Elaine Schweitzer, Alex Siskin, Jody Silvio, Darlene Vanderhoop, Maria Vidal, Lynn Wagmeister, Pam Walker, Nick Wapshott, Barry Weiss, Lauren White, and Donna Yesner.

Thanks to my intrepid interns, Gina Magnuson and Shelby Lorman. Sorry I couldn't pay them, but I promise to write them excellent recommendations when they apply for their next unpaid internships.

Thanks to my fellow book club members, who have made sure I read something other than the Fiske Guide for the last several years: Cindy Bendat, Patty Cohen, Michele Nasatir, Carol Newsom, Deborah Phillips, Sharon Rubin, Susan Stangl, Nancy Steingard and Barbara Zipperman.

Thanks to the calm/competent college professionals in my life: Jennifer Delahunty, Ted Dorsey, Candice Frankel, Veda Robinson, and Bill Wells.

Thanks to Gail Katz, Bruce Wessel, Alex Rockwell, Gigi Mahon, and anyone else who has offered to throw me a fabulous book party.

Thanks to the talented Paul Ryan for his generosity. College counseling is on me.

Thanks to everyone else who has helped with administrative, technical, or tour-related favors, especially Kasue McGregor, Jonah Kagan, Daniel Keilson, Dana Schweitzer, Taylor Schweitzer, Zach Scott, and all the high school and college students who contributed on many levels. I have left out names because of potential embarrassment, but if anyone would like specific recognition in the next edition, or a walk-on in the sitcom, just let me know.

Thanks to my awesome managers, Ellen Goldsmith-Vein and Julie Kane-Ritsch, for the nonstop hand-holding…and, in advance, for the seven-figure feature deal.

Thanks to my kindred-spirit agent, Lisa Queen—I look forward to our sleepover during the book tour.

Thanks to Ana and Larry for all the BB&B coupons.

Thanks to my smart, funny Gen X nieces and nephew, Jen, Mike, and Suzanne, whom I hope will not need this book for their kids.

Thanks to Carol, the most caring sibling on the planet. Anyone who knows her will testify that I'm not exaggerating.

Thanks to Peter, not exactly my *compadre* in college angst, but otherwise my #1 fan and soulmate, whether the nest is full, emptying, or being remodeled.

And, thanks to my remarkable sons, Leo and Ike. Hope we never stop laughing and hugging…and that I never will have to proofread their applications again. May the job market still suck when they graduate, so that they will move back home while they apply for positions as baristas.

ABOUT THE AUTHOR

J.D. Rothman, a former instructor of remedial freshman composition, is an Emmy-winning television writer, children's media producer, and lyricist. A resident of Santa Monica, California, she is the writer of theneuroticparent.com, a favorite blog of exhausted admissions counselors and sanity-seeking parents across the country. The Neurotic Parent blog was previously excerpted in the anthology *I'm Going to College—Not You!* (St. Martin's Press). Rothman prepared for none of her careers in college.

PHOTO BY DAVID BLATTEL